ALSO BY WILLIAM MURRAY

A Fine Italian Hand
Now You See Her, Now You Don't
We're Off to See the Killer
The Wrong Horse
I'm Getting Killed Right Here
The Last Italian: Portrait of a People
The Getaway Blues
Del Mar: Its Life and Good Times
The King of the Nightcap
When the Fat Man Sings
The Hard Knocker's Luck
Tip on a Dead Crab
Italy: The Fatal Gift
Malibu
The Mouth of the Wolf
Horse Fever
The Killing Touch
The Dream Girls
Previews of Coming Attractions
The Americano
The Sweet Ride
Pirandello's One-Act Plays (translator)
To Clothe the Naked and Two Other Plays by Luigi Pirandello (translator)
The Self-Starting Wheel
Best Seller
The Fugitive Romans

PLAYS
The Executioner
Witnesses
Dialogue for a Dead Playwright
Ave Caesar

JANET,
MY MOTHER,
AND ME

A MEMOIR OF GROWING UP
WITH JANET FLANNER AND
NATALIA DANESI MURRAY

WILLIAM MURRAY

SIMON & SCHUSTER
NEWYORK LONDON SYDNEY SINGAPORE

SIMON & SCHUSTER
Rockefeller Center
1230 Avenue of the Americas
New York, NY 10020

Copyright © 2000 by William Murray

All rights reserved, including the right of reproduction in whole
or in part in any form.

SIMON & SCHUSTER and colophon are registered trademarks
of Simon & Schuster, Inc.

Designed by Karolina Harris

Manufactured in the United States of America

10 9 8 7 6 5 4 3 2 1

Library of Congress Cataloging-in-Publication Data
Murray, William.
    Janet, my mother, and me: a memoir of growing up with Janet Flanner and
Natalia Danesi Murray / William Murray.
        p. cm.
        1. Flanner, Janet, 1892–1978. 2. Women authors, American—20th century—
Biography. 3. Women in the book industries and trade—Biography. 4. Lesbians—
United States—Biography. 5. William Murray, 1926—Family. 6. Lesbians—
France—Biography. 7. Lesbian mothers—Biography. 8. Murray,
Natalia Danesi. 9. Mothers and sons. I. Title.

PS3511.L285 Z77 2000
814'.52—dc21
[B]   99-045317
ISBN 0-684-80966-4

ACKNOWLEDGMENTS

Some of the quotations that appear in this memoir are from letters and documents that are now to be found in the Manuscripts Division of the Library of Congress. Some are from the journal that Janet kept between 1947 and 1951. I was also granted access during William Shawn's editorship of *The New Yorker* to the magazine's files, then haphazardly contained in cardboard boxes in a storage room below the editorial floors. Most, however, are from my mother's collection of letters, including those I found after her death in 1994, and from my own notes and recollection of events.

I want to thank my agent, Elizabeth Kaplan, for her unfailing and loving support for this project and during times of stress. Also, my ex-wife and beloved friend, Doris M. Kuhns, who helped me recall the events of our time together and who knew both Janet and my mother well. And, of course, my wife, Alice, who shared some of the best and worst of times with me during my mother's last years.

For my children—Natalia, Julia, and Bill—who wanted to know.

CONTENTS

Like anyone else, she must have wanted different things at the same time. The human heart is a dark forest.

—*This Boy's Life,* BY TOBIAS WOLFF

We all construct ourselves.

—LUIGI PIRANDELLO

ONE

IMMORTALITY

The voices of grief haunt the early morning hours. My mother's voice sounded harsh and broken when she called to tell me that Janet had died. Alice and I had been awake for several hours, ever since her first call to inform us that Janet had been taken shortly after midnight to a hospital a few blocks from my mother's apartment in New York. "I am dying, Natalia, I am dying," Janet had whispered to her, while holding on to a chair in the hall where my mother, awakened by a cry of pain, had found her. And now, a few hours later, she was dead.

I felt stunned and cold, unable to indulge my own grief, as I got dressed and began to pack. I had already called the airline and told my mother I would be in New York by midafternoon. "Do you want me to come with you?" Alice asked, as we sipped coffee together in the kitchen.

I don't remember answering her right away. I wanted her to come, I knew she'd be a great comfort and help to me, but I'd already begun to armor myself against sorrow. "Let's wait a couple of days and see how things go," I said. "I'll call you, of course." My mother's apartment was small, not large enough to accommodate us both, and I knew I could not leave her alone in it, not during those first few days. Alice understood. We had been living together for nearly five years; she was a nurse, she knew about death and grieving. She also knew about mothers, especially this one. We drove in silence from our house near the beach in Santa Monica to the airport, half an hour away. Southern California's pale early November sunlight seemed incongruous to me, almost an insult.

I recall nothing about the trip except my arrival. I rang the bell of my mother's apartment, then opened the front door with my key. A small, distraught woman, whose swollen features I didn't immediately recognize, staggered into my arms. We stood there, rocking together as if nothing could have prepared us for this moment. Over my mother's head I found myself staring at the sympathetic, distressed face of Frank Taylor, an old friend of my mother's in publishing. I smiled at him and shook his hand, as he hastened to leave. "Call me, please, if you need anything," he said, those words we all speak to friends in distress, though not expecting to hear from them and helpless to be of use. He'd been kind to come, I told him, yes, of course, and now goodbye and thanks again.

Tuesday, November 7, 1978. It had been a glorious Indian summer day, my mother wrote about the event later. She had joined Janet in Central Park that afternoon. On their way home, Janet had reached out from her wheelchair to pluck a small branch from a bush full of red berries. She'd always loved flowers and countrysides. At home, later, they'd had drinks and dinner and a last good gossip before my mother had put Janet to bed. There had been much to talk about, because my mother was about to leave her job as the head of the New York office of the Italian publisher Rizzoli. She had been discarded by the new management that would quickly bring the firm to ruin. She'd made her peace with it, but Janet hadn't. So often they had championed one another's causes. That night, when my mother bent over to kiss her, Janet had held on to her and murmured, "I love you, Natalia, I love you so much."

At the hospital, where Janet had been rushed away to an operating room, my mother, accompanied by a friend, had been prevented from following her. "Who are you?" the nurse on duty asked her. What could my mother say? The great love of her life? The person who had meant more to her than anyone else she'd ever known? The woman who had shared her most intimate thoughts and physical tendernesses since they had first met thirty-eight years ago? Does bureaucracy in any form acknowledge love beyond all else? No, of course not. In her distress my mother could not make herself lie and pretend to a kinship of blood, could not be a sister, a niece, even a cousin. All she could think of to say was, "A friend, the only person she has in New York." They lived together, she added, in vain. "Wait in the entrance," the nurse, who had clearly mastered the rules, instructed her.

They sat there, my mother and her friend, in a downstairs waiting room, "for interminable hours, without any information: two women alone in the silence of the night. We didn't speak. We just waited."

Janet had suffered an abdominal aneurysm. The doctors had had to operate, but the young doctor on duty had not held out much hope, "only a ten percent chance of survival." The patient, after all, was eighty-six years old and had not been in good health for several years. In the end it's always a matter of cold statistics.

Shortly after six o'clock, the anesthetist appeared. The heart had failed, he informed them. He handed my mother a small bundle containing Janet's pajamas and red bathrobe, "all that was left of my Janet." The friend took my mother by the arm and ushered her out into the street, then walked her back to her now silent and empty apartment.

I first held Janet Flanner in my arms sometime during the summer of 1941, when I realized that I loved her and that, through her deepening friendship with my mother, she had become family to me. She didn't at all mind being hugged from time to time during the next thirty-seven years, though I think it surprised her when I did so. She would beam with pleasure, cackle, and usually tap me lightly on the arm or shoulder and exclaim, "Why, Bill, dear—how nice!" She was not a woman easily given to public emotion, as her sister Hildegarde observed during the memorial service held for her a week after her death. Janet was in everything "passionate but restrained."

She did love to laugh, though, and she had an unfailingly keen eye for the absurd. The last time I held her in my arms was the morning after that service, when I went to pick up her ashes at the gloomily elegant Madison Avenue funeral home where she had been cremated. All that was left of her then was contained in a small but heavy pewter box, wrapped in brown paper and carelessly tied with ordinary twine. Cradling it, while simultaneously clutching a bouquet of flowers I had bought to ease the dreariness of the occasion, I started off down the avenue back toward my mother's apartment, in what soon became for me the longest ten blocks I had ever walked. Most of the way I was sickened by grief; but, as I turned the corner toward my mother's apartment, I suddenly imagined how Janet would have reacted to the scene—first with a great squawk of indignation at the inappropriateness of death and the lugubriousness of the way we deal with it, then with laughter at the sight of the two of us enmeshed in such a surrealistically comical embrace.

Had she written about it, she would have found some unusual, original way of describing the scene and its effect on her. She'd always prided herself on never saying anything in an obvious or boring way, and she was always outraged by the misuse of language, even in casual conversation. She had made herself over the years into a masterful stylist, the witty and keenly observant writer who had created a literary form with her biweekly Letter from Paris in *The New Yorker*.

At the service, held in the large funeral home chapel, to which so many hundreds of old friends and admirers came that the crowd overflowed, with standees packed along the walls, Hildegarde recalled that Janet had begun her career as a novelist. "I wanted to be Miss Henry James," Janet once said about herself. After some training in journalism in her home state of Indiana, she'd moved to New York, then on to Paris, "her chosen civilization." And there, under the strange nom de plume of "Genêt," which *The New Yorker*'s creator, Harold Ross, apparently thought was the French word for "Janet," she found her true vocation.

"I believe that the greatest event in creativity in the middle of this century," her old friend, the novelist Glenway Westcott, told us, "has been the change and development and refinement in journalism." No one, we all knew, was more responsible for that event than Janet Flanner. Westcott also recalled how she had looked in her later years, "a little like George Washington," with a wonderful beak of a nose, a great shock of white hair, very small hands and feet, and lively eyes.

My mother perched in a front row on the edge of her chair, not scheduled to speak and probably unable to, but ready to pounce on anyone who might falter or stray from the point in a discourse recalling Janet's past and virtues. She owned the memory of Janet now, just as she had finally been able to own her physically in these last three years, when Janet had at last left France to come and live with her in New York. She made Westcott nervous. He dropped his papers, he fumbled with his lines, he wandered in his speech and smiled sheepishly at us; age had caught up with him, too, and his memory was going. "Talk about Janet," my mother whispered fiercely from her seat, so loudly that I felt compelled to put my arm around her. I was afraid she would try to tell Westcott what to say. Alarmed, the novelist rallied, managed to find the relevant part of his discourse, and spoke his lines.

The years had claimed so many of Janet's old friends, crippled others. I had to help the playwright Lillian Hellman up the three short steps to the stage. Nearly blind, she could not rely on notes, but her mind was focused and clear. She remembered how kind

Janet was even while she was being "recognizably witty," two qualities that rarely flourish in company. "I have long thought that most people's deaths diminish the rest of us," Hellman said, "but that certain deaths do more than that. They don't seem to me to have much to do with the talent of the person or how good or bad they were. It's that some strange complex of remarkable qualities that have come together never can be duplicated again. And it's those deaths we feel most saddened by, most grieved by."

Hildegarde—a poet, small, stooped, a more feminine replica of her older sister, with the same fair complexion and crop of white hair—spoke last, in a soft, clear voice that accentuated every syllable and recalled Janet's own insistence on not mangling the English language. She began by informing us that Janet's literary bent had wavered at least once: "My sister, at age seven, desired to be a streetcar conductor." She also reminded us that, though Janet would be remembered primarily as a "superb urban writer," she had always loved the landscape, not only of France and Italy, but of California as well. Whenever she came out to visit Hildegarde and her family, either in the Pasadena area or the Napa Valley, "her chief delight was to be taken for a drive. 'No mountains, please. They're important, but excessive.' "

"How she adored the multitudinous minute bloomings of the California spring," Hildegarde told us, and then read aloud her beautiful "Prayer for This Day," the closing lines of which read: "Kneel down. We ask no vision, no heavenly light / But simple faith, like faith of grass, in earth / And seed's old dream against the night, the night."

During the ten days I spent with my mother in New York, the mornings were the worst time. She slept either heavily or badly or not at all. She wore her grief like a huge stone that had to be raised from her, inch by inch, from the bottom of a well. The telephone saved us. By ten o'clock it would begin to ring, thrusting the outside world

into the gloom of my mother's kitchen, where we sat struggling
with her despair. There were voices of comfort from near and far;
most welcome were the ones bearing news of practical matters, the
small but insistent needs of the day. I seized on them with relief, serving as my mother's secretary and factotum, forcing her to deal
through me with the mundane realities. Friends came and went,
bearing gifts, bringing comfort. Hildegarde, sweet but strong as tempered steel, lingered for several days, long enough to lend support
and also, by her calm acceptance of the event, to force my mother to
maintain a facade of Roman stoicism, at least in her presence.

It was during this period of her life, with Janet obviously failing,
that my mother had begun going to church again. Not on a regular
basis, but from time to time, as if to check in with God and make
sure He was still there, just in case He might be needed. Like most
Romans, she had been raised a Catholic but came from a long line
of *mangiapreti,* priest-eaters, good citizens willing to acknowledge
the spiritual power of the church but impatient with its meddle-
some intrusions into temporal affairs.

Several times during the week after Janet's death I accompanied
her to her unpretentious local church on Lexington Avenue, a couple of blocks from her apartment. We sat in a back pew, meditated,
lit candles on our way out, not only to Janet but also to my grandmother, Mammina Ester, then walked home in silence. It would
have been unthinkable to linger long enough to hear a service, participate in Holy Communion, or subject ourselves to the indignity
of a confession. I had long ago, at the age of twelve, rejected even
the possibility of submitting to the formal doctrine of the church.
My mother, as a native-born Italian, had proceeded through childhood within the ceremonial pattern of a formal religious upbringing, but, like the rest of our family, had throughout most of her life
simply ignored it. You went, perhaps, to some church or other on
Christmas Eve and at Easter, but only to acknowledge such events
as traditional public celebrations of a shared humanity. Even now,
when old age and death had made her more vulnerable to dogma,

my mother could not yield to forces she had resisted all her life. Her brief visits throughout the rest of her time to places of worship signified no retreat in her convictions, nor any sort of conversion. She was not a hypocrite; she was hedging her bets.

Janet had been raised a Quaker in her home state of Indiana, and so had never had to free herself from the formalities of an entrenched ecclesiastical system. She had always had an absolutely open mind about religion—any and all religions. In Rome, on her visits there with my mother over the years, she had willingly accompanied her on those occasional excursions to the great cathedrals or into the recesses of various favorite family temples, but always to gaze at the art on display in them or to experience the shared enthusiasm of some public event. She, too, had little patience with the clergy and had once in Rome shut the door in the face of a priest who had come, as was the custom at Easter time, to bless my mother's apartment. "We are Protestants," she had said, having been tipped off in advance by my mother that the custom dated back to a time when the clerical rulers of the medieval city used this subterfuge as a way of sniffing out criminals, unbelievers, and possible heretics. "I meant with a small *p*," she explained later, as if anxious not to have committed herself to any established order.

On November 16, the day before I was scheduled to come home to California, a memorial service for Janet was held at the American church in Paris. It, too, was attended by a large crowd of old friends and admirers. The novelist and critic Mary McCarthy delivered what she called an elegy, "a poem of lament and praise for the dead," to celebrate Janet's "informal spirit, vigorous, forthright, often speaking out of school, and yet grand in her nature, magnificent like Lorenzo, first citizen and patron of the arts, with some mythic quality in her like a splendid sacred bird." The image struck me as apt, because Janet, "with her sudden grackle cries and ejaculations of wonder, astonishment, alarm," had indeed been not unlike a wonderfully genial eagle. McCarthy's words, read aloud to her over the phone by a friend, pleased my mother and seemed at last to bring her a healing measure of relief, as if they confirmed her own estimate of irreparable loss.

I sat with her that night in the living room of her apartment, and for the first time since Janet's death we talked about the future. I had work I had to get back to in Los Angeles, including the openings of several plays I had to review for *New West,* the magazine to which I contributed a drama column. I would have stayed in New York a few more days, but my mother told me she would be all right and so allowed me to leave. I reminded her Christmas would soon be upon us and urged her to come out to California early enough to spend as much time as possible with us and with her three grandchildren—my two daughters and son, who lived in Malibu with my ex-wife.

I also hoped that she would be present at my marriage to Alice. We had been living together for nearly five years and had been planning to get married two days after Christmas, in a modest civil ceremony to be attended only by Alice's father, a few friends, and, I hoped, my mother and the children. I didn't remind my mother of this event that night; in fact, Alice and I had already talked on the phone about possibly postponing it. In the end, we decided not to, feeling that somehow a positive thrust at life might help assuage grief. My mother and my children liked Alice and would be supportive. Alice and I wrote to my mother independently from California to confirm our plans.

I miscalculated. Something in my mother had been damaged beyond repair. She wrote to me from New York in Italian, the language we used to express our deepest feelings to each other, to tell me that she would come, primarily to see the children, but would be unable to participate either in our happiness or in "the rituals of Christmas."

"With Janet's disappearance I feel the foundations of my existence missing," she wrote.

> I know you love me so much and that you would like to help me overcome my pain. I'm grateful to you. I will not be a presence up

to the events and celebrations, alas. What I would most like would be to lock myself away in isolation and pray over this mystery that is life, tied by a thread that at any moment can snap and leave you suspended, without direction or strength or balance. We are never prepared for death, unfortunately. Therefore, we have to try to live as best we can—I don't mean materially—but lovingly and spiritually. And that's what I wish for you and Alice.

I consoled myself with the fact that at least she would come to California and not sit brooding endlessly in her apartment. I had never seen her in such despair before, even at my grandmother's death. It wasn't like her, and it frightened me. She was seventy-six, but still an explosive force of nature, the independent, vital woman who had been my greatest friend and supporter, as well as my most dangerous antagonist, for a lifetime. I wasn't afraid she would do anything stupid to herself, but I couldn't accept the picture I now had of her in my mind, defeated at last by love and loss. She had always seemed invincible, even long after I had freed myself from her and no longer saw her through a child's myopic eye.

The consolations of a structured faith had never been available either to Janet or to her. Janet's ashes, in their pewter box, sat now on a shelf in my mother's living room where, I began to realize, they would bring comfort, representing a last tangible connection. We had told Hildegarde that eventually one of us would carry them to California, where Hildegarde wanted to inter them close to those of her late husband, the architect Frederick Monhoff, and a stillborn infant son. They would eventually repose in a circular grove of native redwoods and firs that stretches down a gentle slope to a small creek.

This form of immortality was the only kind that Janet could ever make herself believe in. "I regret not having any religious faith," she once told an interviewer. "I'm an agnostic. Of course, if I find out where I'm going that I was wrong, I'll apologize."

THE BEST
SUMMER
OF MY LIFE

Janet and Natalia met at a cocktail party given by my mother in January, 1940. We lived at the time on East Forty-ninth Street, in a section of Manhattan known as Turtle Bay, in a rented four-story house with a small garden in the back. My mother, her mother—Mammina Ester—and I occupied the first three floors, while the top one was sublet to Tom and Beatrice Farrar, a married couple who had become friends of my mother's on Fire Island, where she had a summer cottage. The occasion was to celebrate the Farrars' return to New York. He was a set and lighting designer who had been working out of town for the Ringling Brothers and Barnum & Bailey Circus. Janet came to the party as the guest of John Mosher, a short-story writer and *The New Yorker*'s movie critic. My mother had no idea at first who she was, only that she was elegant and witty.

They did not meet again until the Fourth of July weekend, when Mosher, who also had a summer place on Fire Island, invited my mother to dinner. Janet was his house guest. I was fourteen, home from boarding school and about to spend my summer vacation on the island in my mother's rustic hideaway. Mosher's house was much larger, with several bedrooms and an open deck with a view over the bay toward Long Island. The party was a large one, and my mother insisted that I stop by at least to say hello before I went off with my friend Bobby Munnell in futile pursuit of the teenage girls who would be arriving later on the so-called moonlight cruises from Sayville and Patchogue.

I remember not wanting to go. Not that I disliked my mother's friends—far from it; but I knew I'd be the only kid there and that, out of regard for my mother, some of the guests would fuss over me, force me to answer questions about my life that I knew would not interest them. But to keep the peace, always a tenuous one between my mother and me, I showed up prepared to make the rounds, mumble my responses, and escape.

Janet dazzled me. She seemed to be the center of attention, as if a shaft of sunlight had singled her out from among the crowd milling about on Mosher's deck. She had launched into some story about goings-on at *The New Yorker* that meant nothing to me but which she punctuated with great cackling gales of laughter that were irresistible. I lingered for nearly an hour just to be around her. When I was introduced to her, she looked at me intently just long enough to take me in, asked me no questions about myself, then plunged back into her party mode. The fact that she seemed to take no interest in me at all was a great relief, especially as it enabled her to go on talking uninhibitedly, hilariously, about a grown-up world to which I had only begun to connect.

The next day I asked my mother about her. "Did you like her?" she inquired, without telling me anything about her. "She's the funniest woman I've ever met," I said. "She's wonderful."

Some of the party had gone dancing that night, up at Duffy's, the ramshackle hotel that was the community's social center. It served food and had a bar with a dance floor and a jukebox. My mother and Janet had danced together, had drunk a lot, had toasted their hatred of dictators together, and had fallen in love. My mother was to describe this second meeting as a *coup de foudre*, a thunderbolt that had instantly sent them rushing into each other's arms and forever altered their lives, as well as mine.

I had no inkling at first that anything of the sort had happened. This was an area of her life that my mother carefully guarded from me and never discussed. Janet was not the first woman to have come into my mother's life; but, with one exception, none had ever become part of our family structure. In any case, at fourteen, I was too wrapped up in my own concerns to pay much attention to my mother's love affairs. Most of my life with her had been spent away at school or at various summer camps. And when I was with her, we led separate lives.

This was fine with me. I loved my mother intensely, but I had become used to the freedom that the long separations from her had made possible. Besides, I had passionate interests of my own that summer. I had fallen in love with baseball and, specifically, the Brooklyn Dodgers. In 1936, when the team managed, after many years of mediocrity, to finish in the first division, I had begun to take the subway by myself to Ebbets Field to watch them play. I listened to their games on the radio and memorized their statistics. Bobby Munnell (a Giants fan) and I played endless games of stickball on the beach, using broom handles and old tennis balls. We'd run down the starting lineups of the two teams, emulating each player's batting stance. It didn't matter that Bobby, who was older and stronger, won most of these games. We played two or three games a day, breaking them up with periodic dashes into the surf. In the mornings, I'd be out and gone by sunrise to fish for crabs or snapper off the pier or to go clamming in the bay. Most of the time I ran around in sandals or tennis sneakers and a bathing suit. I turned the color of copper.

All my mother required of me was that I carry out my household chores (helping with the shopping, pumping the water by hand to fill the storage tank, trash disposal), eat my meals at home, and keep her informed of my whereabouts. For the first time in several years, freed from the supervised activities of summer camp, I was enjoying my life to the full. The weekdays were the best, because most of that summer my mother went back to the city, to her broadcasting booth at NBC, and I was supervised only by my grandmother, who thought I could do no wrong and who cooked all of my favorite dishes for me: *mozzarella in carrozza, pomodori al riso, vitello tonnato*. It was the best summer of my life, even though I was now at an age when I had become keenly aware of sex.

My mother's summer cottage was in Cherry Grove, soon to become a largely homosexual resort. She had discovered the place in 1936, when she visited it for the first time with a group of friends, all gay, from New York. They'd driven out from the city (then a four-hour trip through Long Island's coastal towns), taken a speedboat from Sayville, and walked up to the hotel bar, where they bumped into another visiting party that included John Mosher. They were all looking for a refuge far enough away from the city where they could be themselves.

This was long before the advent of gay pride. The word "gay," in fact, had not yet been adopted by the homosexual world to define its lifestyle. Everyone was trapped in the closet, even those who, like my mother and most of her male friends, worked in the arts or the entertainment business. What they all longed for, especially the men, was a place where they could be accepted on their own terms without fear of the law, without endangering their livelihoods or risking social ostracism.

Cherry Grove was the haven they were looking for. The whole of Fire Island is merely a long, narrow strip of sand that forms a sort of barrier reef protecting the south shore of Long Island from the ocean, with the bay as its lagoon. Nearer the city, the communities of Ocean Beach and Point 0' Woods had already been established as summer resorts, the latter as a snooty private enclave for wealthy WASPs; but Cherry Grove had not yet been discovered, much less developed. In the mid-thirties it consisted of a cluster of cottages raised on wooden posts above the sand, with the hotel as its focal point. Most of the houses belonged to Long Islanders from Sayville, the nearest town across the water, who occupied them mostly on weekends during the warm months. There were no roads, only narrow wooden boardwalks linking the village and the hotel to a single pier jutting out into the bay, and no public amenities. Water had to be pumped by hand from underground, and lighting was supplied by kerosene lamps. Only the hotel had electricity, provided by its own gasoline-powered generators.

Although Cherry Grove was only about fifty miles from downtown Manhattan, it might as well have been in the Bahamas as far as accessibility was concerned. Even after Robert Moses, New York's famous parks commissioner and master builder, began launching his parkways out from the city toward the tip of Long Island, it still took at least three hours to get to Cherry Grove. On a Friday in mid-June, 1937, when my mother first brought me there, the only regular service to the village was supplied a couple of times a day by a ferryboat that took a minimum of forty-five minutes to chug across the placid waters of the bay.

What struck me forcibly about the first trip was the almost manic merriment of some of the passengers just off the train from New York. Simply stepping from shore onto the boat seemed to have liberated them from whatever constraints they had been under all week long. One of my mother's pals, a man in his mid-thirties who worked as a stockbroker on Wall Street, sat across from us with a couple of less formally attired friends. He was dressed in a pin-striped business suit and a Homburg and was carrying a leather briefcase. No sooner had the boat begun to move out of the inlet and into open water than he began to divest himself of his protective disguise. Off came the Homburg, his jacket, his tie; out from the briefcase came a small silver flask. Drinks all around. Toasts, jokes, witty remarks, much laughter. By the time we docked, we'd been included in a party that apparently would go on all night, to judge by the festive greetings exchanged between the passengers on board and the swarm of friends in beach attire who had come to meet the boat.

I went off to camp in the Adirondacks later that first summer on the island, but I came back in time for the Labor Day weekend and spent the rest of my vacation there before going back to school. From the first I was fascinated by Fire Island and my mother's friends. Their cottages, including my mother's, were all within a few minutes' walk from each other at the western end of the village, away from the older section closer to the hotel where the locals from Sayville lived. Tom and Beatrice Farrar had the biggest place, a white two-story affair they had just built called Pride House, plus a smaller one they named Prejudice that they rented to a friend, Douglas Summerville, an antiques dealer.

Except for my mother and Beatrice, who was considerably older than her husband and everybody else in the group, most of this newly-formed summer colony were men. My mother's closest friends among them were Arthur Brill, a textile designer; Allen Prescott, who starred in a popular daytime radio program called *The Wifesaver;* and Gerstle Mack, a writer of densely factual historical and art books, who came from a distinguished old Jewish family in San Francisco. Mack was a gentle, loving soul who from the beginning, and for all the time I knew him, took a genuine interest in me and what I was doing; then later in my career and my family. Brill was the most generous of hosts, and Prescott a brilliantly funny talker. I called them all by their first names and felt in a way that I'd been adopted by them as a sort of mascot—undoubtedly because of my mother, whom they adored.

She must have worried during that summer of 1940 that I might get into trouble. I had begun to have vivid fantasies about girls and indulged them by myself, either in the sanctuary of the bathroom or late at night while lying in bed. She never spoke to me about sex, but always wanted to know what I was up to on the evenings we weren't together. I also had the feeling that I was being protected from something. Arthur, Allen, Gerstle, and others of her friends always asked me, nearly every day, what I'd been doing, where I was going, whom I'd been seeing. I realized, after a while, that my mother was using her friends to shield me from the purely carnal aspects of the gay world, her world.

She needn't have worried. Like most kids, I knew far more about homosexual sex than she imagined. At the age of twelve, when my father inflicted a year at a military school on me, I'd been taken to bed by an upperclassman, who had fondled me and tried to make me touch him. I'd refused, but there had been other similar episodes at the other boarding schools I'd attended. We'd all talked about sex a lot and, as I grew older, it became more and more a major topic of conversation among my male schoolmates. Homosexuals were commonly and contemptuously referred to as homos, queers, fags, faggots, fairies; and the effeminate boys among us were ridiculed and pretty much ostracized. This didn't prevent the rest of us from occasionally getting a crush on some good-looking classmate or indulging in hero worship of some glamorous older student, usually a sports star. None of this led to much of anything, apart from an occasional group masturbation known as a circle jerk, but by the age of fourteen I was not the innocent my mother imagined me to be.

I hadn't yet quite grasped the truth about her own involvement in gay life, but I wasn't troubled by it nor very curious about it. The only other woman who had ever lived with us, apart from Mammina Ester, had been almost a second mother to me during part of my childhood in Italy and New York. I had never questioned any of my mother's domestic arrangements. I didn't think of her as a lesbian either. I simply assumed that she shared her life with other women simply because there was no man available or willing to keep up with her. She had high standards, and I couldn't imagine her submitting to any relationship she couldn't dominate, which ruled out most men. The question of whether or not she went to bed with other women didn't trouble me, nor did the fact that for years, off and on, she had shared a bedroom with a female. I had never lived for any length of time in a household with a man; the presence of women in my life was a constant, the only one I had known. When my mother and Janet fell in love, it was easy for me first to ignore the larger implications of this, then to accept the relationship without questioning it or being upset by it.

One of my closest friends at school was alarmed, however, by what must have seemed to him a peculiar situation. He assumed that I knew nothing about it and that something damaging would happen to me when I found out what was really going on. When I was sixteen, long after Janet and my mother had begun their relationship, he decided to talk to me about them. He had recently discovered Freud and had become a disciple; for months he had irritated all of his schoolmates by constantly analyzing their behavior and relating it to their sex lives or lack of same. He spoke to me in the solemn, kindly tone of an elder addressing an innocent. Was I aware that my mother was involved in a homosexual affair with another woman? How did I feel about that? He wanted to assure me that I had no need or reason to be shocked or dismayed or feel betrayed by it. Freud could explain it all to me; I should read his studies on such cases.

I stared at him in amazement. What was wrong with *him*, I wanted to know. Of course I knew about Janet and my mother. What was the problem? They loved each other, wasn't that enough? I had never envisioned them actually making love, but I knew they wanted to be together, that Janet had joined the family. That was all that mattered to me. And I didn't want to discuss it with him or anyone else. My mother had had a lot of women friends over the years, and what people did in the privacy of their bedrooms was their own business.

My school chum was vastly relieved, he told me. He had worried for weeks about how to enlighten me without causing an upheaval. I laughed at him.

Envisioning my mother in bed with anyone, male or female, was not something that preoccupied me. I didn't believe that women, unlike men, could be exclusively homosexual. My mother had married my father and given birth to me, hadn't she? All women were susceptible to the male. I imagined no exceptions.

As I grew older and well into my teens, I'd occasionally get a crush on some younger female member of my mother's entourage. I'd hang around with them, and once I invited one of them out for a drink in New York, when I was seventeen and home from prep school. She indulged me by taking me to an elegant cocktail lounge off Park Avenue and treating me to my first martini, then dashed my hopes by asking me very seriously all about my studies.

Nothing ever happened with any of my schoolboy crushes. I think these older women were amused and touched by my admiration for them; but even if they'd wanted to indulge my puerile fantasies about them, they'd never have done so. The closest I came to ever connecting to any of them was at Duffy's, when I'd stop by my mother's table there and dance with them—though it was always my mother who most wanted to dance with me. She'd take me out on the floor with her and we'd jitterbug to Glenn Miller or Benny Goodman, while her friends laughed and applauded. I was always embarrassed by these exhibitions, partly because I wasn't a very good dancer (this was the tedious era of the fox-trot and the lindy) and partly because I knew everybody thought it was cute to see a mother and son out on the floor together. Nobody else in my mother's circle of intimates, male or female, had children.

It was a relatively innocent time. During the early years at Cherry Grove, the gay community consisted mostly of older men who kept to themselves. If they had younger lovers, the relationships tended to be stable ones. A lot of drinking and partying went on at the hotel, but at first the clientele was about evenly divided between straights and gays, and nothing too outrageous ever happened there. The groups kept their distance from one another and respected each other's turf. The gay men did not dance together, and no one thought anything of it if a couple of women happened to venture out on the floor. Real men didn't much like to dance, everybody knew that, so why shouldn't women get out there on their own if they wanted to?

On the weekends, nobody paid attention to anything that might be going on. The younger single men who tended to show up then in parties of four or five stuck pretty much to themselves, while the moonlight cruises periodically brought crowds of revellers, some of them unaccompanied teenagers, onto the scene. Bobby Munnell and I would meet these boats as they pulled up to the dock to scan the new arrivals for possible single girls, but most of the time we'd be disappointed or ignored. I counted on Bobby to pick up the girls. He was about a year older than I and also a local, the son of a Sayville couple who had a summer cottage near the hotel. He'd know what to say, how to do it. Occasionally he did succeed and we'd go partying with some girls up to the bar, even though we were too young to buy drinks there. We'd dance with them and then, after a couple of hours, they'd go back to their boat and sail off again. The contact would be just enough to keep me in a state of lubricious frenzy for the rest of the night, until I could find the solace of my hand in the comforting darkness of my room.

My mother knew very well what was going on with me that summer, which was why she worried and had mobilized her friends to keep an eye on me.

Though I was unaware of it, the atmosphere of Cherry Grove was changing. The community had been all but wiped out by a tremendous hurricane in late September 1938. Winds of over a hundred miles an hour had sent the ocean crashing over the dunes, tearing up the boardwalks, smashing houses or carrying them out into the bay, where the following day they could be seen bobbing about like bathtub toys. It had seemed to some like the end for Cherry Grove, but actually the storm helped to put the place on the map and brought hordes of new, younger visitors flocking to it.

The hotel and a relative handful of cottages, including the Farrars' and John Mosher's, had survived, as had my mother's more modest rented digs, looking, she told an interviewer many years later, like a "Rube Goldberg contraption, with things sticking out everywhere." Almost immediately the federal government, acting through the Army Corps of Engineers and the Works Progress Administration (WPA), rebuilt the dunes higher than before, created sand fences, and planted beach grass to help shore them up against future storms. At the same time, property prices had plummeted. No bank or insurance company would back anyone incautious enough to build anything in such a vulnerable area. Lots went for as low as fifty dollars and cottages for only a few hundred. The locals who could afford to rebuild had to rent their houses out for the summer to recoup their investments. Cherry Grove began to fill up, especially on weekends, with a younger, more openly homosexual crowd.

I wasn't bothered by what was going on. Although I'd taken part in boarding school in all that homophobic juvenile posturing and would continue to do so into my twenties, the reality was that I liked my mother's gay friends. They were kind and loving and protective of me, and I had no strong relationship with any other older man—certainly not with my father. As for the younger crowd of unattached cruising males, I had almost no contact with them. They mostly partied together up at the hotel, on the beach, or in their rented cottages, and their nighttime activities were well hidden from me.

I'd heard about a so-called meat rack, where men came together in the darkness to have sex anonymously with one another, but its location shifted from night to night and, that summer at least, no such activities ever took place near my mother's house. A couple of years later, when the meat rack went into operation one night along the secluded boardwalk next to the house my mother had bought, not far from the Farrars' Pride and Prejudice, she stormed outside, flashlight in hand, and levelled a torrent of indignant protest at the participants that sent them fleeing into the darkness. The word went out, and no such incident ever occurred again near her place.

Bobby Munnell and I used to talk about what went on that summer, but he wasn't upset by it either. His mother, Camilla, a plump jolly woman with a great raucous laugh, liked the gays, helped to find summer rentals for them, and had been adopted by them as a queen mother. Like me, Bobby was left alone to live his life pretty much on his own. We bonded, not only because we liked each other, but because we were almost the only straight boys our age spending the summer there. Secretly, I envied the gays because they at least had a sex life, whereas Bobby and I were floundering around in hopeless pursuit of these naive, mostly Catholic teenage girls from Patchogue. The gays could get laid whenever they wanted to; we had only our imaginations and the beast with five fingers.

Although I may have been fairly sophisticated about homosexuality in men for a fourteen-year-old, I couldn't imagine what the women might be doing with one another. If I'd understood it at all, I'd probably never even have thought about bedding any of my mother's circle of friends. Only a few were young enough or feminine enough to be attractive to me anyway, so the question rarely troubled me at all. The conventional view at school was that no attractive woman could possibly want to be a lesbian, not when so many splendid young studs were available to take care of them. Any man could convert a woman to the correct sexual coupling, if just given the chance. Also, everybody knew that while most men were either hetero or homosexual, women were basically bisexual.

This dogma enabled us to fantasize about "threesies" and orgies, a major topic of dormitory and locker-room conversation during my prep school years. Whenever I thought about my mother in this connection, the theory seemed to make sense. She was beautiful and both men and women tended to fall in love with her. Beyond that incontrovertible fact, I made no judgments. I loved her, I was proud of her, and she could still frighten me into obedience with the intensity of her emotions.

I don't remember Janet coming back to the island that summer. She may have, but she wouldn't have stayed with us. My mother's rented cottage was too small to accommodate a weekend guest except in her own bedroom, and she would not have permitted that in my presence that year. Janet had not yet become a permanent part of our lives.

She was spending the summer in Croton, up the Hudson River from New York, and coming into the city from time to time to her Manhattan apartment and her office at *The New Yorker*. She was also still living with Solita Solano, the woman with whom she had left New York for Europe in 1921. They were no longer passionately involved with each other, and Janet had had other affairs, but Solita was very protective of Janet and fiercely possessive. Solita had pretty much abandoned her own career as a novelist to become, in effect, a housewife and part-time secretary to Janet. Natalia, only thirty-eight, very attractive, with an aggressive personality and very strong desires and ideas of her own, represented a formidable threat.

Janet and Natalia must have met frequently that summer. I became aware of it when I came back to the city after the Labor Day weekend. I spent about ten days there before I had to leave for my freshman year at prep school, at Phillips Exeter Academy in New Hampshire, and I saw a lot of Janet. She seemed to be practically living with us, although I never saw her at breakfast. Solita was around quite a bit, too, and I liked her. She was warm, talked to me like an adult, and seemed to be interested in what I had to say. I

asked my mother about her, but she didn't seem to share my enthusiasm for her. "She's an old friend of Janet's," she said, not bothering to tell me anything else about her.

Sometime after I left to go back to school, my mother wrote to
tell me that the Farrars had moved out of the top floor of our
house and that Janet had moved in.

THREE

GENÊT

By the time Janet came to live with us she had already become a minor literary celebrity, well known to the half-million or so readers of *The New Yorker* who read her reportage from Paris. She had not yet achieved the larger recognition and acclaim that would come to her later in her career, but with her regular biweekly Letter from Paris she had established herself as the creator of a new style of journalism—the highly personal, elegant, often witty essay through which she conveyed to her readers an impartial, acutely observed view of events and personalities in the news of the day. At first this reportage had been gossipy and essentially frivolous, reflecting the hedonism of the twenties, but with the coming of the Depression in America and the rise of Hitler and fascism in Europe during the thirties it had darkened and deepened in tone and content, so that no one who cared about what was going on abroad could afford not to read her. Her editors at *The New Yorker*, which had been born as a humor magazine, regarded her with admiration as the correspondent who had most influenced the magazine's style and contributed to altering its tone, making it a serious publication. Even I had heard of her, though I had just begun to read the magazine, after being hooked by looking at its cartoons. Most of what Janet wrote about failed to connect with anything in my teenage view of the world.

Janet had been living in Paris since the fall of 1922, when she arrived there in the company of Solita Solano. The two women had become lovers in New York and had been traveling for months around Europe, mostly in Greece, Turkey, and Italy, before settling into a small hotel on the Left Bank in what became for Janet her chosen civilization. For less than a dollar a day, they rented a large, oddly shaped room on the fourth floor of the Hotel Saint-Germain-des-Prés on the rue Bonaparte and remained there for the next sixteen years. Solita had been writing articles for the *National Geographic* and Janet had a small income from her father's estate. Both women were working on novels and aspired, as Janet recalled many years later, to become famous as quickly as possible. By then, Paris had already become a mecca for aspiring expatriate artists, especially Americans fleeing from the prejudices and restraints imposed on them by a less tolerant society. Janet and Solita had been sharing a secret life together in New York, but only in Paris did they feel free to be open about their relationship.

Janet was a product of the Midwest. She was born in Indianapolis, Indiana, on March 13, 1892, the daughter of a prosperous undertaker and dabbler in real estate named William Francis Flanner, better known as Frank, and Mary Ellen Hockett, a beautiful woman with theatrical aspirations. Janet was the second of three daughters, all of whom were gifted. The oldest, Marie, studied to be a concert pianist and later taught at the Mannes School of Music in New York; Hildegarde became a published poet and essayist. From the age of five Janet aspired to be an author, even though she couldn't yet spell the word. At a private school named Tudor Hall, which she began to attend in the sixth grade, she became fascinated with literary construction. "Diagrammed sentences looked like beautiful architectural drawings of horizontal, vertical, and angled lines on which the sentences' words roosted like birds perched on various lengths of wire," she wrote in the introduction to the reprinted 1974 edition of her only novel, *The Cubical City*. It was a fascination that became a constant; as a writer she spent hours over the construction of her sentences, on the nuances of a single metaphorical phrase. When she enrolled at the University of Chicago in 1912, the only courses that interested her were the writing classes taught by Robert Lovett, whom she called "the only man in western colleges who actually taught writing." She spent two years there, until asked to leave her dormitory for being "a rebellious influence." She later confided to my mother that this may have been because of a passionate involvement with a female gym teacher.

Back in Indianapolis in 1916–17, she began to write pieces on the movies for the *Indianapolis Star*, making her, perhaps, the country's first movie critic. She also worked for a year at a girls reform school and made speeches in favor of women's suffrage. But there was little to hold her in Indianapolis, which she had come to despise for its stifling, uncreative atmosphere. Her father, deeply depressed over the failure of an investment and by his troubled relationship with his wife, killed himself on February 17, 1912, by swallowing poison. He left an estate of about one hundred and fifty thousand dollars, enough in those days to provide his children with small incomes to launch them into the world.

Janet was twenty-five when she arrived in New York shortly after the end of the First World War. She was not alone, because on April 25, 1918, she had married Lane Rehm, a young investment banker who had fallen in love with her back in Chicago. The couple moved into a small flat in Greenwich Village and Janet began to frequent the city's literary and artistic hangouts. She wrote short stories and her wit quickly brought her to the attention of Franklin P. Adams, whose regular column, The Conning Tower, in the *New York World* recorded the comings and goings and bons mots of the literary crowd.

She became a regular at the studio of Neysa McMein, a successful magazine illustrator whose door was never locked and whose quarters were a daily gathering place for artists, writers and Bohemians of all varieties. There Janet met the songwriter Irving Berlin, the columnist Heywood Broun, the actress Ruth Gordon, the violinist Jascha Heifetz, the writers and celebrated wits Robert Benchley and Dorothy Parker. The whole of New York's literary and artistic world seemed centered on McMein's studio. "Neysa was a magical kind of person," Janet remembered. "She attracted all sorts of people to her studio. . . . It was all very giddy and guffy."

One of her earliest champions and admirers was the enormously influential critic Alexander Woollcott, who, along with Benchley, Parker, the playwrights Robert Sherwood and George S. Kaufman, and a gangling would-be magazine editor named Harold Ross, also frequented the Algonquin Round Table, the luncheon group whose exploits and wit Adams celebrated regularly in his column.

McMein fascinated Janet. She was a free spirit, beautiful, glamorous, and generous. She was married but had affairs. She was talked about, envied, admired. Janet felt she could never emulate her openhearted lifestyle, but she was captivated by it. McMein, in fact, was to become the model for Delia Poole, the heroine of Janet's novel, *The Cubical City*.

Despite her acceptance into this new world of artists at work and at play, Janet never felt completely at home in it. Her married life was not going well and she felt guilty about what she considered her almost criminal behavior toward Lane. She wanted to flee from her duplicities and this increasingly untenable situation. Falling in love with Solita, whom she met that winter of 1918–19, turned out to be the answer. Solita had arrived in town as the drama editor of the *New York Tribune* and had solid journalistic credentials; but she, like Janet, was essentially a romantic. She was put off by what she considered the flippancy of the Algonquin crowd and longed to succeed as a serious artist. Fleeing to a place where they could both begin a new life together seemed irresistible to them. So when the *National Geographic* provided the means for escape, they seized it.

In Paris, Janet and Solita immediately felt at home. They ate breakfast every day around nine at the Deux Magots, the soon to be famous café in the nearby Place Saint-Germain-des-Prés, and worked in the afternoons. In the evenings they frequented the gathering places of the expatriate artistic colony, and they soon became regulars on the scene. Janet had friends already living there and she quickly made many others, though mostly not in the world of the small magazines and publishing ventures that had begun to flourish in the heated postwar climate. They did drop in fairly frequently at Sylvia Beach's Shakespeare & Co., the cluttered little bookstore at 12 rue de l'Odeon, where they met other writers and which was soon to become celebrated for publishing James Joyce's *Ulysses*. Janet proved to be shy about meeting literary personalities, but she did become friends with Ernest Hemingway and, later, Scott Fitzgerald, both of whom would occasionally drop in on her at all hours to gossip and talk about writing.

Among Janet's other friends and acquaintances were Djuna Barnes, whom she considered "the most important woman writer we had in Paris," and Gertrude Stein, about whose own work Janet had reservations but whose salon was the central gathering place for the American colony. Margaret Anderson, the editor of *The Little Review*, became a pal, as did John Dos Passos, E. E. Cummings, Glenway Westcott, Monroe Wheeler, and Kay Boyle, all of whom came and went, sometimes spending no more than a few weeks at a time in the city. For Nancy Cunard, the beautiful and highly eccentric English dabbler in the arts and hearts, Janet developed a lifelong attachment. They met in the autumn of 1923, after which Nancy became a fixture in both Janet's and Solita's lives, almost certainly sexually as well as spiritually, and the attachment lasted until Cunard's death in 1965. Cunard was deeply involved with French writers and artists and provided an entrée into French intellectual circles, which was greatly facilitated by Janet's growing mastery of the French language. Within a matter of months, she had taught herself to speak fluent, precisely accented Parisian French.

Janet adored her new life and felt entirely at home among the French. Her mother, however, in letter after letter, urged her to come home. She and Hildegarde had recently moved to Berkeley, California, where they survived the terrible wildfire of 1923. Shortly afterward, Janet told her mother in a brief note that she didn't want to come home. "I can live here without hack work: do not like California because of the absence of art, which I really hunger for," she wrote. "Can't live in New York without extra working. My novel is my life work, then another and another. It is all I have, darling."

That was soon to change dramatically. During the summer of 1923, the writer and fierce feminist Jane Grant, newly married to Harold Ross, came to Paris, where she and Janet saw a lot of each other. After Jane's departure, Janet wrote her a number of letters full of witty gossip and commentary on Parisian life. Grant showed the letters to Ross and suggested he recruit her for his new magazine. Janet was to be paid forty dollars for a fortnightly column about life in the French capital. "I don't want to know what *you* think about what goes on in Paris," Ross instructed her. "I want to know what the French think." "All I really know about what Ross wished me to write, and what I wished for me to write," Janet recalled, "was that it must be precisely accurate, highly personal, colorful, and occularly descriptive; and that for sentence style, Gibbon was as good a model as I could bring to mind, he having been the

master of antithesis, at once both enriching and economical
through his use of opposites."

Janet's first Letter from Paris appeared in the October 10, 1925,
issue of *The New Yorker*, then only a few months old and struggling
to establish itself. The piece had been edited into a single column
out of the first two attempts Janet had made. It was gossipy and
tart and covered a variety of events, from the weather and a strike
by bank clerks to the lectures of Sir Arthur Conan Doyle, the latest
fashions and the popularity of a new nightclub called the Florida. It
set the style for all of Janet's early Letters, although as she grew in
confidence and skill, she began to write about fewer topics and to
cover them in more depth.

Her working methods were exhaustive. She read a minimum of
eight French newspapers a day, clipping out items that interested
her with a pair of shears. Then she would go have a look for herself
at the goings-on and interview the people at the heart of them. She
adored artists and theatrical types, but deeply distrusted politicians
and their official spokesmen. As the political situation darkened in
Europe in the nineteen-thirties and she was compelled more and
more to write about large public events and personalities, she relied heavily on her friends to provide insight and guidance, most
notably Doda Conrad, a transplanted Polish concert baritone who
seemed to have useful connections in high places and had a vast
fund of historical knowledge at his fingertips.

When Janet began to write longer pieces for the magazine, in
the form of Profiles, as they were called (her first one, in 1927, was
on the dancer Isadora Duncan), Conrad was enormously useful to
her, both in her selection of subject matter and in the sorting out
of pertinent material in her research. In fact, whenever Janet
bogged down and despaired of being able to make sense of what
she was about, which was quite often, she would meet with Conrad and other intimates to discuss the possibilities and alternatives
confronting her. She never acquired the self-assurance of an established pundit, and writing was often a slow, agonizing business for

her. She struggled with her style, and in her effort to be original she sometimes stumbled into what one of her editors back in New York described as "Flannerisms"—a phrase or sentence struggling to be born from under the weight of excessive metaphor. Because she was naturally self-effacing and modest about her abilities, she eschewed the personal pronoun and was outraged whenever some editor added the word "I" to her copy. She was enormously proud of her work, and it sustained her whole life; she felt her work gave her life both meaning and a noble purpose. It was the anchor to which she would cling all of her life, which, in her darker moments, she considered a failure, especially in regard to her personal relationships.

The Cubical City was published in New York in 1926 and was respectfully if not enthusiastically received. The critic for the *Herald Tribune* noted Janet's penchant for overreaching herself linguistically, but others praised the story and took note of the author's wit. Sales were modest; but, undiscouraged, Janet immediately set about starting a second novel, which she hoped to complete in a few months by turning out four thousand words a day. This soon proved to be an impossible task for her, especially as she was becoming more and more deeply involved in her work for *The New Yorker.*

Meanwhile, the letters from her mother continued to urge her to come home and in 1926 she did go back for a visit, though she made it clear that her well-being and career were now connected to her life in Paris. Her last link to New York was severed when Lane showed up in early 1926. Janet had been nervous about meeting him, but he proved himself to be understanding and accommodating. He had moved, so Janet was able to divorce him on the grounds of desertion, and all the legal and financial matters were swiftly and fairly settled.

The pressure that Mary Ellen Flanner exerted on her middle daughter was constant and it was to be three years before Janet went back to visit her again. She remained close to her, however,

and invited her to come to Paris for as long as she liked. Janet both
loved her mother deeply and felt guilty about having, in effect,
abandoned her, though she knew she was in good hands in the care
of Hildegarde. She confided in her, except about her unconven-
tional love life, which Mary never inquired about and resolutely
chose to ignore. Her letters to her daughter were full of advice and
consolation whenever Janet admitted to her darker periods of
doubt about her career. "I know I must try to conquer my periods
of gross despair," Janet wrote to her on July 24, 1927. "When I
can't work, I want to die and weep, that's all. I've been so terribly
ambitious and have done nothing. It's a constant grief to see myself at thirty-five of no consequence to public or art. I am pleased
with the entirely new ms of which I have already five thousand
words done. The worst is over since I have decided what kind of
book to do and I feel my *New Yorker* Letters have afforded me a facility in writing that will aid me infinitely." She asked her mother
to forgive her. "You've given us all every chance to be artists—Result?—We are 'talented women,' which is something."

Janet constantly tried to explain herself to her mother, feeling
undoubtedly that she needed her approval in order to feel at ease
with herself. "When I can't work, I have a guilty conscience," she
wrote her that same year, "and when I have that, I can't write you.
It's something old and secret and subconscious, perhaps."

Janet's relationship with Solita remained close during all the years
they were together, but by then in Paris it was an open relationship.
They both felt free to see other women, and Janet in particular had
a roving eye. She liked to go dancing, and frequented dance halls
and nightclubs where she could meet other women; her attitude
toward casual sex was essentially that of a single young male.
None of these affairs lasted very long, but when Solita was once
asked whether she and Janet were still together, she replied that
Janet did still live with her whenever she remembered to come

home. Sometime in the early nineteen-thirties, however, Janet met a woman named Noel Murphy, and by early 1932 she was deeply in love. She remained a resident of the fourth floor at the Saint-Germain-des-Prés, but her emotional life became completely bound up with that of her new lover. Like all of Janet's deepest attachments, it was to last a lifetime.

Noel Haskins Murphy had been living in France since 1920, when she and her husband, Fred Murphy, moved there. Fred had been seriously wounded in the war and had hoped that his health could be restored by living in a part of the world that he already knew well and liked. However, he was subject to nightmares and was often delirious. His health deteriorated rapidly, and he died in May. Noel was almost inconsolable and couldn't bear the idea of losing him. She bought a house in the village of Orgeval, northeast of Paris and not far from where Fred was buried. It was to become Janet's second home.

Noel came from a distinguished New York family, and Fred had also been socially well-connected. His sister Esther was a brilliant conversationalist and his brother Gerald was an aspiring painter. Gerald and his wife, Sara, became famous as the most elegant and generous of hosts, and were to become the models for Scott Fitzgerald's protagonists in *Tender Is the Night*. But Fred had been considered the most brilliant of the talented Murphys, and Noel had adored him. Janet was impressed by Noel's feelings for him and the fact that she rarely talked about him except to say that she still loved him. Noel had an aristocratic disdain for excessive surface emotion, but at the same time she was down-to-earth and unafraid of demeaning herself with household chores or the work of running the small farm on which her house rested. Janet used to imitate her tony New York accent and referred to her as a Park Avenue peasant.

Noel was tall, blonde and slender, every inch the aristocrat. She liked to entertain, and her three guest rooms in Orgeval were usually full on weekends with friends, including, occasionally,

Gertrude Stein and Alice B. Toklas. Noel did much of the cooking herself, and for Janet Orgeval became her weekend refuge. The two-story stone house behind a high wall shielding it from the street was cool and quiet, bordered by a magnificent rose garden of which Janet was especially fond.

Solita, though not a great friend of Noel's, was accepted by her and also spent time there. After the publication of her third novel, which, like the earlier ones, had little success, Solita had stopped writing and began spending more and more time as Janet's unpaid assistant. She clipped and saved everything Janet wrote, and helped Janet with her research and in setting up interviews. She also helped to edit her copy and checked for errors. This role she chose for herself was to become her main function in Janet's life, and it lasted well beyond their final breakup in New York. There is no doubt that she and Noel, along with Conrad and two or three other close friends, were enormously helpful to Janet in those early years of *The New Yorker* Letters, when Janet was still feeling her way and developing her technique to eventually create the style of journalism, elegant and profound, that became identified with her. Janet never again was to think of herself as a writer of fiction, and though she persistently denigrated her talent, unsure until very late in her career about the lasting value of her magazine work, she secretly took enormous pride in it. Her whole life became so inextricably bound up with her work for the magazine that it became for her the entire raison d'être of her existence. It gave her the happiness and sense of achievement she had longed for. As early as 1931, during the course of a letter to her mother in which she complained about her lack of money and her health, Janet also expressed, perhaps for the first time, her satisfaction with her work. "I love my life," she wrote, "and am succeeding at it, late, it's true, but I like [my] work increasingly."

FOUR

ITALIAN
VOICES

The earliest voices to dominate my life were those of women: my mother, her two sisters, and my grandmother. They spoke to me in Italian, because I spent most of my early childhood in Italy and they were native-born Romans. In Italy we were always on the move, from Rome to Taormina to Capri, even to Paris, and back to Rome, so that home was never a fixed geographic entity for me but simply wherever we happened to be. I didn't mind it; I felt sheltered and warmed within the radius of those female voices praising, cajoling, scolding, correcting, teaching, admonishing, always urging me onward to tasks and achievements they deemed worthy of this inconvenient young male in their charge.

The basic problem I posed for them was what to do with me, because my mother had begun to pursue a career in the theater and couldn't take care of me much of the time. She would be off on tour somewhere or other, and I would be left with Mammina Ester or one of my aunts for weeks, occasionally for months. I didn't mind that very much either, because I never felt unwanted and my mother's moods were unpredictable. She could be warm and full of laughter and high spirits, a tremendous source of joy and strength. But sometimes she alternated between excessive concern and overwhelming love for me, on the one hand, and bouts of nervous irritability on the other, the sources of which I could never seem to pin down. I only felt entirely secure in my grandmother's house, even though, as I learned much later, she was herself a formidable presence, with a solid history of willful actions and a trail of men discarded in her wake.

Ester was living at the time with Federico Nardelli, a pale, gloomy-looking journalist who fancied himself a disciple of Luigi Pirandello and wrote a hagiographic biography of the great Sicilian playwright. I remember Nardelli as a lot of fun. He kept a pair of large black snakes on the roof terrace of their house and fed them live mice from time to time. He had also had the small toe of one of his feet amputated, to prove, according to him, that the appendage was useless; he preserved it in a bottle of formaldehyde on a shelf in his studio, where it bobbed gently about for visitors to admire. He also liked to fry buttered noodles for me in a pan, and had once turned a garden hose on a couple of neighboring older boys who had been giving me a hard time. His was the only male presence I recall from this period of my life.

Mammina Ester had been widowed at the age of thirty-five. One of four sisters, members of a noble family of Ravenna called the Traversari, she had married a painter, lithographer, and printer named Giulio Danesi, whom my mother described as "a very handsome man with dark eyes." He parted his hair in the middle and sported a splendid handlebar mustache. By all accounts he was a charming, vivacious sort who loved to socialize and play tennis, but he was a very poor businessman. With his brother, he inherited a studio and printing plant in Rome specializing in photographic reproductions; the firm printed elegant art books. Solvent at first, it was already losing money by the outbreak of the First World War. By the time Giulio died suddenly in 1915 of septicemia, at the age of thirty-seven, the business was in trouble. He had not written a will, and the forced liquidation of the firm left Ester with very little money to raise her three daughters.

Natalia was thirteen at the time. Until then, she and her younger sisters, Lea and Franca, had enjoyed a comfortable upper-middle-class existence in various houses and apartments on both sides of the Tiber. There were garden parties and weekends spent at a private tennis and swimming club along the riverbank. In an old family album, there is a picture of the three girls bathing in the Tiber, then unpolluted. They traveled around town in a private horse and carriage driven by their own coachman. They had been privately tutored in English and French and spent summer vacations at the seashore. Their father's sudden demise threatened to end all that and compelled Ester to go to work.

She had always wanted to have a career, but had been held back by the men in her life. In school she had studied harder than anyone else, sometimes until late at night by candlelight, but her efforts had failed to impress the males of the family. At university in Rome, she had been unable to claim a coveted prize she had won because she could not attend the ceremony unaccompanied; her only brother refused to escort her. Before and during her marriage, she had written magazine and newspaper articles and had been published here and there, but her attempt at a separate career had always been opposed by Giulio, who one day burned the only copy of a lecture she had given on Russian literature. He also objected to her involvement in the women's liberation movement. Nice Italian girls from good families did not do that sort of thing, but Ester had nevertheless persisted. Even motherhood had not stopped her, because servants and nannies had always been available to women of her class, and she had chosen to go on with her journalistic and literary career despite Giulio and a society in which women had no voice and no vote.

When I first learned all of this history from my mother many years later, I noticed that all the men who had opposed Ester's drive for independence had somehow disappeared from the scene. They had died prematurely of disease or in tragic accidents, or had been cast aside. Perhaps they'd become winded in their efforts to keep up, so diminished in their self-love, so threatened in their inherited concepts of manhood, that they had fallen by the wayside like spent refugees in flight from a conquering army.

Ester had never even cooked for her children, nor did she intend to begin doing so now. With the money she earned from her articles and essays in various publications, as well as by taking in boarders, she was able to pay a cook and a maid. Late in the war, on assignment for *Il Messaggero*, then as now a leading Roman daily, she became the first Italian female war correspondent ever to visit a front, where Italian troops faced the Austrian lines. She was given a personal tour of the area by a couple of snappily dressed Italian army officers in jodhpurs. I have a photograph of her, elegantly attired in white shoes, a long white coat, a beret and a scarf, posed in a trench between parallel rows of sandbags. I've always wondered whether the subsequent Austrian breakthrough and Italy's defeat at Caporetto might have been caused by her sudden appearance in a hitherto exclusively male domain.

With her life of ease and being cared for by a man behind her, Ester blossomed and quickly became a force on the Italian cultural scene. In addition to her journalistic work, she gave lectures, promoted women's causes, and took part in cultural activities sponsored by public arts councils and private clubs. In 1919, she became the founding editor of *La Donna*, an elegant, slick new magazine devoted exclusively to women's causes, fashions, and the arts. It became an instant success, and her regular Thursday-afternoon salons, held at the offices of *La Donna* on the Corso, in the heart of Rome, attracted most of the city's best young writers and artists, several of whom fell in love with her. Among the latter was Carlo Tridenti, a brilliant young critic with whom she began a passionate affair.

As a girl, she had been a beauty: small, with long, curly brown hair, full lips and large, almond-shaped brown eyes, a face full of intelligence and resolution. Men fell very easily in love with her and, after Giulio's death, she had as many suitors to contend with as Homer's Penelope. Tridenti, like most of the men who pursued her, including Nardelli, was younger than she, but it seemed to make no difference. Though she had become a bit stout and no longer could benefit from the advantages of youth, what she always scornfully referred to as *la bellezza dell'asino* (the donkey's beauty), she cut a sizeable swath through male ranks wherever she went. Nor were these casual involvements. When *La Donna* was bought by the Milanese publisher Arnoldo Mondadori, who wanted to shift the editorial offices to Milan, she refused to move to the city she referred to as "the moral capital of Switzerland." She resigned, not only because she didn't want to leave Rome, but also because she was still involved with Tridenti.

She became the editor of another women's magazine called *Foemina*. A colleague recalled her working at her desk there. She was elegantly dressed, "her pen held in her right hand from which she had removed a long white chamois glove, her upper torso immobile under her feathered hat, a picture of impassive elegance." (Later, in New York, at NBC, she also worked at her desk every day attired in silk or velvet, with a hat and a veil and in full makeup, a cigarette clamped between her lips as she typed, the smoke curling up into her eyes.)

That she was able successfully to continue supporting herself and raise three small children in the Italy of that postwar era seems incredible in retrospect. Italy had failed to grab much from the peace negotiations at Versailles, and the country had been in turmoil ever since the end of hostilities. The economy was in poor shape, with workers striking and crowds agitating in the streets. In 1922, Benito Mussolini and his black-shirted Fascists took over the government. They immediately clamped down on the press.

Ester somehow managed to continue working during all this,

probably because she had never delved much into politics but instead had concentrated largely on the arts. Among her friends were
Pirandello and the composers Ottorino Respighi and Alfredo
Casella. Gabriele D'Annunzio—poet, novelist, playwright, war
hero, and by far the country's most celebrated literary figure—had
also become an admirer and had made her an honorary legionary
in a superpatriotic organization he had founded to celebrate his
own achievements. He had also become a more than casual admirer, though by then his satyr's gaze had focused itself more
firmly on my mother, only twenty and a beauty.

Ester managed to navigate serenely and triumphantly through
all these tricky and potentially compromising relationships without
either betraying herself or using the men who admired her merely
to advance her career. She may have had lovers, but never more
than one at a time—and they all played second trombone to her
fierce concentration on raising her daughters to become as educated, cultured, and liberated as herself. "She was so modern in her
ideas," my mother told me. "And marrying in Italy after the war,
you can imagine, wasn't a very easy thing." Not only were potential husbands confronted by having to undertake a relationship
with a fiercely independent woman with no money and three children, but also by the realization that theirs was not to be a dominant role in it. This was too large a burden for the average Latin
male. It's no accident that Ester's three daughters would all wed
foreigners. Nardelli, whom Ester did finally consent to marry, was
soon to find the pace too exhausting for him, too, and would also
collapse in a heap after a few years in the dust of her active career.

Natalia and my father, William Murray, met in Rome during the
summer of 1922, when he was traveling in Europe to recruit concert artists to perform in the States on his company's product,
Baldwin grand pianos. He had a background in music, having studied the piano and worked for a couple of years as a music critic for

the daily *Brooklyn Eagle* before accepting a job with Baldwin. He had come to Rome to talk to artists and to see an agent named Palotelli, who represented a celebrated but eccentric Polish concert artist named Vladimir de Pachmann, a noted interpreter of Chopin. If he could recruit him for Baldwin, it would be a coup. Palotelli persuaded his client to sign a contract to play in the U.S. for Baldwin, after which he and his wife threw a dinner party to celebrate the event. They invited their friend Ester Danesi Traversari and her beautiful older daughter, Natalia, then barely twenty.

"It was a marvelous night," my mother remembered, "at a restaurant on the Palatine and overlooking the city. And here was this American." After a lovely dinner, they drove to the Vatican and strolled about the great piazza in the bright moonlight. The setting was highly romantic, but nothing transpired. Bill Murray went back to New York, soon followed by the Palotellis, who lived part of the year there. My mother heard nothing from him.

A year later, she was crossing the Piazza del Popolo and passed in front of the open door of a hotel just as my father emerged. He greeted her warmly, told her he had meant to write, and asked about Ester. Natalia brought him home for lunch, then spent most of the next few days showing him around the city. He was on another of his recruiting and scouting tours for Baldwin, but seemed to have plenty of time for sightseeing. "Then we came home for lunch one day and we were drinking coffee in the salon and suddenly the cup started to tremble in his hand and he asked me to marry him," my mother recalled. "This was surprising to me, because we had never kissed, nothing. So I said, 'It's very nice, I'm very flattered, but I hardly know you. How can I say that I will marry you?' "

He invited her to New York for a visit. She could stay with the Palotellis until they could get to know each other better, "and then you can make up your mind," he told her. She accepted his invitation. "He arranged everything and paid for the trip." Natalia and her sisters, Lea and Franca, were to leave for Paris together, though the two younger girls were only traveling as far as Lausanne, where they were going to spend the winter studying French. The trip was delayed by the theft at the railroad station in Rome of Natalia's luggage, which contained her passport and visa. She took it as a bad omen and told Mammina Ester she ought not to go, but my father rushed back to Rome from Paris and helped her obtain a new passport and visa as well as boat tickets, after which he hurried back to the U.S. Three weeks later, my mother and her sisters left again, and she sailed for New York from Le Havre.

Natalia was bowled over by New York. Never in her entire life had she imagined such a city, with people living and working at a pace that struck her as frenetic. She responded to it enthusiastically. Her older American suitor seemed to know everyone in the arts and cultural life. He took her to concerts, to the Metropolitan Opera, to art galleries, and to parties attended by artists, performers, reporters, editors, critics, promoters, and patrons of the cultural scene. They spent very little time alone together and never made love, but that didn't strike my mother as strange. She was awed by him and tried to imagine herself in this world he had unfolded for her. After a few weeks, she returned to Rome engaged to be married.

She didn't know very much about Bill Murray. His late father had been a railroad conductor and the family had settled in Brooklyn after emigrating from Scotland sometime in the late nineteenth century. Margaret, my paternal grandmother, of Northern Irish descent, was still alive. She was a tiny, cheerful woman who immediately fell in love with Natalia and marvelled that her son had succeeded in finding such a jewel of a girl as a potential bride. She pushed hard for him to marry her and lavished attention on her prospective daughter-in-law, who returned her affection. She was a simple, honest, straightforward woman from a modest background who had saved and sacrificed to educate her only son at Cornell and Columbia. She was proud of him, but was puzzled that he still had not found a bride for himself. The arrival in New York of this petite Italian beauty with her large dark eyes and black curls delighted her.

She became Natalia's champion. By the time my mother sailed back to Italy a few weeks later, the wedding arrangements were already being discussed and plans were being made.

They were married the following year in New York in a modest formal ceremony at the old Trinity Church in downtown Manhattan, where on Sunday mornings my father played the chimes. Alexander Woollcott, portly, acerbically witty, acted as best man. Ester and Lea, who attended the wedding, returned to Rome after the ceremony, leaving Natalia to embark on this new life in a strange country thousands of miles away from home.

From the beginning the marriage was not a success. The atmosphere in New York during Prohibition dictated an active social life consisting of frequent parties and heavy drinking. The couple never spent an evening at home; at the very least they would dine out with friends and then drop in afterwards at various popular speakeasies. Whenever they went to the opera or to a concert, Natalia was entrusted with carrying a flask of hard liquor in her purse; it was inconceivable to go anywhere without one. Most of their friends seemed to be hung over during the day and drunk at night. At the first party to which they were invited after their wedding, the host himself opened the front door. "Well, well, Bill Murray and the little woman," he sang out, as he proceeded to topple through a glass-topped table in the entrance hall.

There were weekends in the country during which everybody seemed to be high all the time either on booze or drugs. During one outing to Harlem for an evening of dancing and jazz, my mother sat next to a young actress named Tallulah Bankhead, who sniffed every now and then from a small silver box containing a white powder. When my mother asked her what she was doing, Bankhead told her it was cocaine and offered her some. My mother expressed alarm and informed her that the habit could become addictive. "Don't be silly, darling," Bankhead replied, "I've been doing it for years."

Worst of all from my mother's point of view was the sex. Bill

Murray proved not to be a tender, solicitous lover. He would simply grab her when they came home from somewhere late at night, penetrate her, ejaculate, and fall asleep. She was not experienced enough to know that there were other ways of making love, and the subject was never discussed between them. He seemed satisfied, and she thought that in time she would grow used to it. Besides, in every other way, he was a good husband—kind, witty, charming, proud of her and anxious to show her off to his friends. Also, she was impressed by his standing in this new world he had opened up to her. He seemed to know everybody, and his friends were the most talented and brilliant artists and writers in the city. He was on the road much of the time for his concert business; during these trips, he would tour Europe while my mother would flee back to Rome until it came time to return together to New York. To an outsider, this could have seemed a glamorous life; but to Natalia, still so young and inexperienced, it was a gypsy's existence, cut off from her roots and a mother she adored.

I could never get my mother to talk much about her marriage. I am certain that she loved my father, but the sexual part of their relationship was troubling. Quite apart from the fact that her husband was not a considerate and gentle lover and that he was drunk much of the time, the mechanics of lovemaking itself disgusted her. She could never understand exactly what it was in the basic act that any woman could find pleasurable. In Rome, as a teenager, she had had boyfriends, but she had never gone to bed with any of them. She was a virgin when she married my father.

Her most ardent and dangerous suitor had been Gabriele D'Annunzio, the celebrated poet and national hero, whom she had met while still in her teens through her mother. D'Annunzio had a wife, whom he almost never saw, and a mistress, the concert pianist Luisa Baccara, but he was an insatiable seducer. He had retired in his sixties from public life and lived alone in his huge villa, the Vittoriale, on Lake Garda in the north of Italy. From there he summoned friends, acquaintances, and potential conquests with boldly hand-written notes scrawled expansively on private stationery bearing his private mottos, including his favorite one, "I have what I have given." He was short, bald, and blind in one eye, but few could resist him, certainly not a relatively innocent young girl in awe of his fame and reputation. Still, it is unlikely she would have yielded to him then, even though, with Mammina Ester's consent, she had allowed herself to be summoned to his presence and had at least spent some hours, if not an entire night, in the villa. She had come, too, as an emissary from the Italian publisher Arnoldo Mondadori, who had been negotiating with the poet for the rights to all his works. It was well known that the easiest way to approach the hero was by send-ing him a beautiful woman. When Natalia showed up with Mon-dadori's proposal, D'Annunzio promptly christened her Sister Chiaretia. (He assigned special names to all of his women.) "Now I also love the little great soul of Sister Chiaretia," he wrote to her on March 1, 1923, soon after their first meeting. He signed the note "Gabriel," though later he was to find another of his religiously in-spired pseudonyms by which to address her.

After my mother's death, I found among her papers a cache of letters to her from the poet. One, dispatched to her hotel soon af-ter their first meeting, bemoans the fact that she had left him sooner than necessary. "Your 'anxiety' caused you obstinately to maintain your departure time of four o'clock!" he wrote. "The train leaves a little before six. You could have given me another beautiful *three hours*. Because you didn't want to give them to me, I didn't want to ask them of you. Oh divine swiftness, mine! Oh puerile haste, yours! I am very unhappy." He signed it "Ariel," an-other of his favorite names for himself.

Forewarned by Ester, who some years earlier may have had her own brief fling with the poet, Natalia appears to have resisted his casual advances during these early meetings. But D'Annunzio was not to be put off so easily and he did not forget her.

●

After I was born, on April 8, 1926, in New York, my mother fled
back to Italy with me. I was a sickly child and nearly died of pneumonia before I was a year old. My mother insisted that I could be
properly cared for only in her native land, where she also had her
mother to help her. We spent winters in Taormina, summers in the
mountains. My father visited as often as he could, but his career
was rooted in New York. Two or three times my mother returned
with him to the city, but never for long. I have no recollection of
any life as a family in New York, except for a large apartment on
East Ninety-sixth Street from which a nanny would spirit me away
into Central Park. I have old snapshots showing my father, mother,
and me dressed to go out—my mother in furs and a cloche hat, my
father sporting an elegant Homburg. What I do remember are departures and arrivals on various ocean liners, romps around the
decks in even the roughest seas, large gatherings of adults in various shipboard dining rooms and salons. We were always traveling,
always in flight, it seemed.

My mother could not stay away from Italy for more than a few
months at a time, always with the excuse that my health was her
paramount concern and that I needed the clean air and superb diet
of her native land to get well. The truth is that she was terrified by
her life in New York. Her early fascination with the city had given
way to a horror of the casual but constant drinking, the rounds of
parties, the days when my father would be away on business and
she would be alone to fend for herself in a milieu she found unfamiliar and strange. Used to working with her mother on various
literary and journalistic projects, on moving serenely and confi-
dently in a world she was familiar with, she found herself alone
and helpless in a society that seemed barbarous and strange. There
were so many parties, so many weekend gatherings at various
country houses, but the pace was always frantic. Everyone seemed
to be making a great deal of money in the stock market without

working for it, which to my mother's conservative European eye seemed immoral, almost as if people were stealing it. At heart, she felt it couldn't last. Only at home in Italy, close to Ester and her sisters and old friends, did she feel in command of her own destiny.

She was in Rome with me in October of 1929, when my father, like so many other Americans, suddenly found himself broke, wiped out by the stock market crash that ushered in the Depression. He wired my mother to stay in Italy until he could sort matters out and salvage what he could from the wreckage. "I was fifty thousand dollars worse than broke," he told me many years later about that period of his life. The party was over.

Having spent most of the past three years in Italy with me, my mother found it was no hardship for her to remain there indefinitely. Also, she may have had another reason not to come home. Soon after her flight back to her native country with me and that first winter in Taormina, D'Annunzio had come back into her life. Again at the behest of Mondadori, she had gone to see him at the Vittoriale on a publishing matter, but this time she stayed in the villa. After their first night together, he wrote her, on October 13, 1927, another of his expansive, seductive letters that read like proclamations from a world entirely divorced from the mundane matters of mere flesh. "Chiaretia," he wrote, "sleep tonight departed from me as if dancing. You went away from me *dancing*, between the great walls of silent books! And I was overcome by one of those depressions—which I know—blacker and more impenetrable than death. Depression, oh perverse sister, is the secret wound of the Invulnerable One. But I just had in my hands your small nubile breasts, fresher than the dawn over the waters of the still sleeping lake." He tells her how insomnia kept him up all through the night until dawn and how he finally awoke after noon to find her wedding ring on his nightstand entwined with his own. He returns it to her, along with an elixir he calls "drops of the Abruzzi, which cure or alleviate every ill." He deals briefly with practical matters, then concludes that even as he writes he sees only her face at his knees. "The whites of your eyes, oh dark Chiaretia, sometimes invade your entire body, so that you see and express yourself with a single look, from your forehead to your big toe. And from the nape of your neck to your heel you are a desirable youth of the time of Praxiteles. I take you. 'Burn me!' I told you last night. I am burning." Again he signed it "Ariel."

The last of D'Annunzio's letters to her were written in 1930, and I doubt that the affair lasted more than a few weeks or months. In any case, she was only one of the many women the poet seduced and who flitted through his life like migrating birds. For her, however, the experience must have been far more significant, introducing into her life an element of intrigue and high romance. Her generation had grown up during the years of his dominance of the Italian literary scene and in the glow of his patriotic exploits during the First World War, when the poet had flown a small unarmed plane over Vienna to drop propaganda leaflets and driven a torpedo boat into the bay of Fiume to sink an Austrian warship. Then there had been the postwar occupation of Fiume on the Yugoslav border, when D'Annunzio, at the head of a few hundred volunteers, his so-called Arditi, had occupied the town in protest at its being turned over to Yugoslavia by the peace treaty and had remained there for sixteen months before being forced out. No other literary figure had ever established himself as such a man of action and national hero. Benito Mussolini and his Fascists imitated his bombastic style and copied his uniforms, with their black shirts, braid, and ceremonial daggers. What could going to bed with such a man have represented for her? It was a subject that she chose never to discuss with me. "After I am gone, you'll find out," was all she ever said about it.

It was also during this period of her life that my mother began to have relationships with women. They alone seemed to provide for her the warmth and affection, as well as sexual satisfaction, she needed. Certainly, the men she knew had never offered her much of a choice. D'Annunzio at least had the reputation of being a passionate lover, but by the time she went to bed with him he was well past his prime and sinking into an eccentric and degenerate old age, his glory years well behind him. My father and the new world he represented had turned out to be disillusioning. She was happiest in Italy with me and Ester and in a new relationship with an English-born woman named Joan du Guerny.

Growing up in Italy, surrounded by extraordinary women, I had no idea who my father was or even if he existed. I never asked about him, and no one ever told me anything. Bouncing about from one household to another, with one full year, at the age of six, spent in a boarding school in the French part of Switzerland, I grew up as a little Italian boy, speaking only Italian and French. No one ever informed me I was a native-born American, and I wouldn't have known what to do with the information if I had been told. I had a child's instinct for survival and adapted like a chameleon to every new surrounding. The longest uninterrupted period of time I spent in any one place during those very early years was at Chaperon Rouge, near Chesières in the Swiss mountains, a school to which I became so attached that I tried to hide when my mother showed up one day to pluck me out of there. She was dressed all in white and accompanied by Joan du Guerny, tall, elegant, and also all in white. I was dazzled by the two of them, but I had to be literally pried away from the playhouse on the side of a mountain slope where I had taken refuge, after being told by one of my teachers that my mother had come to take me away.

We went back to Rome and, a few months later, on to the island of Capri, where my mother had rented a small whitewashed stone house high above the main harbor and only a short walk from the central piazza. My grandmother and my Aunt Franca periodically came to stay with us. Then, one day, Joan du Guerny reappeared. We took the funicular down to the port to meet her, waving her ashore from a launch in the prow of which she stood, again dressed all in white, like Lohengrin arriving in his swan boat.

Joan was a tremendous addition to my life. She had beautiful green eyes, a great scoop of a nose, and seemed to bound through life like a big cat. She was also bright, funny, outspoken on every subject, and she immediately appointed herself my friend and champion. She had married a French count and spoke fluent French, but with an English accent that seemed irresistibly comical to me. The count had long since been discarded, another in the long list of males dumped overboard by the women I knew. My mother and Joan had met the summer before on the French Riviera and had been more or less living together ever since. On Capri, they seemed to be always going off to picnics, lunches, dinners, and parties, while I led an idyllic boy's life romping on the island's pebbly beaches, swimming, kicking soccer balls, riding donkeys, stealing grapes from neighboring vineyards, and generally enjoying myself. I must have studied, but I don't remember a single day spent in a classroom anywhere. All the women, especially Joan, read aloud to me, and I began to acquire a library of my own. My favorite publication was an Italian children's magazine called *Girotondo,* to which my mother had begun to contribute when she was still in her teens, long before I was born. Much of the time I was cared for by Teresina, a local peasant woman with a delicious smell of warm earth about her and a nephew, Carmine, a local fisherman, who would often take me out with him on his boat. I soon mastered the local Caprese dialect and once again blended into my scene as invisibly as I had in all the others.

For much of the year that I had spent in Switzerland, my mother had been touring the Italian provinces as the ingenue lead in an Italian repertory company, with Joan tagging along. The company put on a new play every week, so my mother was always in rehearsal during the day and on stage at night. It was an exhausting schedule, but she was determined to find out whether she could have a career as a full-time professional actress. She could also play the guitar and sing in a dark untrained alto voice that car-

ried well even in a large theater. (It was in Rome, while singing in a
musical variety show later that year, that she met and became
friends with Anna Magnani.) By the time I was rescued from Chaperon Rouge, however, and we went to live in Capri, she must have
decided that a performing career was both too chancy and time-
consuming.

"I had to work, because your father lost all his money in the
crash of 1929," she told me some years later. "I was in Italy with
you when it happened and he sent me a telegram telling me to remain abroad until he could begin to earn money again." He must
have begun to do that and was helping to support us by the time
we went to Capri, because during the year or so we stayed on the
island my mother, deeply involved with Joan, apparently kicked
back into a sybaritic lifestyle once associated with the roaring
twenties. The rest of the Western world had tumbled into the Depression, but on Capri the dancing and singing went on uninterrupted. The Fascist era had not yet clamped down on the good
times, and Europe was still at peace. "People gave the most wonderful parties," my mother recalled. "It was such fun and all so gay.
It was living in a dream."

The dream ended abruptly one day when a letter arrived from
my father asking for a divorce. My mother was stunned. She apparently hadn't thought much about what the future might hold,
but my father's letter hit her very hard. Her attitude changed. Despite her bohemian upbringing, she proved at heart to be a true
Roman bourgeoise. Marriage was not an arrangement to be conve-
niently discarded at the first crisis. It never occurred to her simply
to accept my father's demand; it was her duty as a wife to rejoin
him and try to patch up their marriage. If she hadn't made the decision to return to New York, I might have grown up as an Italian
with an oddly Anglo-Saxon name, destined perhaps to surrender in
the Second World War to the Allies in North Africa or to vanish
forever on the Russian front.

FIVE

A CONSCIOUS FOREIGNER

Forced to deal more and more during the nineteen-thirties with politics and public events as Europe began its swift slide toward another world war, Janet, from her advantageous perch in Paris, became for *The New Yorker* the correspondent who most influenced the changing editorial shape of the magazine. Her columns evolved away from her early quirky, gossipy style to deal in much greater depth with the riots, scandals, and political crises that were toppling French governments and threatening to destroy the republic itself. She had no idea, nor did anyone else exactly, what shape some new form of government might adopt, but she was convinced that a big change of some sort was coming. "The French are so filled with fear of Communism on one side and hatred of Hitler on the other," she jotted down in a note to herself, "that they cannot even go Fascist to save themselves from Bolshevism. I think the country will go Fascist in some form, but they must have one man to follow; maybe he isn't even born yet. Maybe America has in Roosevelt a *faux grand homme;* well, a *faux* is pretty satisfying. He becomes a figure to follow and love. *People remain pilgrims;* they love to love, they yearn to follow, to believe, to put trust in. It's a human necessity which democracy, ironically, has deprived them of, in seeking to serve everyone."

As this sort of thinking began to infuse her writing and her Letters took on an increasingly political tone, Janet worried that her editors, and especially Ross, would object. When no one did, she felt reassured, though she remained troubled by the editing to which her copy often was subjected. As early as 1929, she had written to Katharine White, with whom she engaged in a brisk correspondence over the early years, protesting changes. "Who in God's name is my editor now, if not you?" she asked. "Do drop me a note, at least, to tell me your news and promise you have slain whoever cuts my Letters: the castration of the few bright lines they contain is really *idiotic* editing: it's so much simpler and sensibler to cut out one whole paragraph and leave the others intact. (If you did the editing, darling, I'll have to start cutting my throat!)"

Katharine White did, in fact, do much of the editing of Janet's copy, though others had a go at it as well, and it's unlikely White would have been the culprit in the above complaint. Younger, more ruthless types, such as Wolcott Gibbs, would have been more likely to manhandle a writer's copy than she. White, then in her early thirties and newly married to the writer E. B. White, had become almost since the founding of the magazine Ross's most trusted senior editor. It was always she who dealt with the larger issues of what the magazine's staff writers were up to and the overall editorial procedures to be followed. Gibbs and others were entrusted with the copy itself. On January 12, 1932, Gibbs tried to fend off a possible Flanner protest by a preventive apology for having had to heavily edit Janet's profile of the soprano Lily Pons as well as a Letter from Berlin. "I had to be particularly drastic with the Berlin thing, because it was almost twice the length we could take care of, mechanically," he explained. Not only had he had to cut and rewrite, however, but he had also had to add some material, "probably even more unfortunate." This was the trouble with having to edit copy from abroad in an era when communications were still relatively primitive and *The New Yorker* was up against weekly deadlines. Whatever agonies Janet may have suffered during this period, it was always Katharine White who wrote to reassure, encourage, suggest and placate, after conferring with Ross as to what they wanted her to write about and from where.

On the whole, however, Janet accepted *The New Yorker*'s editing, and there's no doubt that she was becoming a far better writer because of it. Her letters to Katharine are full of local news and observations about what is going on and who is doing what to whom, as if testing her material by subjecting its possible pertinence and significance against the anvil of the editor's judgment. Both Ross and White had strong ideas about what guidance, and how much, the contributors needed from them, and Janet, at this stage of her career, was one of the writers who required the most nurturing.

As life in Paris became more difficult and expensive, with the value of the dollar plunging against the franc, Janet branched out and began to contribute an occasional Letter from London. She was barely surviving financially and had been casting about for additional sources of income. She'd been approached by other American magazines to write for them, and had tried her hand at it; but obviously any such assignments tended to conflict with her *New Yorker* work, and she was soon forced to give up the idea, especially after Katharine White, who had discussed this development with Ross, tactfully poured cold water on it. Her efforts from London were initially well received, especially a profile she wrote of Queen Mary, and the new arrangement looked as if it might work out. Janet continued to reside at the rue Bonaparte, between her visits to London, where she had rented a small flat in a house on Clarges Street, near Shepherd's Market. The arrangement improved her finances, but soon began to put too much pressure on her. It became evident to her editors in New York that, though the London essays were competent, they lacked the piquant brilliance of her Paris writings. Luckily for Janet, by the time she began the London correspondence she had acquired a new editor at the magazine, the man who first understood her true potential as a journalist and who was for the rest of her career to watch over and guide her through the stylistic changes both she and the magazine were to undergo.

This was William Shawn, who joined the staff of *The New Yorker* as a reporter in 1933 but who quickly found his true niche there as an editor. He contributed ideas and synopses for possible stories and soon began to take a direct hand in the actual editing procedures. One of his first tasks was to take on Janet's Letters, primarily because at the time she was one of the few staff writers the magazine had under contract. He saw even in her early efforts a depth of talent and abilities the writer herself was unaware of. As time passed and she began to improve, he became an admirer. "Her style, which had so much humor in it, seemed to be brilliant and stylish, and because it was so brilliant and stylish, it was not taken as seriously," he told me a few years before his death. "She never pretended to be a big intellectual or heavyweight in any way, but her light reporting was better than most of what was being done at the time."

Shawn had been born William Chon in Chicago in 1907. The family, of Russian Jewish descent, was solidly middle class; Shawn's father owned a cutlery shop. The boy changed his name because he wanted to be a writer and didn't want to be mistaken for Asian. He worked in various newspaper jobs and in 1928 he married Cecile Lyon, a reporter on the Chicago *Daily News*. When the photo agency he was currently employed by folded, Cecile took a leave of absence and the couple went to Paris, where they stayed for nearly a year. Shawn, an excellent jazz pianist, earned some money playing in nightclubs. Janet remembered catching a glimpse of him in 1929, when he was playing every night in a bar called La Chaise.

The editor, however, did not recall meeting her, and there's no real evidence they ever did meet before 1939, when Janet showed up in New York and was finally introduced in person to this shy, self-effacing young man who had become her principal editor. Shawn was short, already quite bald, with bright pink cheeks and so ex-quisitely polite that he seemed always to be about to apologize for his existence. Behind that unprepossessing exterior, however, was a shrewd, brilliant mind and a character as tough as tempered steel. He was never confrontational, but he always seemed to get what he wanted from his writers, which, essentially, was the best they had in them. For Janet, insecure about her status and unsure of her technique, there could have been no more perfect a professional re-lationship than the one with Shawn. Even after he succeeded Ross to the editorship of the magazine, after the latter's death in De-cember 1951, he continued to edit all of her longer pieces, the ones she signed with her own name.

From the earliest years of this collaboration, Shawn had no doubts about Janet's true potential. "Her style threw people off," he explained, "the fact she had so much wit and such a dazzling way of writing. People didn't realize how sound her reporting was. It went beyond mere entertainment, though it was entertainment most of the time. Having started in the nineteen-twenties, her writing reflected her times."

The success of the magazine coincided with the Depression that followed the financial crash of 1929. Few people connected to the publication's fortunes, however, were even aware that there was a Depression, partly because *The New Yorker* had begun as a humor magazine and its social commentary mostly ignored politics and economics. Ross himself was ignorant about the rise of fascism in Europe and wasn't at all sure as late as 1935 that Adolf Hitler was important enough to merit the long Profile that Janet wrote about him that year.

This attitude began to change as it became clear even to Ross that the country was in a mess and that in Europe forces were at work that threatened to plunge the western world into another major war. And as the tone of the magazine began to change, so did Janet's writing; her pieces became models for the sort of serious but brilliant reportage that established the magazine's reputation. "Her style evolved in conjunction with how the magazine was changing," Shawn recalled. "The most dramatic change could be traced from September 1939, the start of the Second World War, but prior to that there had been the Spanish Civil War, the Italian invasion of Ethiopia, a lot of very unfortunate world events that passed by and were hardly noted in *The New Yorker*. As soon as Janet began to pay attention—and the impulse came from her, not from her editors at the magazine—there were automatically changes in the sort of stuff that began to appear in the magazine, not only in Janet's copy. It became a more socially and politically responsible magazine." Shawn found working with her one of the most satisfying experiences of his career as an editor. "I can't remember ever having an argument with her, nor her ever having an angry exchange with anyone," he said. "She was also unfailingly kind to the secretarial help, the fact checkers, even the humblest employees on the staff."

In January 1936, Janet went back to America on a visit, although apparently she spent no more than a few days in New York and for some reason did not meet Shawn. She went on to Indianapolis, where she received a hero's welcome, and then to California to see her mother and Hildegarde. She told Katharine White that she wanted to give up the London Letter, but that she also needed to make more money. Other publications, including Time, had again contacted her about coming to work for them. White was alarmed. Whatever the problems with the London pieces, they were still far superior to anything anyone else was writing from there, and the possibility of losing Janet's French reportage was unthinkable. White and Ross ended up persuading Janet to stay on with the London correspondence, while also assuring her that she would be given the freedom to spread out a bit in order to contribute articles and Profiles from elsewhere in Europe. Her basic schedule would consist of some forty pieces a year, enough to keep her very busy for *The New Yorker* exclusively.

It was a backbreaking arrangement. Just shuttling back and forth from Paris to London by train and Channel ferry, the latter very rough in bad weather, was a major nightmare. Nevertheless, Janet persisted, and her work continued to be appreciated in New York. She herself, however, was becoming increasingly uneasy with her situation. Mussolini's flouting of the League of Nations to invade Ethiopia, the Fascists triumphant in Spain, Hitler's successful bullying tactics and saber rattling—all these developments had convinced Janet that war was all but inevitable. She didn't think she'd be able to function as a reporter in such circumstances. Her habit was to sit at her desk reading, clipping, and pondering, or to venture out for the one-on-one interview; she knew she wasn't the type to hustle down a quick story in a hectic onrush of events. She was too old, too set in her ways for that, she told Katharine White, and asked if there weren't some way she could work for the magazine in the States. When *The New Yorker* insisted that it wanted her to remain in her present role, she resigned herself to the task and set about figuring out how to go about it.

On April 14, 1939, Janet wrote to St. Clair McKelway, then the magazine's managing editor, saying that in case of war she might hole up in Orgeval, where she had her own room and had just helped pay to put in an extra bathroom. "If things get bad, I will try to come home on a warship or whatever they will be taking us off on," she wrote. "Noel says she will stay. She feels she can't leave, that is her home; she is a fatalist and has great physical courage and vitality and strength." Janet didn't think she'd be able to survive under a continual bombardment, and she had no doubt that the Germans were capable of subjecting entire populations to this sort of terrorism, having witnessed at first hand in 1935 a four-day military air show in Nuremberg featuring superbly trained troops. "I love German language, food, baroque art," she confessed, "I have always disliked the Germans as people, from 1909 when I first lived in Berlin, till tonight, and through tomorrow to the end of my days. They are bullies, whiners, ferocious obedient organizers and organized men; they are out of their century, are still medieval, with a lust for combat, conquest, capture and seduction. God help us all."

On June 29, Janet wrote McKelway again, telling him that she was planning to come back to the States in September. Her mother was in poor health and she'd have to stay with her for at least several months. She had begun to feel that perhaps "the strange and private diplomacies" of Neville Chamberlain, the British prime minister, might succeed in preserving the peace, at least for a while, though she recognized that Hitler's continued demands would dictate the actual course of events. She viewed her forthcoming trip home as a visit, but that all depended on whether war broke out or not. It had become clear to her that she would not make a good war correspondent and that she might be unable to remain in France.

One of her problems, she confessed to McKelway, was that she couldn't write fast enough. It was all she could do to maintain her present schedule, although she thought she could always earn some extra money by occasionally turning out pieces "for other people who now pay me, thanks to my being on *The New Yorker,* those high prices which are the reward for our virtue." But she assured McKelway that she "could never abide to work for anyone else, because I could never find the same mixture of lunacy and leniency."

At this stage of her life, with the crisis in Europe threatening to shatter her world, Janet continued to worry about her writing. "As a writer I fear you have to wash behind my ears more than for the rest of the staff," she told the editor. "I have a passion for complicated sentences, but I struggle against my vice more than I used to. . . . The trouble with me is that I really adore to write and I go into a kind of séance with every page."

Janet spent much of that summer in Orgeval, with occasional trips into Paris to sniff out the news. It was a strange, disordered, almost lunatic time. Restaurants, cafés, and nightclubs were full and everyone seemed to be giving elaborate parties, as if there were something to celebrate. When French and British troops paraded on Bastille Day to celebrate the hundred and fiftieth anniversary of the French Revolution, huge crowds of revelers turned out to watch them and afterwards milled about the streets and squares, turning the city into a giant outdoor party. It was hard to know what to make of such scenes. Many people had already begun to evacuate the city and others were crowding the stores to lay in supplies of food and other necessities, but in some quarters there was an attitude of devil-may-care, as if nothing would or could happen just so long as enough people denied the reality of the situation. Janet's own feelings wavered from day to day between the certainty that war was inevitable and the possibility of at least several more months of peace based on Chamberlain's program of appeasement.

On September 1, however, Hitler's armies invaded Poland, and two days later France and Britain declared war. The long party was suddenly over and Paris shut down, with shops and restaurants closing up early and people scrambling into air raid shelters during the frequent drills punctuated by the wailings of sirens. The Germans were much too busy laying waste to Poland to spend any time on France at the moment, but everyone knew this period of false tranquility could not last. In the meantime, Janet still had no idea exactly how to cope with her situation.

The New Yorker wanted her to stay on, at least until October, when Janet had arranged to spend three months in the States, mostly to be with her sick mother in California. After that she would presumably return to Paris; America was not going to war with Germany, and the magazine wanted somebody on the spot to report on goings-on during the hostilities. On September 4, the day after war was declared, Janet wrote McKelway that she was making arrangements to send her copy by mail only, since it had become impossible to telegraph anything without having it censored by local authorities. She said she already had enough material for two Letters, but confessed she might have nothing to say worth sending after that. "I cannot compete with the American newspaper men in Paris, who have not only a vast organization at their command, but also a newshound instinct," she wrote. "My being only a commentator puts me in a curious isolated corner." She pointed out that she had "always written to one side (or behind or around the corner from) the regular news," but she assured him she would do the best she could. She planned to remain in Orgeval, with occasional forays into the city to find out what was going on.

By the middle of the month, however, it had become clear to both Janet and Solita that they couldn't stay on in France. Quite apart from her doubts about being able to write anything worthwhile under wartime conditions, Janet was also clearly afraid of what might happen. She had no stomach for heroics and wondered if she'd be able to stand up under bombardments and shellings and a German occupation. Early on the morning of September 16, Noel drove Solita and Janet out of Orgeval to Bordeaux, taking along four suitcases and thirty-five gallons of gasoline. When they arrived there, they found thousands of other Americans all trying to book a passage home. They managed to get a hotel room and settled in to await their turn, which came three weeks later, on October 5. Noel, true to her commitment, remained behind, which filled Janet with admiration and some anguish.

Safely back in America, she spent a few days in New York, then hurried on to Altadena in California to help take care of her mother. *The New Yorker* soon wanted to know what Janet's plans were and whether she intended to return to France. The war in Europe seemed to have settled into a stalemate, with nothing of much note happening. The Germans seemed content to consolidate their easy conquest of Poland and, except for the occasional air raid warnings, life in Paris appeared to have become quite livable. No one knew what the spring would bring; it was even possible to believe that the stalemate would be permanent.

In mid-February, Janet wrote to Shawn that she did want to go back to France, but not before late April or May. This decision would be conditioned by what might happen there. "If there is the big bloody push, with Paris bombed, gas, measle germs in parachutes, etc., which some, indeed, may now envisage, I shall not, should not return there because I would be of no use," she said. "The kind of work I can do wouldn't be that kind of reporting; for that work would be needed, as I've told you, a writer who is male, young, fighting-minded; my age, sex, Quaker upbringing would make me a poor leg-man in those conditions." Foreigners were not wanted in France now and she did not want to go back to become a useless body on the scene of a catastrophe. Unlike Noel and other friends still there, she did not feel French. "I have never had a strong sense of nationalism, either about Indiana or the USA or France or even Jerusalem, as a Christian," she continued. "I like the French mind better than any other, that's all I have to say about geography, and that resides in the head; I think I think more clearly, as a mortal activity, than if I'd remained in Indianapolis all my life, or even in Greenwich Village where I first resided in New York. But for this I owe nothing, since these cannot be debts but participations. Maybe the only helpful notion at this moment is seeing France as clearly as the French see it, too; and I know I have lived there as a stranger and a foreigner for nineteen years. But I was a conscious foreigner; in California I feel an unconscious one, a kind of immigrant, without thought."

Janet was depressed by having had to watch her mother's descent into an infirm old age, requiring constant attention, and she told Shawn that it had affected her ability to make decisions about her own future. "My answer is one of my characteristic, snail-horned, slow, progressive, mica-like affirmatives," she explained.

"Indeed, on goading myself, I see my answer is yes, even if there is a Hitler push; for then all decisions would be taken from my hands. . . ."

She said she would live in Paris, because it would be much easier there, with gas rationing and disrupted public transportation, to be on top of events and she outlined several possible subjects to write about. She would sail back to Europe on an Italian ship, possibly linger long enough in Rome to do a Letter from there, then proceed into France via Cannes for a possible article from the Riviera. "A Swiss Letter would be interesting," she observed and added that she was dying to go down into the Balkans, to Bucharest or Belgrade. Yes, there would be all sorts of things and scenes to write about, war or no war.

No one imagined that Hitler's war machine would soon sweep across Belgium and France in a matter of a few weeks, pushing the Allied armies into the sea at Dunkirk. Not even Janet foresaw the efficient devastation the Germans were capable of. In the spring of 1940, back in New York and with no plans any longer to go back to Paris, she settled into an office at *The New Yorker* for the duration of the war. With the fall of France and the creation of the Vichy regime, with no interruptions in the form of biweekly Letters, she found in Pétain, the head of the Vichy government, the subject that established her at last as the serious chronicler of events she had always aspired to be.

SIX

A GOLDEN AGE

My mother and I arrived back in New York early in the fall of 1934 and settled temporarily into a small hotel off Washington Square. I had no idea why we had left Italy, even though my mother had informed me that I had been born an American and was coming home to live in my native country. I certainly didn't feel or look American. I was a tall, skinny kid with a great mass of curly hair who dressed in perfectly tailored suits with wide collars and big buttons. I was painfully well mannered and had been raised to believe that my role was to remain quiet and respectful in the presence of adults. When my father showed up at the hotel to see me the day after our arrival, I was as unprepared for the meeting as he was and I had no idea what he expected of me.

He was forty-three years old, but to me he seemed ancient. He was bald, somewhat overweight and accompanied by a small brown dachshund on a leash. My mother had insisted I embrace him, but it was not a success. Did I speak any English, he wanted to know, addressing my mother in barely serviceable French. "He knows 'yes,' 'no,' and 'ham-and-eggs,' " she told him.

My father then took me out to lunch, during which we communicated awkwardly mainly in French. After the meal, he took me into a nearby barbershop, where a sheet was tied around my neck and the barber set to work on me with a pair of clippers. The great mass of curls my mother had tended through my childhood soon tumbled to the floor at my feet. I emerged feeling stripped, but for some strange reason some of the tension between my father and me was eased. We were able to talk to each other more intimately, as if we were actually related. What I wasn't prepared for was the rage my mother flew into when he delivered me back to our room a couple of hours later. They had a short but savage argument, after which my father gave me a quick hug and left.

I couldn't understand what my mother was so angry about. Hadn't we come back to the U.S. because she wanted me to become an American? Wasn't I supposed to blend in and become like everybody else? To please her I began to spout all the new words and phrases my father had taught me during lunch, but nothing seemed to mollify her. She actually cried, which appalled me, because she was not the sort of woman to shed tears frivolously.

I realize now that those first few months in New York must have been very difficult for her. It was only a matter of weeks before I was converted from a well brought up, polite little European boy into an American street urchin. At the Dalton School, a private school which I began to attend that fall, my new friends introduced me into the intoxicating subculture of the comic book and the bubble gum card. I was whisked out of the world of Greek and Roman mythology and the traditional fairytale into the dazzling universe of Buck Rogers, the Lone Ranger, Mandrake the Magician, and Flash Gordon. I learned to flip G-Men cards in the boys' room and toss a football, and my newly fluent English was salted with the hot slang phrases of the hour, all expressed in an accent my mother identified with gangster life in Chicago. I rejoiced in the freedom from my past and its traditions that my new life had suddenly conferred upon me, but to my mother it must have seemed as if the whole fabric of her own life was being torn apart.

She had come back to New York, after all, not just to restore me to my heritage, as she continued to maintain throughout her life, but to salvage her marriage, if possible. When I displayed such a chameleonic talent to become the sort of barbarian she had always despised, a reader of funnies and a chewer of Tootsie Rolls, she must have rued the decision she had made to return. After all, the marriage had not been a success from the start, and what did this new world have to offer her, if she couldn't make her marriage work? She was a Roman at heart, not yet in love with America and uncertain of her relationship with this man who had plucked her out of her milieu, foisted a child upon her and left her dangling between two worlds.

To her dismay I quickly became an American, so committed and fiercely proud of my new status that I even refused to speak Italian or French at home. I adored my new school, where classes were taught on a progressive system that allowed pupils largely to choose their subjects and concentrate on what they displayed the most aptitude for. There were certain basic requirements that had to be met—so much of this subject, so much of that—but essentially we were allowed to master knowledge at our own pace and without the periodic pressure of exams to establish how we were doing. So many assignments in each category had to be completed every month, but no one forced us to accomplish our goals in any particular order. I plunged myself into history, English and French literature, and writing. By the time I was twelve I was editing my own in-house newspaper, which I called *Murray's News*, and had turned out dozens of comic strips and pieces of short fiction, based mainly on historical events and mythical personages. My newspaper, however, dealt exclusively with events at home, under such headlines as "Natalia Murray to Star in Broadway Musical" or "Mammina Ester Flees Fascism and Persecution in Italy."

I also began to sing and act, after discovering that I had a nice soprano and loved to perform. I did most of my singing at the morning assemblies, whenever I was asked, and scored minor triumphs with several of the Roman and Neapolitan songs my mother had taught me. I think now, as I look back over my life, that everything I've loved best I was allowed to indulge and develop at Dalton.

We lived during this period on East Forty-ninth Street, in a railroad flat on the top floor of a brownstone between Second and Third Avenues. Joan du Guerny arrived to live with us soon after we moved in and stayed for four years, until she and my mother reached an amicable parting and Joan went back to France, where she had always been happiest. My mother went to work in the theater again, this time in a Broadway musical called *Revenge with Music,* with a score by Vincent Youmans. Also in the cast was the woman my father was living with, Ilka Chase, who was soon to become a Broadway star as the bitch Sylvia in Clare Boothe Luce's play *The Women.* My mother and Ilka had no idea they would find themselves in the same show, but they managed to keep their distance from each other and remain frigidly cordial. After the musical, which received lukewarm reviews and ran for only one season, my mother appeared in two other Broadway plays, *To Quito and Back,* a melodrama by Ben Hecht, and a drawing-room comedy starring Roland Young. None of these ventures amounted to much, so my mother was happy to be able to accept a job in 1938 with the National Broadcasting Company to beam a daily news and talk show to Italy. The opportunity provided work for my grandmother, who had been forced to leave Italy by the Fascists and had also come to live with us. Although she had always shunned politics, her outspoken contempt for Mussolini's regime had made it impossible for her to function any longer in Italy as a journalist or editor in any field. Also, her relationship with Nardelli was breaking up, and fleeing to the U.S. seemed an opportune move.

I was unbelievably content with this period of my life. I was watched over and indulged and adored by these women I loved most. As for my father, I managed to achieve an uneasy but friendly relationship with him, which consisted mainly of weekend visits. He and Ilka lived next door in a big ground-floor flat with access to a large private garden in back. Ilka and I got along fairly well and even became friends after a while. She was a tall, slender brunette, not beautiful, but witty and attractive to men. She informed me that she loved my father very much and that they planned to get married. This surprised me, because I knew that my mother had hoped to effect a reconciliation and that, as noted previously, her main reason for returning to New York had been to salvage her marriage to him. When I told her what Ilka had confided to me, she became visibly distressed. She had had a meeting with my father, she informed me, at which he had promised not to rush into a divorce. This woman of his was obviously a scheming witch who wanted to break up a sacred relationship. What was sacred about it? I asked her. Marriages were breaking up all the time. Half my friends at school lived with divorced mothers. Besides, I told her, I wasn't going to live with him, no matter what. I would stay with Mammina Ester and Joan. "You don't love him," I said. "You love Joan and Mammina Ester. Why shouldn't he marry Ilka? She loves him, at least." I remember so vividly the odd look of bewilderment that came over her face as she stared at me. Then, without a word, she walked swiftly out of the room, as if I had broken a taboo or said something personally insulting to her. We never discussed the subject again, until some months later when all she said about the situation was that a divorce was indeed taking place and that my father and Ilka were going to be married. I did not go to the wedding.

The weekends with my father were fairly pleasurable, mainly because he opened up an entirely new world for me. He had ceased to be the art- and music-loving intellectual who had so impressed my mother in Rome. He no longer played the piano or the chimes at Trinity Church, and none of his close friends were from the arts or even journalism. While he was looking around for a job after the 1929 crash, he had been offered the chance to run a small radio station by its founder, William Paley, but had turned it down, since he wasn't sure that the Columbia Broadcasting System would ever amount to much. He had accepted instead an offer to run the New York branch of William Morris, a big talent agency with its home office in Los Angeles. The country was entering the golden age of radio broadcasting, and the William Morris clients were among the biggest stars in vaudeville: Sophie Tucker, Al Jolson, Ed Wynn, Eddie Cantor, Archie Gardner, Fanny Brice, and a host of others. My favorite among them was Fred Allen, whose Sunday night one-hour broadcast was the funniest, most sophisticated show on the air.

On the weekends that it was being broadcast from the NBC studios in New York, I would go with my father to the Sunday rehearsals in Radio City, then listen to the show live on the air that night. I never tired of it, and I worshipped Allen, whose cynical outlook on the American scene delighted me. He was also a gentle, kindly man who always acknowledged my presence and asked what I was doing, what I thought of this scene or that act, just as if my opinion mattered. He wanted to know if the jokes were funny, and I think he trusted my reactions, even at the age of eleven and twelve, more than those of his employees, who were well paid to laugh at his stuff and tell him how great it all was. He was the only comedian I ever met who seemed to have no ego to contend with, though he was as insecure about his talent as most performers, who need applause and approval as humbler folks need oxygen to survive. Allen's ability to play second banana to his cast and guests on the show stamped him as unique in a world in which ego is dominant.

My mother had told me that my father had moved in a world of serious musicians and fine artists, but I never saw any evidence of it. His closest friends were his colleagues at the Morris office, most of whom seemed to be tough, wisecracking New Yorkers under five and a half feet tall. My father was an inch or so under six feet, which at his office made him seem like a giant among midgets. "You're Bill Murray's kid, right?" one of the younger agents said to me one day, when I had gone to the office to meet him for lunch. "Your Dad's a great guy. He scares us to death, sits behind his desk and reads stuff in ancient Greek. We need him here because he's the house goy." I had no idea what this man meant until my father laughingly explained the remark to me. I knew by then that he did occasionally read texts in ancient Greek, a holdover from his college days as a classical scholar, but I had never heard the term "goy" before. As for his background in the classics, he never discussed the subject with me, even though I had told him I had read both the *Odyssey* and the *Iliad*, in English, of course, and loved them. He didn't seem interested, and I became convinced that his occasional readings in Greek were staged primarily to awe his colleagues, who had all clawed their way up in show business from one ghetto or another.

Our other activity on weekends was to attend sporting events. My father always had the best seats at Yankee Stadium or at the Polo Grounds for New York Giants football games. We'd also go to boxing matches, Ivy League football games, and the yearly tennis tournament at Forest Hills. Afterward he'd take me to dinner either at 21 or Toots Shor's, restaurants frequented by showbiz and sporting types. When I reported on all these activities to my mother, she often became indignant. Why wasn't I being taken to concerts, the opera, the theater? Why had my father become such a philistine, after all those years as a player in the worlds of the arts and the intellect? "Something died in him," she said one day. "When he lost all his money, he became another person. I don't know him anymore. Those tough agents and terrible comedians he knows now." I think she tried to speak to him once about exposing me to higher culture, but it didn't take.

He did whisk me off one summer for a week of touring the Civil War battlefields and Williamsburg, but the trip wasn't a success. I wasn't as interested in American history as in that of the ancient Greeks and Romans, but my father seemed to have no desire to discuss those historical periods with me, even though his knowledge in those areas was presumably vast. We always had a hard time communicating. He felt uneasy around me, as if I presented a threat of some sort to his own life, while I didn't know what to make of him. We never touched except to shake hands, he never asked me what I most cared about or what I thought about anything, and I didn't love him. He was a stranger who had suddenly assumed a role of importance in my activities that I felt he hadn't earned for himself. My mother's distress at his behavior toward her had also prejudiced me against him. He must have sensed this and so retreated from intimacies he felt would make him vulnerable to judgments he didn't want to acknowledge.

In 1938, we had a major falling out. He had decided that I wasn't being properly educated at Dalton and that, if I remained there through the primary grades, I'd never be able to get into any good prep school or Ivy League college, much less Harvard, which is where he had decided I was destined to enroll. So, without any discussion or forewarning, I was suddenly taken out of Dalton and sent to a small military boarding school in Litchfield, Connecticut, run by an ex–West Point colonel and his wife. I was miserable there, with the regimentation, the hazing, and the brutality common to all such institutions. I ran away from it twice and spent much of the year fighting and fleeing from my tormentors. I lost a year academically, which my father blamed on Dalton, but which was due entirely to the time I wasted trying to survive or escape military school. I never forgave my father for inflicting this needless trial on me, which effectively ended the happiest four years I had known, when I had lived at home and, among other benefits, enjoyed a family life in the company of the women I loved.

I was able to extricate myself from Litchfield, but this time was

dispatched to Fessenden, a boarding school in West Newton, Massachusetts, that specialized in preparing students for the major East-
ern prep schools. It was a more humane institution, and I managed
to fit in there and eventually flourish. Scholastically, the school was
first-rate, and the education I received there ultimately enabled me
to catch up on my lost time and to sail through Phillips Exeter
Academy in New Hampshire in three years. But my father and I
never really patched up our quarrel, and I infuriated him years later
when I pointed out to him that my closest friends at Dalton had
also all successfully gone on to prep schools and colleges without
difficulty. At a dinner he and I had alone at his house one night I
delivered a vivid denunciation of all military schools and the sort
of people who thrived in them. My father, well aware that I was in
effect denouncing him for having caused me so much suffering, finally arose in anger from his seat. "You young whippersnapper!" he
shouted. "Get out of my house!" Which I did, slamming the front
door behind me.

For a long time afterward I felt badly about this confrontation,
although he and I never discussed it. He was alone at the time. Ilka
had left him for another man, the family doctor, and had moved
with the doctor to an apartment exactly like the one she had
shared with my father, but five stories above it. This had enabled
her to take with her not only most of the furniture, but also the
drapes, blinds, and carpeting. My father had kept his books, the
dining room table and chairs, and his grand piano, which now sat
alone in his living room, unplayed and out of tune. The place
looked abandoned and our footsteps rang loudly on the bare
wooden floors. I felt sorry for him and regretted that I had made a
scene during a time in his life that must have been unrelievedly
dreary, but I couldn't forgive him for what he had done to me at
the age of twelve. Nobody can be as cruelly vindictive as a
wounded child.

SEVEN

LOVE ON A ROOFTOP

My mother had a genius for finding odd but often charming places to live. My earliest memories of home are of a rambling apartment in Rome, with a rooftop studio looking out on a huge terrace with a view over a public garden, and of a tiny house in Capri clinging to a steep hillside overlooking the harbor and the Bay of Naples. In New York we had lived first in a small hotel off Washington Square, then in a dark ground-floor flat with a gloomy courtyard in back, followed by subsequent moves to the top-floor railroad flat in the old brownstone on East Forty-ninth Street and—the grandest find of all—the whole house at 212 East Forty-ninth, with its art-deco interiors and small garden.

We never stayed in any of these places for more than three or four years, so it was no surprise to me when shortly after Janet came to live with us, we moved again, this time into a duplex penthouse on the southeast corner of Fifty-eighth Street and Madison Avenue. I never knew why we were always moving, but it didn't trouble me very much. My entire boyhood had been nomadic; I had been shuttling between countries, across oceans, in and out of boarding schools and camps, bouncing from one set of rented rooms to another. Wherever we went I had always had a room of my own, well-stocked with my books and toys, and never felt unwanted. I hated being sent away to school and summer camps, but I loved coming home on vacations. My life was punctuated by departures and arrivals. In between, I lived a fairly ordered existence in the shadow of my mother's sometimes tempestuous involvements and careers.

The apartment on the corner of Fifty-eighth Street was by far the most eccentric of my mother's discoveries. To get to it you took an elevator to the top floor, walked along a corridor toward the rear of the building, turned right onto a covered terrace leading to a staircase ascending one floor up to the penthouse. The first floor of this duplex consisted of a kitchen, bathroom, dining room, and living room, with two bedrooms at opposite ends. Another short flight of stairs led up to a third bedroom, a tiny sitting room and bath perched on the rooftop like a large chicken coop.

Janet and my mother occupied the chicken coop, while my grandmother and I lived below. On the rare evenings when we were all home, we ate together the splendid Italian meals both my mother and Mammina Ester seemingly were able to whip up out of leftovers even at the last minute. Janet and I, both helpless in the kitchen, ate with gusto, then sometimes helped clean up afterward. I was used to this chore, but Janet clearly wasn't and was vocal about her distaste for the whole necessary procedure. "It's exactly like uneating the meal one has just consumed," she once protested. "Not unlike ancient Roman behavior at orgiastic banquets."

"She can only boil an egg," my mother explained. "She has lived in hotels all of her life."

Much of the time, however, even when I wasn't around, Janet

and Natalia were out on the town somewhere. I was too wrapped up in my own teenage social life to pay much attention to their activities, but I knew they had between them a huge circle of friends and acquaintances in the arts and literary world that kept them deeply involved. My mother periodically gave parties and frequently invited people over for cocktails before going out to dinner. On those evenings I'd have to thread my way through the dining room and living room to get to my bedroom, a minor ordeal that compelled me to have to greet everyone, shake hands, or share a kiss before I could retreat to the sanctity of my own quarters. Once inside, through my closed door, I could hear a buzz of conversation and laughter. Finally, after they'd gone, I'd emerge to have supper with my grandmother. On vacations I, too, would dash off afterward into my own social life of movies with friends, dating, and dancing. From a small balcony off my bedroom I could look down over Fifty-eighth Street and directly across to the canopied entrance of Larue, a nightclub that catered to high society types and upper-middle-class teenagers. If I had nothing else to do and I spotted friends or a covey of unattended girls on their way in, I'd rush off to join them, leaving my grandmother alone.

I accepted Janet immediately into our family, just as I had accepted the other friends and lovers who had moved in and out of my mother's life as I was growing up. In some ways I regarded her as an ally in my constant struggle to free myself from the often overwhelming dominance my mother exercised over my life. This contest became more intense as I lurched clumsily into my teenage years, with their unfulfilled yearnings, sexual gropings, and egotistical male posturings. My mother and I were capable of staging tremendous scenes, and sometimes days passed when we'd hardly speak to each other. When I was still a child, calm was usually restored by my grandmother, whom both of us adored and who was always a source of comfort to me, a strong and tranquil presence throughout my boyhood. In my teens, however, not even she could act as a buffer between us, partly because, as a European gentlewoman, she could no longer understand me either. I had cast off, I hoped permanently, all the remnants of my continental up-bringing, and had blossomed into what both she and my mother considered that most appalling of phenomena, the American teenage lout.

Janet kept apart from this ongoing fray. I'm sure she was as re-pulsed by my self-centered arrogance as my mother, but she was also able to cast an objective eye on the situation. She understood that often my worst behavior and most extravagant outbursts were the result of a growing need for independence, that my rages were fueled in part by my mother's refusal to let go of me. My mother would alternate between long periods of basically ignoring me, while I was away from her, to bouts of attempting to exert control over all my actions. The first battle I ever won with her was man-aging, at the age of thirteen, to banish her from my bathroom, which she used to invade to make certain I was washing myself properly and to scrub my back.

Janet, who had never wanted children, was uninterested in them, and claimed not to understand them, nevertheless was, at least from a distance, sympathetic to my plight. Her whole career had been founded on a need for freedom and independence. Her only impor-tant relationships had been with women, but her outlook on self-ful-fillment was essentially masculine. I sensed it and counted on her for support, though not until long after her death did I discover for cer-tain that she had indeed, on more than one occasion, intervened on my behalf. "You're a curious mother," she wrote to Natalia, after an-other of the many crises that were precipitated in my late teens by some action of mine that my mother regarded as idiotic. Janet went on to point out, with exquisite tact, that although Natalia obviously wanted her son to become a strong, self-sufficient, and independent human being, she tended instinctively at first to smother or thwart every attempt I made to become one through my own efforts, how-ever misguided they might seem.

My main defense against my mother's attempts to impose her will on me was secrecy. I told her as little as I could get away with about what I was up to. Mostly she was so occupied by her own affairs that she was unaware that I was leading a rich, full life under her very nose. But Janet knew. She suspected that I lived spiritually in a dark cellar where I was cultivating small, obscene vices like a Republican businessman with an underage mistress. She worried about me, partly because she liked me and partly because she had no idea what I was up to or might be capable of. Janet liked men and had many male friends, both straight and gay, but she deeply distrusted the male ego and its capacity to inflict pain and misery on the world.

In between the occasional dramatic scenes which my mother and I staged, from which Janet would flee to the upstairs bedroom, life on the rooftop for me during those years was a delight. At the age of sixteen I had finally managed to lose my virginity, to a wonderfully considerate and beautiful prostitute who specialized in teenage boys from certain East Coast prep schools and a few Ivy League colleges, and I had acquired enough self-confidence to pursue girls of my own age, though never with much success. The short-lived sexual revolution was a generation off, and the casual lay was an inconceivable possibility. I did have girlfriends, however, with whom passionate necking was acceptable. During those vacations when I was home from school, I remained in a state of perpetual lust, which also blinded me to most aspects of civilized discourse. Apart from the theater, movies, sports, and my sudden discovery of opera, I had no other enthusiasms. Politics and the state of the world were of no fundamental interest to me; they were things I could do nothing about, which effectively eliminated me from participating in the one paramount concern that animated our household. Apart from their direct connection to me as family, I had no idea who these women were whose lives I shared.

My mother was thirty-eight when she met Janet, who was ten years her senior. Since 1938, the year Hitler annexed Austria and the Sudetenland, a region that comprised about a third of Czecho-slovakia, into the Greater German Reich, my mother had been broadcasting her shortwave news and talk program five days a week to Italy, part of an overall effort by the NBC network to in-trude the voices of America into the developing crisis in Europe that would lead to the Second World War. At first my mother had no idea whether anyone was listening to her. Before long, however, she began receiving letters and other communications from Italy indicating that, to the anti-Fascist Italians, she represented a lonely voice of freedom. She began every program by announcing in Ital-ian that "this is the voice of NBC speaking to you from Radio City in New York," followed by the three-note chimes that identified the network. She delivered the news, and eventually began reading some of her mail aloud over the air and answering questions from her fans, without, of course, identifying them.

One of her most frequent callers was Maestro Arturo Toscanini, who would pick up her broadcasts on his powerful shortwave re-ceiver at his home in Riverdale, New York, and call to confirm or comment on what she had been telling her listeners, especially about developments indicating America's possible involvement in the goings-on abroad. Every Sunday afternoon she would also broadcast the maestro's NBC Symphony concerts; he was an out-spoken anti-Fascist and a living symbol for all Italians, at home and abroad, of resistance to Benito Mussolini's dictatorial regime. By the time the United States finally entered the war, after the Japan-ese attack on Pearl Harbor on December 7, 1941, my mother had been venomously singled out by Roberto Farinacci, a high Fascist official, as "the voice of Italo-American anti-Fascism." If the Axis had won the war, she would have been among the first to be elim-inated, a consideration we used to joke about, but only after it be-came clear we were not going to lose. Occasionally I'd refer to her as "Tokyo Rosa."

After the NBC shortwave broadcasts were incorporated into the activities of the Office of War Information (OWI) and the conflict

finally turned in our favor in late 1943, with the German defeat in
North Africa and the Allied invasion of Sicily and the Italian main-
land, my mother volunteered to serve overseas, specifically in Italy.
If approved, she would receive the honorary rank of captain and
be sent to a newly-liberated Rome to help in the creation of a free
Italian press and the revival of the country's artistic and cultural institutions. On a personal level, she was also eager to go find her
two younger sisters, my aunts, from whom we had had no news
for many months. Mammina Ester, who had been working part-
time at NBC but who was too old to go back home, was suffering
from the silence abroad and increasingly anxious about the fate of
her two other daughters, both of whom had married foreigners, a
Hungarian journalist and screenwriter and a Swiss businessman.
We didn't know by then whether they were even in Rome, which
had at least been declared an "open city" and thus was not subject
to the bombings that were in the process of destroying much of
Europe.

Janet had also been talking about going back to Europe ever
since she'd moved in with us, but it seemed far more likely that my
mother would go first, as Italy would be liberated long before the
Germans would be chased out of occupied France. Janet, I knew,
had old and dear friends in Paris and often declared that she felt out
of place in America, the country she had fled from twenty years
earlier. In retrospect, I realize now that her love for Natalia was
what made her New York life temporarily acceptable to her. She
continued to write articles about France under the occupation for
The New Yorker and other magazines, turned out profiles of
Thomas Mann, Wendell Willkie, and others, and produced one
major piece that I read with fascination.

This was her long four-part profile of Marshal Philippe Pétain,
the so-called hero of Verdun in the First World War, who now, at
age eighty-seven, was governing what was left of France after the
German victory and occupation, and who would later be tried for
treason. I was away at college that winter when I idly picked up a

copy of the magazine one afternoon and began to read. Here is how Janet's article began:

> Historically, the octogenarian Marshal Philippe Pétain is unique. He is the only Frenchman who ever survived a hundred and seven French governments and then founded one of his own, the hundred and eighth. Because he is so old that he was a youth at the beginning of the period of French history over whose end he now presides, and because during his long life, the decades have drained away the glory of France, the world has assigned to him a curious chronometrous quality; it has made of the Third Republic a sort of hourglass whose sands, in the person of Pétain, have finally run out.

I was galvanized by the simplicity of style, the elegance of the writing, the sheer beauty of it. I had never read any magazine piece quite like it, and it suddenly established Janet in my eyes as not merely a journalist but a writer. This was an important distinction to me at the time. Her earlier Paris Letters, some of which I had read after I'd met her, had seemed gossipy and remote to me, dealing with people and events in a country I knew little about, even though I spoke French fluently and had been to Paris. But by the time she wrote "La France et le Vieux," as the series was titled in the magazine, I had become serious and passionate about writing, overwhelmed by my discovery of Hemingway and Fitzgerald. Here was an American woman who wrote nonfiction with the poetic sensibility of a novelist and whose style elevated reportage to the level of art. I was about to turn eighteen in February 1944, when the first installment of this piece was published, goofing off at Harvard while waiting to be called into the army. I had already decided I wanted to become an opera singer, but I intended also to write. For the first time I realized that this woman, who had been living with us and acting as a sort of surrogate father to me, was someone I could also look up to. It was a revelation that ultimately deeply influenced my life, although I didn't realize it at the time.

Janet was also a regular panelist that year on a radio show called *Listen: The Women*. It was a talk show featuring prominent women discussing the issues of the day. I went to hear her in person a couple of times and again was struck by how witty and charming she could be, how easily she dominated the proceedings simply by the sheer force of her personality. She did it so effortlessly that I couldn't understand why she seemed reluctant to pursue it. She was a natural public speaker and entirely fearless when confronted by a microphone as well as a live audience. But she seemed contemptuous of the medium, as if she were betraying her real vocation, which was writing. "I loathe the radio program," she told Natalia, calling it "silly and futile." I had never met anyone so totally dedicated to the word (or anything, for that matter), and it impressed me. I wasn't surprised when I heard that she happily gave up all radio appearances when her contract ran out after twenty-six weeks that October and the program went off the air.

By then my mother had left for Italy. Sometime in early May she was told to report to an army camp in Delaware, where she was assigned her rank of captain, issued uniforms, and inducted into the communal joys of life in a barracks. I didn't even have time to come down from Boston to see her off, but said my goodbyes to her over the phone. I wasn't surprised. We'd always parted from each other like that, suddenly, swiftly, with not much preparation and no long-range planning. I thought it was the way most people lived.

She and Janet managed to stay in touch, even though no one knew exactly where she was. She even managed to call Janet on May 17, the night before her departure, but couldn't reveal any details of her whereabouts or specific destination. All we were told was that she would be leaving on a troopship as part of a convoy heading across the Atlantic for North Africa. Small consolation, since we knew the route would be full of mines and German submarines. Still, I never doubted she'd make it. At eighteen I believed as strongly in her immortality as in mine.

●

I came home from Harvard at the end of the spring term to spend
my last few weeks as a civilian with Janet and Mammina Ester on our
Manhattan rooftop. The house, empty of my mother's forceful personality, seemed strangely quiet, even though daily life continued in
it just as if she were present. The routines remained basically the
same. Janet occupied the chicken coop and left every morning for
her office at *The New Yorker*. Mammina Ester had been let go from
NBC after my mother's departure and the takeover by the OWI, so
she remained at home to manage the household and await news
from abroad, which came irregularly in the form of my mother's letters. I had nothing to do but enjoy myself. The trouble was, I didn't
really know how to go about it and secretly was frightened by the imminent prospect of being whisked out of my comfortable boyhood
into the real adult world of the military at war.

My father had wanted me to enroll in a navy program that would
have kept me in college for at least two years, after which I'd have
been commissioned an ensign and gone on to serve an additional
period of time, probably as the war was ending or perhaps after it
was over. Partly because I distrusted all of my father's plans for me
and always resented what I regarded as his periodic intrusions into
my life, I had enlisted instead at seventeen in the U.S. Army Air
Corps' preflight cadet training program. Sometime after my eighteenth birthday, in April 1944, I'd be called up and sent to some
camp somewhere for basic training; then, if I qualified, I'd be dispatched to an officers school to become either a pilot, a navigator, or
a bombardier. I didn't give a damn about flying; I just wanted to get
into the service and out as quickly as possible. The idea of lingering
on campus in a military uniform, with perhaps years of service
ahead of me, seemed dismal. I had already enjoyed Harvard as a
civilian, one of about a thousand in a sea of uniformed recruits who
marched to and from class in formation and had to live as if in a military school. I wanted no part of that. I'd already had a year at a mil-

itary school, thanks to another of my father's brainy interventions in my affairs, and had hated it from my first day there.

Basically, we waited. Janet was impatiently looking forward to the liberation of Paris, which seemed imminent after the Allies landed on the Normandy beaches on D-Day, June 6, 1944. She expected to return soon to France. Her editors at *The New Yorker* had already taken steps to secure press credentials for her that would enable her to go. Travel anywhere in wartime was difficult and the military authorities restricted the number of correspondents allowed to be anywhere near a front. The magazine already had a war correspondent, A. J. Liebling, in France that summer, and it began to look as if Janet wouldn't be able to go until the fall, as his replacement. She fretted about it and, as the Allied advance continued, worried whether she'd ever be able to go. A primary reason to leave, I knew, was her desire to resume her normal role as *The New Yorker's* person in Paris, but a secondary one was her hope that, once in Europe, she and Natalia would be able to see each other again. Rome and Paris were not that far apart, war or no war.

Mammina Ester lived day to day for the news from abroad. She scoured the newspapers and listened for hours to the news dispatches on the small radio next to her bed. She and Janet fed each other the bits and pieces of information they could garner from anywhere, including all the gossip of their many friends and acquaintances with connections on the Continent. Mainly, they waited for my mother's letters, which brought them the personal news they thirsted for. Natalia's accounts of her landing by air in Naples, of the destruction she saw everywhere in the city and around it, and, later on, of her drive in a jeep up to Rome, after the capital's liberation, past the wasteland around Cassino and all along the ancient Via Appia, would reduce my grandmother to tears. Janet once heard her sobbing in her room and rushed in, alarmed that she might have received bad news, but was told she was crying for joy. She was at last in contact with her beloved Italy, living vicariously in her homeland through her daughter's reports.

The letter that brought the most happiness into our home was my mother's account of finding and reuniting in Rome with her two sisters and their husbands, as well as other members of the family. Everybody seemed to have survived the war and the German occupation, even though there had been hairy experiences when they'd had to hide out in the country. My Uncle Akos, a Hungarian married to my mother's middle sister, Lea, had actually been arrested in a roundup and held for a few days for questioning in Rome's Regina Coeli prison. He had been sprung by Lea's energetic intervention on his behalf; she had found someone who knew someone who managed to get him released. After this news, Janet referred to Rome as the ex-capital of the world, but still the capital of the formidable Danesi women. It made perfect sense to me. I had tried to imagine my mother's entrance into Rome. What I suspected was that she herself had singlehandedly broken through the German lines at Monte Cassino and sent the Nazis flying north so she could make her entrance into the city at the head of the troops. It was during this period that I began to refer to her as "the General," a nickname that stuck to her.

Those last few weeks in New York and Cherry Grove before I was called up remain in memory as a jumbled blur of absurd events. Neither Janet nor my grandmother could control me, and I shuttled back and forth from the beach house to Manhattan in endless pursuit of girls and pleasure. After I had all but demolished the interior of the Fire Island cottage during a two-day spree involving a friend of mine from school and a couple of women from Patchogue we had picked up at the hotel bar, Janet gave me a tongue-lashing that literally reduced me to tears. What my mother referred to as my worst qualities at the time—my aggressive appetites, lack of discipline, and ignorance—were evidently in full flower. I was going to eat, drink, be merry, and sexually harass as many girls as I could before marching off to serve my country. I even managed to fall briefly in love, with the younger sister of my Exeter roommate. Luckily for her, she lived in West Virginia and didn't hang around long enough to become too deeply involved with me and suffer any serious aftereffects from my ruthlessly boorish behavior. All I could think about was getting into bed with any girl incautious enough to risk it. My roommate's sister told me she loved me, too, but never quite went all the way to prove it. On our last date I promised to write her faithfully, told her that I would always love her and that when I came home we would meet again, presumably for life. I wrote her once, she wrote me back once, and that was it. I never saw her again.

The war seemed very far away. Every morning the newspapers brought us news of death and destruction all over the world, pictures of the dead and dying and the wounded, atrocity stories from prison camps, devastated towns and villages, ravaged countrysides. It might as well have been happening on another planet. No one I knew had been killed or maimed or had disappeared. My mother's accounts of her adventures in Italy read like dispatches from a frontier so distant that I could barely imagine the scenes she described. As for my Italian relatives, I hadn't seen any of them for a decade. I no longer spoke Italian or French at home; I had rejected all that to become an American. I didn't even want to know about that lost world of my early childhood. It seemed unconnected to me, irrelevant, almost an intrusion into my present sense of who I was, what I wanted, where I might be headed. The once familiar names of people who had known and loved me and whom I had loved, as a child loves, out of trust and dependency, rang only faintly in my consciousness. I was totally wrapped up in my own selfish needs. My grandmother forgave me everything, but Janet was exasperated not only by my behavior, but also by my insensitivity to anything and everything not directly linked to my immediate desires.

It must have been an enormous relief to her when I was finally summoned to appear at nine A.M. on a Monday morning in mid-August at Grand Central Terminal. I was told to report early enough to be able to identify my unit, bound for Fort Dix, in New Jersey. Janet wrote Natalia to tell her I was bright and cheery about it all, laughing and joking through what I called "the warrior's last breakfast at dawn." She noted, however, that I couldn't eat anything. Out in the street I heard Janet call from above. She and Mammina Ester were leaning over the railing of my little terrace to see me off. I smiled and waved. Another departure, another change of scene, separated once again from the women in my life.

EIGHT

COMINGS
AND
GOINGS

On Christmas morning, 1945, newly discharged from the Army, I took a ferry to Ellis Island in New York Harbor to meet my mother coming home from the war. I hadn't seen her for over a year and a half, not since she had departed to help liberate her beloved Italy from the country's native Fascists and its Nazi occupiers. I had been waiting impatiently for her in New York and had just received word that she'd be arriving on an aircraft carrier, along with thousands of other servicemen and women returning from the European theater. Evidently, she had succeeded beyond even my expectations; Mussolini had been shot and strung up with his girlfriend by the heels in a piazza in Milan, and Hitler had perished in his underground bunker in Berlin. I suspected that my mother had had a hand in both events.

The ship, the *Franklin Delano Roosevelt*, had been hastily converted into a troop carrier, after having spent most of the war fighting the Japanese in the Pacific. It was ferrying the boys and girls home from the Mediterranean. The ship made a tremendous impression as she moved slowly, surrounded by tugboats, toward the dock where I stood waiting, jammed in among hundreds of other people, mostly civilian dignitaries and brass, who had managed to gain privileged positions toward the front of the expectant crowd. Plumes of water spouted into the air, car horns and sirens blasted a welcome, as the great, gray hull loomed closer, its decks packed with cheering sailors and soldiers. I couldn't spot my mother anywhere, but waved anyway, hoping she'd be able to see me.

The *Roosevelt* had sailed from Naples on December 15 and should have arrived a couple of days earlier than she did, but had been delayed by heavy storm weather in the north Atlantic. She looked battered but impregnable, a floating fortress with a row of rising suns, each one representing a downed Japanese plane, painted on her hull. The sight of her exhilarated me, and I laughed and shouted as she seemed to inch toward her berth.

My enthusiasm caught the attention of a high-ranking army officer next to me. He was in his forties or early fifties and his chest was plastered with medals and decorations from all the action he had seen during the war. He was accompanied by his wife, a well-dressed woman in a fur coat, and was obviously among the favored elite who had been whisked into the front ranks for the event. I had felt him eyeing me earlier, probably because he hadn't been able to figure out what I was doing there. I was in my recently discarded Army Air Corps uniform, which I had salvaged from my closet for the occasion and donned in order to bluff my way past the MPs guarding access to the front rows. It had been easy, but my presence must have puzzled the officer. My chest was devoid of decorations and my sleeves sported a single chevron, indicating that I had managed to attain the not so exalted rank of private first class. But as I stood there, laughing and waving, he suddenly thought he'd understood. "Your brother coming home, eh," he said, beaming at me. "That's fine, soldier, that's swell."

"No, sir," I said. "It's my mother."

"Your mother?"

"Yes, sir. She's been in Italy."

"In Italy? She's Italian?"

"No, sir, American. She was born in Rome, but she's American."

He looked amazed, but I decided not to explain anything to him. It would have taken too much time, and I was too excited and too busy looking for my mother to want to bother. Besides, I had had my fill of military life, anyway, and I didn't have to answer his questions. I was even a little annoyed at myself for having reverted to military subservience out of some kind of reflex action from having once more donned my uniform. I had been out of the service for nearly two months by then, and this was the first and last time I was ever to put the uniform on again. I eased myself away from the officer, leaving him and his wife to figure out by themselves how it was that I was almost certainly the only soldier on the dock that day who had come to greet his mother returning from a battlefield.

It was another couple of hours before anybody began to disembark, but I knew that my mother would manage to be among the first off the ship. She was always in the vanguard of people coming and going on and off trains, boats, airplanes, buses, never one to drift along with a crowd, arrive late anywhere, or be left behind. So it was no surprise to me when she appeared with the first contingent of officers on the main gangplank. A tiny figure festooned with military gear, including a helmet and canteen, she struggled to carry a heavy duffel bag down the ramp. I maneuvered my way toward her to give her a hand and reached her just as she managed to step onto the pier. I came to attention and flashed her my snappiest salute. "Welcome home, General," I said, grinning. She looked up. "Bill!" she cried. She dropped her bag and I swept her into my arms.

By the time we were finally able to get away from Ellis Island and onto a ferryboat back to Manhattan, it was mid-afternoon on a gray day, and lights had begun to come on along the shore. My mother couldn't get over the spectacle. She had just come from a continent plunged into darkness by nearly five years of war, where people were only beginning to think about recovery, their daily lives devoted mostly to survival. The lights of New York dazzled her. All the way back to our house in mid-Manhattan, she couldn't stop commenting on it, even as she held my hand and told me bits and pieces of family news back in Rome and the difficulties of the crossing that had turned even most of the ship's crew green with seasickness.

When we stepped out of the cab in front of our apartment on East Fifty-eighth and Madison, my mother hurried on ahead, leaving me to cope with her gear. She swept out of the elevator, rushed along the outside landing to the short flight of steps leading to our penthouse, and bounded up the stairs. Mammina Ester was waiting for us, with a bottle of chilled champagne and a welcome-home cable from Janet. My mother hugged Ester, then caught sight of the small Christmas tree my grandmother and I had decorated a few days earlier for the occasion. To my amazement, she began to cry, with happiness, I realized later. But it startled me, because I couldn't recall her shedding tears more than two or three times during my childhood. Since that day, yes, many times, especially in her old age, but not then. I hadn't nicknamed her the General for her weaknesses, but for her strength and commanding character. I was shocked and a little embarrassed.

Sometimes it seems to me that my entire life—divided between two continents, two cultures, two sets of relatives and friends—has been little more than a disconnected narrative fiercely punctuated by dramatic scenes of farewell and reunion. Even as we sat there on that Christmas afternoon in New York, sipping champagne, opening presents, and catching up on one another's news, I knew that we were all preparing to abandon each other again.

Ester, then nearing seventy, wanted to go back to Italy. It would be hard to see her go, because she had been the warmth and light of my life all during the years of my American childhood, an unfailing source of comfort and support. When my mother went off to war, Ester had remained behind to watch over me, even though so much of the time during those war years I had been away at boarding school, college, and then the service. Janet, too, had been around the past couple of years, but she had returned to Paris in November and resumed her Letters for *The New Yorker*. It was Mammina Ester who had loved me unreservedly and without judgment all these years, who had always been there for me alone, and now she, too, would leave. Her two younger daughters, Lea and Franca, were in Rome, as were most of the rest of my Italian family, and her roots were still deep in the Italian earth. I knew that I would miss her terribly, but that she had to go. I wasn't sure yet what I was going to do with my life, but I knew I wouldn't be staying on forever in my mother's house. Comings and goings—the standard operating procedure of the Danesis and the Murrays and of all the people who passed through my early years. Some lingered longer than others, but none stayed put, neither in New York nor abroad, in any of the houses, apartments, villas, hotels, spas, schools, and camps I lived in. I was used to it.

My mother, too, would soon be gone again. She was overjoyed to be home, but her conversation was full of Italy—of Rome, of her sisters, of her work, and of what she had accomplished there. Her first days back in New York were filled with friends and parties, but after the holidays she began to organize herself to depart. Her main hope was that the State Department would send her back to Rome to resume the work she'd been carrying on for the past eighteen months. There was so much still to do, and she was clearly the right person to do it. At first she didn't doubt that that would happen; like any other soldier, she had come home on furlough and expected to be returned to duty at the end of it.

She was enthusiastic about what she had accomplished. She also told us about how she had finally managed to get to Rome from Naples, at a time when travel conditions were chaotic and there was no train or bus service. She had persuaded a navy officer to let her ride with him in his jeep up the Appian Way to the newly liberated capital. "I couldn't speak all the way there," she recalled. "The ruined country, the empty bombed villages—terrible." Her only conversation with the navy man occurred as they neared the city and he caught his first sight of the ancient Roman aqueducts below the Alban Hills. He thought our bombers had done a terrific job there.

Her first task had been to find her sisters and other members of our family, after which she immediately went to work. She imported books, newspapers, and magazines; organized lectures, round-table discussions, and cultural and educational events—all designed to open up Italy, after twenty years of fascism, to the heady pleasures of freedom. By the end of her stay, her work had been demilitarized and the activities of her Special Projects Division had been made part of the overseas operations of the U.S. Information Service (USIS), a branch of the State Department.

All these details I found out much later from her. All I knew at the time, preoccupied as I was by my own concerns, was that back in New York she was full of enthusiasm and projects that she expected our government to fund. She would be sent back to Italy to resume her work, which she saw as a way of winning the peace while helping Italy to recover from the physical and spiritual desolation of the war.

I had my doubts. Nobody in Washington seemed to know about her and what she had done. She complained all that winter that her letters and phone calls went unanswered. When she went to Washington to make inquiries, she was bounced from one office to another, the victim of some sort of bureaucratic runaround. I was home one day when somebody from Washington actually did call to ask for her. "Natalie Murray there, please?" a woman's voice inquired.

I told the caller that she wasn't, but that she'd be back later. I took down a phone number. "By the way," I added, "it's not Natalie. It's spelled with an *a* on the end."

"Oh, Nat*a*lia," the woman said.

Something in the officious tone of her voice irritated me. "No, Nata*li*a," I corrected her. "It's Italian. The accent is on the third syllable. Her maiden name is Da*ne*si, accent on the second syllable. It's Natalia Danesi Murray." I had suddenly become proud of my Italian heritage for some reason and could be pompous about it.

"Fine," the woman said and hung up on me. She was obviously a secretary in one of the offices my mother had been pestering, but it didn't bode well, I thought, that the people she was supposed to be working for couldn't pronounce her name correctly.

The strongest reason my mother had for wanting to return to Rome was to be closer to Janet, who had been back in Paris since the last week in November 1944. Janet had checked into the Hotel Scribe near the Opéra, then the headquarters of the foreign press, and had immediately resumed her work for *The New Yorker*. She and my mother had finally managed to spend a couple of weeks together when Janet had flown to Rome at the end of June. They had gone on to Naples and Capri, "just fun and relaxation," my mother later recalled, "like two proper tourist ladies enjoying their first vacation abroad."

In the fall, my mother had wangled her way to Paris for a week, where they had not had such a happy time together. For the first time my mother had had to confront the fact that Paris was Janet's home, that she would never leave there to come back to New York. She had her work and another world she had created there for herself, full of old friends and lovers my mother hadn't even met. Janet had told Noel about Natalia, or so she had assured my mother, but continued to spend weekends at Orgeval. My mother had not yet met Noel, but she wanted to share that world, to be a part of Janet's life forever. It would not be easy. There was no place in Paris for her, nothing for her to do there, no way to earn a living. She was reassured by Janet's visit to Rome in early December, just before my mother's departure for New York, when Janet promised to come for a long visit after the New Year. But she wouldn't stay; she was first and foremost a writer who lived for her work, and she had structured her life to leave herself unencumbered by possessions and people.

My mother knew this about her and understood it intellectually, even sympathized with it, but at heart it filled her with anguish. New York was too distant; they would be able to see each other only once or twice a year. If she could get back to Rome, she felt that their prospects would be better. Rome was closer, only an overnight train ride or a few hours' flying time from Paris. It seemed like the only possible solution to her, which was why she continued to batter away at the Washington bureaucracy in an effort to be sent back to Italy. The struggle went on for weeks, then months, as no one in Washington would either commit himself to her return or explain to her why she wasn't being reassigned there. Finally, she was summoned back to Washington, where an official she had never met or spoken to before handed her a letter of resignation to sign. No reason was given for this termination of her service, but there was no appeal from the decision. She was baffled and angry, and was further distressed by the fact that, contrary to her promise, Janet did not show up in New York after the first of the year. There were too many stories she was working on, Janet said, too much for her to write about to permit herself a holiday. The letters now flowed back and forth between them, with my mother obviously becoming increasingly alarmed and distressed by their separation.

She began to talk about going back to Italy on her own, but I wasn't paying much attention. I was used to her departures and long absences, and I figured she would find a way to leave. I was nineteen and I'd been on my own by then for nearly two years. My time in the Army Air Force had been largely wasted. I had spent it being shuttled from one military camp to another in Mississippi, South Carolina, and Alabama. The army couldn't figure out what to do with me or with the roughly hundred and thirty thousand other young men who had volunteered for the cadet program. We were all supposed to proceed after five weeks of basic training to flight school to be trained as pilots, navigators, or bombardiers, after which we were to be assigned to one war front or another. But long before the war had formally ended it had become obvious that there was no longer any need for us; the Germans and Japanese had already lost the air war. We had spent months at various bases performing meaningless chores, and had even been made to repeat basic training. By the terms of our enlistment, we couldn't be reassigned as enlisted men to any other branch of the services, where we could at least have been used as occupation troops. Finally, it was decided that we would be discharged back into civilian life, with the prospect that those of us who had served less than a year would be drafted back into some other branch. I had been in for fourteen and a half months and had just enough time to escape being called back. What the army had left me with was an education in evasion, mendacity, and manipulation plus enough money to support myself back in New York until I figured out what I wanted to do with my life.

No sooner had I set foot back in the city that November, after being discharged at Westover Field in Massachusetts, than I was to be dazzled by a whole new world my father had incautiously opened up for me: Hollywood.

NINE

GOING
HOLLYWOOD

I was surprised when my father invited me to come with him to California in early December. He went there a couple of times a year on business, but had never before asked me to come along. His timing was good. I was just hanging around New York, not knowing what to do with myself and waiting for my mother to come home. I had some discharge pay and I was going to the racetrack in the afternoons and partying at night, mostly with some old buddies from the service.

On the morning my father called me up to suggest I come along, I had had only four hours' sleep. He asked me what I'd been doing. I told him that four of us had picked up some chorus girls from the Latin Quarter, a big nightclub near Broadway, and taken them to a few late-night boîtes. I didn't tell him that it had all been relatively innocent. One of my friends knew a girl in the chorus line from having gone to school with her and had arranged the whole thing. We'd met them at the stage door and taken them to a late supper at a small club on the East Side, where we'd been unlucky enough to sit down near a table occupied by Peter Arno, *The New Yorker's* sophisticated and ribald cartoonist. He knew all the girls and within half an hour had managed to detach one of them from us, leaving us in the difficult social situation of four on three. Arno, who smoked cigarettes out of a long holder and looked like one of his own creations, a lethal seducer exuding an aura of irresistible savoir faire, had already done me in two years earlier. He didn't remember me, of course, but he had shown up one summer weekend at Fire Island, when I was seventeen and in love with Nellie, the teenage blonde daughter of a liquor store owner in Sayville. One look at Nellie's long legs, and Arno had set out in pursuit of her, spending several hours with her on the beach. He caught sun poisoning and had to be carried off the island on a stretcher, but not before he had succeeded in turning Nellie's big blue eyes away from me. I heard later that she had gone to New York and modeled for him; her face cropped up in a number of his drawings. I considered him my nemesis, now that he'd stuck it to me again.

I didn't tell my father this story. As far as he was concerned, I allowed him to think I was leading a life of spectacular debauchery. I'm convinced that otherwise he might not have invited me to California. He was worried about me, but not because I was alone in New York and dating chorus girls. He'd done a lot of that sort of thing himself, I'd been told by my mother. He wanted me to go back to Harvard, where I'd spent an academic year prior to being called up into the air corps. He did not want me to become an opera singer, which was what I had begun to long to become above all else at the time. Now that I was displaying an interest in chorus girls and the sybaritic pleasures of New York nightlife, he must have reasoned that a taste of southern California would complete my undoing and set me up for the agenda he had in mind. At least, that's the way I saw it.

I'd learned by this time how to manipulate my father pretty well, during those periods of my life when I wasn't actively opposing or ignoring his plans for me. It never occurred to me that he may have merely wanted the pleasure of his son's company when he went out to the West Coast. Only once before in our troubled relationship had he ever taken me anywhere for that reason, and he'd given me no cause since to think otherwise. I'd never been to Hollywood. All I knew was that my father was a big wheel in show business. I'd have a good time and there was nothing to hold me in New York except the Metropolitan Opera, which I couldn't afford to attend regularly. The racetracks had shut down for the winter and the horses had all gone south.

We left on a late afternoon in early December on the Twentieth Century Limited for Chicago, where my father had to spend a day seeing some colleagues and clients, after which we'd board the Super Chief for the three-and-a-half-day trip across the country to Los Angeles. We walked down a red carpet in Grand Central Terminal to the train and, with the aid of a cheerful black porter carrying our bags, found our compartment. No sooner had we settled down for a drink in the club car at the rear of the train than my father bumped into three men he knew who were also on their way out to the coast. Two of them joined us for dinner, then my father went off with them somewhere to play cards. I returned to the club car and sat alone for an hour or so, watching the darkened countryside flow past.

The William Morris Agency had a branch in Chicago. My father spent most of the next day there, while I wandered about the city. He came back to the hotel for dinner and we ate with a group of agency men and their consorts in a restaurant that featured skewered meat and flaming desserts. Like all of the restaurants my father patronized, it was luxurious and overpriced. After dinner, we all went to a large nightclub called the Chez Paree, where Danny Thomas, one of the agency's clients, was performing. The show was much like the one I'd just seen at the Latin Quarter, with beaded, bangled, and feathered chorus girls dancing and featuring a headliner, in this case Thomas, whose act depended largely on ethnic humor. After the performance, the comedian joined us, and he, my father, and the other men at the table talked business, leaving me to chat and dance with the women, all of whom declared themselves delighted to have at last met Bill Murray's son.

By the time we boarded the Super Chief the next day, I had a cold and a nasty sore throat. I didn't bother to tell my father about it until we were halfway across the great plains, passing towns that all looked alike to me, distinguished from each other only by the names painted on the grain silos that periodically sprang up like sentinels out of the vast prairie. I was alone in our compartment most of the time and, as I began to run a fever and feel worse, the trip seemed as endless to me as the flat landscape outside my window. My father had been spending most of his time in the club car, where he had met other friends and acquaintances headed for the coast, or in somebody else's compartment playing high-stakes gin rummy. It wasn't until I told him I wouldn't make the dining car for dinner, because I didn't think I'd be able to swallow anything, that he realized I was sick.

Luckily, there was a doctor on board. He diagnosed a probable strep throat and put me on sulfa tablets, which I swallowed along with huge quantities of liquids. It was another twenty-four hours before my fever, which at one point topped a hundred and four, broke and I began to feel a little better. The last day before we arrived in L.A. my father spent more time with me. We sat up reading books together and I even managed to persuade him to play a couple of games of gin with me, though the absence of a wager on the outcome took most of the fun out of it for both of us. I suggested a tenth of a cent a point, but he refused to gamble with me. We also chatted about baseball and football and tennis. What we didn't talk about was anything that might possibly cause friction between us. We were being very careful with each other at that stage. Since my enlistment in the air corps, my father had lost the only direct control, the power of his money, he'd ever been able to exercise over me, and he knew it.

We got off the train in Pasadena and were whisked by chauffeured limousine to the Beverly Hills Hotel, where I immediately went to bed. I still had a fever and I was told, on doctor's orders, to stay inside for at least two more days, or until one full day had passed after my temperature returned to normal. My father saw me settled into my own room, told me to order anything I wanted from room service, and disappeared. I didn't see him again for three days, except in the late afternoons, when he'd drop in on me for a few minutes between the end of his business day and the beginning of his social life, which seemed to consist of dinner parties at the homes of famous friends and clients or evenings out in well-known restaurants, such as Romanoff's and Chasen's.

My only other visitor during this dreary period, when I could only sniff the balmy California air outside my window and gaze at the palm trees lining the street below, was Gilbert Seldes, who was the father of one of my two oldest friends in New York, Timothy. Gilbert, a brilliant commentator and jack-of-all-trades in the arts, was also staying in the hotel and had bumped into my father in the lobby. He smilingly stuck his head into my room one afternoon, then sat down at the foot of my bed and began to tell me colorful anecdotes about the peculiar social habits of the people he was dealing with in the entertainment industry. He made me laugh, but mostly he made me want to get well so I could join the fun. I had grown up, thanks to my mother, thinking of Hollywood as a quintessentially trivial milieu in which unworthy people were making vast sums of money while the rest of the country suffered through the Depression and the war. At that point of my life, it sounded exactly like the sort of place I wanted to be.

I had my first taste of this cheery new world when I finally was able to emerge from the great pink palazzo on Sunset Boulevard where my father and I were staying. I took a taxi and joined him for lunch at the Brown Derby in Beverly Hills, a restaurant built in the shape of a hat. I thought this was entirely appropriate; on my way there I had gazed out of the taxi window at rows of enormous houses reflecting the architectural styles of at least three continents and a thousand years of history.

My father arrived at the same time I did and we walked into the Brown Derby together. Our table was located at the rear of the room, but it took us nearly half an hour to reach it because everyone in the place seemed to know my father, and he had to stop to greet people and chat a few minutes at every table. He introduced me around and I dutifully shook hands, then stepped back and waited for him to conclude before moving on to the next group. I didn't recognize anybody, and I had no idea who any of these people were, though I knew they all had to be connected to show business. Nobody seemed interested in me at all, which was only natural and fine with me, but at one booth a man rose smilingly up to clasp my father's hand, then expressed surprise and pleasure at my presence. "Bill, this is a great-looking kid you've got here," he said, clapping me on the shoulder.

"I hope he looks as well as I do at my age," my father said, laughing.

"Yeah, you're looking great, too," the man said. "It's wonderful to see you. How long are you in town?"

"Another ten days," my father said and proceeded to make a luncheon date with him. I gathered he was the producer of a radio show starring one of my father's clients.

I was surprised by this conversation. I had never thought of my father as a handsome man, and I didn't think he looked particularly good. He was fifty-five at the time and bald, with only a fringe of short gray hair above his ears. He was an inch or so shorter than I was, and pale. He smoked and drank heavily and his face would turn pink from liquor toward the end of the day. I wasn't a health fanatic and I didn't disapprove of his smoking and drinking, which seemed perfectly natural activities at the time; I drank and I smoked five or six cigarettes a day myself, though I didn't inhale because of my desire to become a singer. Nor did I concern myself with the fact that my father never exercised. But I had seen him naked and I was embarrassed by the pallor and flabbiness of his body. I knew he had once been an athlete, but he always seemed old to me.

I wanted to ask my father about all these people I had just met, but two other agents and Abe Lastfogel, the head of William Morris and my father's boss, also had lunch with us. I liked Lastfogel. I had met him in New York several times while I was growing up and I knew him as a warm, kindly bullfrog of a man who had always taken the trouble to express what I sensed was a genuine interest in me and what I was doing. He was no different in California than he had been in New York. No sooner had we sat down than he asked me what I'd been up to, what I'd done in the service, what I thought of California, and what my plans were for the future. "He's going back to college," my father said.

"That's fine," Abe said, "that's good. Come around and see me before you go back. Call up my secretary and make a date."

I assured him I would, though I had no intention of doing so. I had a feeling my father wouldn't approve. And then, what could Abe Lastfogel tell me about opera or singing in general? The rest of the lunch was devoted to business, after which my father went back to the office and I returned to the hotel, where I lay around the pool for a couple of hours, then read in my room until my father showed up again.

He took me to my first Hollywood party that night. We had a drink in the Polo Lounge, after which we were paged to the front entrance, where one of my father's colleagues was waiting for us in another of the chauffeured limousines my father used to get about. This agent was a spiffily dressed tiny man named Johnny Hyde, whose little feet, clad in shiny black pumps, barely touched the floor. Most of the William Morris agents were short men, but Johnny could have been a jockey. Next to him in the back seat was a spectacular-looking blonde actress named Carole Landis, who had already starred in a few B-movies and who, my father told me later, was being groomed to become another in Hollywood's long line of platinum-haired bombshells.

The party was held in a huge villa somewhere up in the Hollywood hills above Sunset Boulevard. I spent almost the entire evening pursuing Carole Landis around the premises. I was the only person under forty who bothered to talk to her and I soon discovered that I could make her laugh. She told me who some of the celebrities were in the room, but I was not impressed; I had already met a lot of them in New York. Only one of the great opera singers I admired, a Lauritz Melchior or a Beniamino Gigli, would have dazzled me sufficiently to divert me from Carole. She liked to laugh and she exuded sex appeal in such abundance that I began scheming to whisk her away from there, though I had no means of doing so.

It wasn't until my father and I were riding home in a taxi much later that night that I realized I had committed a serious social gaffe. "What were you doing, hanging around that actress all night?" my father asked.

"She liked me," I said. "And I liked her."

"Don't you know who she's with?"

"Johnny? You don't mean Johnny? He's a midget," I said, appalled.

"No, not Johnny," my father answered.

"Who, then? Somebody who was at the party?"

My father didn't answer. He simply stared glumly out the window until the taxi pulled up in front of the hotel. I wondered who it could have been and why my father wouldn't tell me. I never found out, but obviously there was a good deal about his backstage life in show business that I didn't understand.

After that night, my father made certain I wouldn't become an embarrassment to him. He provided me with a car and a potential girlfriend. The former was a Ford convertible, the latter a chesty brunette named Gloria, who worked as a secretary for one of my father's clients, the star of a popular radio show. She was a sweet, cheerful person who lived with her mother in a small apartment below the Strip in West Hollywood. I took her out several times, and through her I met a number of people closer to my own age, most of whom were actors or studio workers.

With Gloria I began really to enjoy myself and to envy the relaxed, casual way these slightly older contemporaries of mine lived. They all dreamed of making it in the movies in one capacity or another, and there was even some talk about the possibility of television one day becoming an important new medium of entertainment. I didn't care about that, but I loved going to their parties and loved the talk about movies and the gossip about what was going on at all the studios. None of these new acquaintances of mine seemed to have an inkling of what was going on anywhere else in the world; the talk was exclusively about what everybody called "the industry." That was fine with me.

When I wasn't with them, in a studio commissary or out to dinner somewhere or at a party in someone's house, I drove all over the Los Angeles basin. There were few freeways then, but traffic moved easily. I revelled in the broad sweep of the boulevards and the junky eclecticism of the architecture, with palm trees everywhere and a blue, cloudless sky day after day. Downtown Hollywood Boulevard sparkled with Christmas decorations, and I almost got a ticket for driving through a red light I had mistaken for one of the bulbs on a huge, illuminated wreath hanging directly over the street. The cop laughed at my explanation and let me off with a warning. My life back East, with its cold winters and grimy city streets, began to seem remote and irrelevant. Did I really want to become an opera singer? Why couldn't I just become a movie star and make tons of money and bask forever in endless sunlight?

I went late one afternoon to have tea with a friend of my mother's named Marguerite D'Alvarez, whom I'd known and liked very much since childhood. We Italianized her name and called her Margherita, although she was half French, half Peruvian. She had been a great international diva, a famous Carmen, but, according to my mother, her career had been relatively brief. By the time I knew her, in my early teens, she had become a voice teacher in New York, but apparently not a very successful one. She did not have good breath support, my mother informed me, and so had developed a tendency to sing off-key; how could she be expected to teach? She was a highly dramatic personality who had once been a great beauty and had been photographed by Cecil Beaton and Carl Van Vechten. She spoke half a dozen languages fluently and could be devastatingly funny in all of them.

She had come to Hollywood during the war to make a movie, in which she played the part of a flamboyant Resistance fighter, and had been well reviewed by the critics. She had elected to stay in order to make a new career for herself; she had very little money, my mother had told me. She lived in a two-room Hollywood apartment filled with priceless antique furniture and objets d'art, as well as a grand piano that took up half the living room. She seemed unchanged from when I had known her in New York: Her long, black curly hair was still combed straight back from her face, and she still wore large, dangling earrings. She gave me a big kiss and gazed at me out of soulful eyes. "Billino," she said, "incredible! You're a man now!"

We talked about opera and singers, and then I told her I'd seen her in a movie and thought she was wonderful in it. "How is your new career going?" I asked. "Have you been offered any other parts?"

An expression of vast disgust came over her face. Yes, a director had come to see her a few days earlier, she informed me. He wanted her to appear in his new movie in a part very similar to the one she had already played. "These people have no imagination," she said. "They don't dream what it is to be an artist." While talking to her about the role, the director had picked up from her coffee table what must have seemed some sort of paper cutter to him and idly began to clean his nails with it. "I threw him out,"

Margherita informed me. "I told him I could not possibly perform for a man who could not distinguish between a nail file and a sixteenth-century Florentine *poignard*."

I laughed and asked her what she planned to do next. "I don't know," she said. "Perhaps go back to Europe. I will never stay here amid such vulgarity. This is not a place for artists."

This assessment of Hollywood was shared by many of my father's friends, especially the actors and creative people. I went to two other parties with him before we left. At one of them, given by the director George Cukor, a soft-spoken, civilized man, and attended by well-established entertainment figures, there was much talk about the misuse by the studios of the talent under contract. The moguls couldn't seem to understand that great Broadway and vaudeville stars like Sophie Tucker and Fanny Brice, both of whom were present, didn't need to be surrounded by lavish production numbers and a chorus line of beauty queens in order to succeed in the movies. I knew Fanny Brice as the star of a radio program, in which she played the part of an obnoxious child named Baby Snooks, but my father assured me she had been a great live performer. "Movie producers don't know much about talent," he said. "They think in terms of stars and box office."

At the second party the complaints were similar, but were also social and political. This party was held in the actress Sylvia Sidney's house and the guests were mostly writers, among whom were Abe Burrows and Dalton Trumbo. I was impressed that my father knew these people, because they were witty and told funny stories and talked about world affairs, the sort of subjects I was used to hearing discussed in my mother's house. They were scathing not only about the philistinism of the people who employed them at the studios, but also about their insensitivity to the plight of the workers and the poor all over the globe. My father seemed to be in agreement with them, which amazed me, because I had never discussed politics with him; I had always assumed that he was a Republican.

The only person in the room who didn't agree that Los Angeles was a cultural wasteland and Hollywood a corrupter of mores and ideals was a young director who, my father told me later, was Sylvia Sidney's new lover. He was much younger than she, dark, good-looking, with a pleasant smile. He informed the room at large that he was absolutely delighted to find himself in Hollywood and happily employed at a major studio. "That's because you haven't been here long enough," somebody told him. "You'll find out."

The director laughed. He'd spent the last few years staging road companies of such corny classics as *Blossom Time* and *The Student Prince* for the Schuberts in New York. He'd been overworked and underpaid. Suddenly he'd been whisked away to California and signed to a long-term contract quadrupling his income. He saw nothing wrong with making lots of money directing B movies. And, he untactfully pointed out, he was by far the least well-remunerated person in the room. He suggested they could all quit and go back to New York if they were so worried about their integrity.

This suggestion was coldly received, and nobody talked to him the rest of the evening except me. I thought he'd made a good deal of sense, but on our way home my father dismissed him as an untalented hack who would never amount to much.

The day before we left California, my father took me to Metro-Goldwyn-Mayer to meet one of these reviled studio moguls, Lou Sidney, and his son George, who directed many of the lavish musicals MGM was then producing. I wasn't certain why my father had invited me, though I guessed it had to have something to do with his plans for me. All he had asked me a couple of days earlier was whether I was enjoying myself in California and how I felt about the movies. I told him I was having a very good time, that I loved movies, and that I couldn't imagine a better way to live than in perpetual sunshine. This seemed to satisfy him and he dropped the subject.

Lou Sidney was a large, heavyset man who sat behind an enormous desk and issued pronouncements, mostly on the state of the industry. George was a smaller version of his father, but quiet and unassuming. After a few minutes of show biz talk, my father came to the point. He told the Sidneys that I wanted to work in the movies and especially in musicals. He asked if there might eventually be a place for me at the studio.

George nodded and smiled, while Lou pondered the request for a few moments. "Well, Bill, I think we could find a place for him here," he said at last. "I think George might be able to use another good young assistant."

"Sure," George said. "There's always room for talent here."

"But the competition for these jobs is tough," Lou Sidney said. "A college degree is a pretty good thing to have these days." He looked at me intently. "Your dad says you're just out of the army."

"He's going back to college this winter," my father said. "He's at Harvard."

Lou Sidney looked pleased. "That's great," he said. "Now, you get your degree from Harvard and there'll be a spot for you here. Right, George?"

George nodded and grinned. "You bet," he said.

We lingered in Lou Sidney's office for another few minutes, after which my father thanked Lou and George and we left. On the drive back to our hotel, my father told me what a great opportunity I had just been given—to be able to work at MGM, a major studio, and for a top director of musicals. I'd be a fool to pass it up. Of course, it all depended on my going back to Harvard to get my degree.

I didn't argue with him and I didn't ask him any questions. I knew I had been set up, that the Sidneys had been incorporated into my father's plot to get me back to school. The fact is, I wasn't sure anymore what I wanted to do, so I kept quiet. My father and I never discussed the matter again. It was his last intrusion into my life.

TEN

BONES

I did go back to Harvard that winter, but only to mark time until I could figure out what to do with my life. I now wanted above all to become an opera singer and I needed to take voice lessons from somebody competent to train me. My father would not pay for the lessons and my mother couldn't afford to. Besides, I didn't want to ask them for help. I had earned my freedom by establishing my financial independence from them. (My father did pay my college tuition, because he thought that was part of the bargain he had struck with me in California.) At Harvard I would at least be far enough away from them to manage my own affairs.

I settled back into my old dormitory, Adams House, then went to the New England Conservatory of Music in Boston, where I began to take singing lessons twice a week from a very nice middle-aged woman who had had a minor career as a concert soprano but had acquired a reputation as a good voice teacher. She may have been a fine teacher of women, but she knew very little about how to train the male voice. Unfortunately, it took me several months to figure this out, during which I nevertheless managed to enjoy myself. I was learning Italian art songs and practicing scales. I never went to class at all in Cambridge, but went to see every touring Broadway show. I also sang around town whenever I got the opportunity, mostly in local productions of Gilbert and Sullivan operettas. I could handle the light baritone roles, and I had a gift for comedic acting, so I managed to appear in several shows. As the young poet Grosvenor in *Patience* I even managed to get a good review from a critic on the *Boston Herald*. For the moment I was reasonably satisfied with my life, although I knew it couldn't last. At some point someone at the university was bound to inquire why I never went to class, and I was sure to flunk my exams.

My mother, feverishly trying to figure out some way to get back to Italy, had no idea what I was really up to. She sympathized with my musical aspirations, but she agreed with my father that I had done the right, sensible thing by going back to college to get my degree. During the time we had spent together in New York she had been much touched by my indignation over the treatment she had been receiving from the State Department in Washington, and we had spent some happy weeks together going to the theater and the opera. It was the first time we had seen much of each other since she had left for Italy, and for once we found nothing to argue about. As I had apparently agreed to conform by returning to college, she made no attempt to run the rest of my life, and we were able simply to enjoy each other's company. I didn't even mind squiring her to parties and dinners given by her old Fire Island friends, even though I now felt like an outsider in that world.

She had written Janet about this favorable development in our often troubled relationship and told her how proud she was of me, now that I had matured and become a man. "You are a curious mother," Janet had answered, "less maternal than most, far less than your mother. It is a final reward for your purely physical maternity that finally you have some spiritual companionship with your child at last. Does he still look merely like your best beau when you go out together?"

Janet could not yet get away from her work to come back to New York that winter. In addition to writing her biweekly Paris Letters, she had been spending time in Germany to turn out pieces about the concentration camps. "Buchenwald—a horrible shock," she wrote Natalia. "The news from the concentration camps seemed to me the most important news of all the years of war. Hitherto the struggle had been mainly military. But with the concentration camp emergences of dead and dying, what lay behind the war, vaguely perceived but not so important as the military figure of Nazi might, suddenly became the great, horrible, shocking protagonist. It must never be forgotten."

Later she attended the Nuremberg trials, at which Hermann Göring, Hitler's right hand, whom Janet described as looking like a fat soprano, and other Nazi bigwigs were being charged with the crimes against humanity for which some of them were to be hanged. Then she had embarked on a series of articles about the Nazi looting of Europe's art treasures, which would eventually be published as a book entitled *Men and Monuments*.

Janet worked slowly and laboriously, by her own account at a snail's pace, and occasionally she would fail to deliver her copy on time. Soon after returning to Paris she had failed to submit her second Letter because she had felt, as she wired Shawn, that "it was no good." She cited the difficulties of having to work in a chaotic postwar atmosphere in which the simplest daily tasks, such as making a telephone call, became chores because of the physical discomforts of insufficient heating and inadequate public services, along with a sort of dull resentment on the part of the French, who had survived the occupation and now found themselves subjected to what they perceived as an Allied one. "Another reason I failed to write a decent illuminating Letter is the fact that I have never learned to be a reporter in the muscular sense of going out and hunting news the way a hunter hunts rabbits," she confessed. "That is now necessary. Thus I am being scooped by every energetic male in my hotel. It will not happen again, but in the meantime some valuable first reports, which I should have been competent to obtain better than anyone, I have lost, such as the Gertrude Stein interview. I will never forgive myself, because *au fond* all I care about is my job and with our magazine [*sic*]. It has been more of a domestic relation than any other in my life."

Despite her self-confessed inadequacies, the fact is she had been contributing frequently and brilliantly an astonishing amount of copy, almost all of it first-rate. Katharine White, now installed at the magazine as its full-time fiction editor, wrote her admiringly in late January 1946. "I have long been owing you a fan letter about your work," she said. "It is magnificent and it makes me proud that *The New Yorker* has you in Europe."

What was really bothering Janet most about her return to Europe was not her work, but her personal life. Noel had heard about her involvement with "an Italian woman," as Hemingway had put it to her, but apparently Janet had not had the courage to break off her relationship with Noel. Janet confided in a letter to Solita Solano that Noel simply accepted "without question like a hind that is beaten [the] fact that I have an Italian friend. What a coward I am, but how can I deliver that blow which she so obviously cowers [at] in order not to receive?"

Janet had found Noel gaunt and wasted from the hardships of life under the German occupation, but was also irritated by Noel's continuing admiration for German culture and art. After all that had happened, Janet had come to hate the Germans and everything about them, a view reinforced by her tours of the concentration camps. "Europe is a charnel house," she confided to Solita.

Janet, however, continued to spend the weekends in Orgeval, where Noel would meet her faithfully at the railroad station. In Paris, Janet lived at the Hotel Scribe, the headquarters of most of the foreign press corps, where she became a popular and admired figure among her colleagues, who were charmed by her wit and her interest in their own work. She saw a lot of Hemingway and spent some evenings with him at the Deux Magots, where the novelist liked to read his poems to her. "I've seen a lot of him and love him far more than ever," she told Solita.

Back in New York, my mother sensed what was going on. She had never underestimated Janet's commitment to *The New Yorker* but had been hoping that somehow Janet would manage to find a way to include her within the pattern of her living arrangements. She was afraid that Janet would resume her old relationship with Noel and forget about her. It was becoming clearer and clearer to her that only her return to Europe could salvage the situation. After my grandmother left on April 5, even before my mother had received her final answer from the State Department, she began to line up freelance magazine assignments and to look for other ways to earn a living from Italy.

Lea's husband, Akos Tolnay, a journalist and scriptwriter, had worked also as an actor in the first great postwar Italian film, *Rome—Open City*, shot by the director Roberto Rossellini in the streets of Rome while the war was still going on. It had been smuggled into New York by a U.S. army sergeant, who had taken it to Joe Burstyn, a leading distributor of foreign films. Burstyn had realized immediately that he had a potentially lucrative property on his hands, but had no idea yet how to launch it. By Hollywood standards the movie was crudely edited and scored, with most of the roles played by amateurs Rossellini had plucked off the streets. *Open City* would become a classic, the first in the series of so-called neorealistic films that came out of Italy after the war and established the reputations of such directors as Rossellini, Vittorio De Sica, Luigi Zampa, and Alberto Lattuada. It also made a star out of Anna Magnani. When my mother, whom Akos had originally contacted months before in an effort to get her to help distribute the film, showed up in Burstyn's office and suggested that he put on a special preview showing of it to benefit an organization for Italian war orphans, the distributor saw the occasion as a perfect way to launch it. My mother, for her part, also saw the chance to create a job for herself as Burstyn's Italian contact, someone who could funnel many more such films from Italy toward the American market. Burstyn wasn't sure what the Italian movie industry might be up to in future, but he agreed that she would be the right person for the job, if anyone else was producing films of that quality.

In addition to her movie distribution work, my mother had her magazine assignments. She had already written two articles from Rome after the liberation, published in *Harper's Bazaar* and *Mademoiselle,* and had been assured by her editors that they would be happy to have other pieces from Italy from her. Then she had proposed a book on the history of the House of Savoy to Frank Taylor, then the editor in chief at Reynal and Hitchcock. He, too, had been encouraging, though he had not yet offered her a contract. All in all, she had begun to feel confident she'd be able to support herself abroad, at least for a while.

Janet was excited about the possibilities. They could spend more time together in the summer, then perhaps come back to New York together in the fall. Janet, too, was struggling to find a way to keep herself in New York for longer periods, should Natalia be unable to make a go of it in Europe, and had come up with a book idea of her own called *One Hundred and a Half: 1800 to 1950,* covering a period of history that had always fascinated her. She had already had an enthusiastic initial response from a New York publisher, though nothing yet in the way of a formal contract. Still, the possibilities for all of these projects seemed favorable, and Janet kept urging Natalia to get Frank Taylor to commit, especially since the House of Savoy itself had just been rejected in Italy by a national referendum that prevented Prince Umberto, the last of the line, from inheriting the throne abandoned by his disgraced father. "*Stop worrying,*" Janet wrote. "I'll come to New York—or I'll come to Rome. Now take your decisions calmly. My daily new colleague and writer—I think it absolutely marvelous you have those writing jobs offered you—and you can do them splendidly."

It seems only natural to me that I should have been the sole shadow cast over the joyous proceedings as my mother prepared to leave for Paris at the end of July. She had sublet both her Fire Island cottage and the top floor of the penthouse when I suddenly announced that I was leaving Harvard for New York. I was dissatisfied with my vocal progress and I'd been placed on probation because of my absence from classes, so there was nothing to hold me any longer in Cambridge. My father stopped speaking to me and I didn't receive much support from my mother either. "Attempting to become a tenor without Caruso's basic equipment seemed rather foolish to me," she observed, but at least she didn't fight me openly. There was no question of cancelling her plans or delaying her departure. I told her I'd be all right, that I planned to enroll at the Manhattan School of Music to study with a famous Wagnerian baritone named Friedrich Schorr, that I'd get some kind of part-time job, and that I had enough money to live on. Because of my military service, I was entitled to a year of unemployment insurance—only twenty dollars a week, but enough in those days to get by on—and my tuition would also be paid by the government, under the provisions of the so-called G.I. Bill of Rights. I told her not to worry about me.

She informed me that the upstairs had been sublet to a very nice Fire Island pal of hers, but that I could move into Mammina Ester's room. I had made a very big mistake in leaving Harvard, she warned me, but then she knew better than to try and tell me anything I didn't want to hear. "You are so contrary," she said to me in Italian. "Since when have we ever denied ourselves anything we wanted to do?" I answered. The truth is, I was looking forward to being on my own in New York.

That summer and fall of 1946 were among the happiest of Natalia's life. She spent the rest of the summer in Paris with Janet and was introduced at last to Noel and others of Janet's circle. To Janet's surprise, Noel and Natalia liked each other from the start, and they all spent weekends together at Orgeval. This was a tremendous relief to Janet, who had worried about the situation and felt guilty about what she sometimes considered a betrayal of old loyalties. Solita was still suffering from having lost Janet, and the two corresponded in secret so as not to trouble my mother. Janet could not let go of any of her old lovers and friends, but regarded that as a weakness and blamed herself for not being able to do so. I thought it was an admirable quality, and once told her so, when I had become aware of her guilt over Solita and that they were still in touch. When Noel, who by then had also become involved in another relationship, could so easily accept Natalia's presence in Janet's life, it enabled Janet to be more forgiving of herself.

In September the two women went to Italy, where Janet wrote for *The New Yorker* from Trieste, Capri, and Rome. By the end of the year she was back in Paris, settled again into her digs at the Hotel Scribe with the other foreign correspondents. Her favorite hangout there was the bar, an ugly but convivial room where she did most of her entertaining while sipping dry martinis, what my mother called her favorite "cocktailino." Natalia remained in Rome in her small apartment on the Via Piemonte, four blocks from the Via Veneto. She had liberated the flat from a fleeing Gestapo officer soon after her wartime entrance into the city and had hung onto it. Like all of her houses over the years, it made up in charm for what it lacked in conveniences. There she began to work on her own magazine assignments, to research her book and to scout around the renascent Italian movie industry for other films in production that might be suitable for American distribution.

I was on my own in New York, not sure of my future but determined to give my musical aspirations a try. I enrolled at the Manhattan School of Music on the Upper East Side and again found myself taking only two half-hour voice lessons a week, one of them with Schorr, whose interpretations of Wotan in the Ring cycle I had admired on recordings. Unfortunately for me, Schorr seemed to know even less about how to train the tenor voice than my teacher in Boston, and his assistant, another retired soprano, matched him in ignorance. I was learning very little about how to sing in my range, but at first I blamed myself. I went regularly to my lessons, practiced all of my exercises and also took on courses in *solfeggio* and music history. I assured myself that eventually I would learn how to sing; all I had to do was keep at it and not become discouraged.

Financially, I was making out quite well. In addition to my weekly income from what ex-G.I.s called the 52-20 Club, I had a part-time job in a book and music store in the East Fifties that paid me another twenty or thirty dollars a week in cash—in all, enough to survive on as a young single male, especially as I was installed rent-free in my mother's apartment. Moreover, I still had some money saved from my time in the army and discharge pay. I wasn't going to starve to death.

Nevertheless, my mother worried about me. She had heard from one of her Fire Island crowd that I had been seeing a lot of an artist named Corrado Cagli, and it worried her. Cagli, a Jewish Italian who had served in the American army during the war, was in his mid-forties and a homosexual. She began to write me obliquely warning letters, not so much about Cagli specifically as about the perils of being young and fairly naive on one's own in the big city. I knew, of course, that she was referring to Cagli, but I couldn't believe that she thought I was still a wide-eyed innocent about sex. I wrote her back, assuring her that I knew all about Cagli but that she was not to worry about me. Corrado was just a friend who liked me for myself (I had met him at one of my mother's parties) and was just being nice to me about inviting me along to art shows, the ballet, and special musical events. He had taken me to the premiere of Gian Carlo Menotti's new opera, *The Medium*, which I had been fascinated by, and afterward we had gone to a big party where I had met Menotti and the members of his cast. I was having a terrific time and she was not to worry about me. I was in no danger of becoming a homosexual.

I was not being honest with her, and she knew it. My relationship with Cagli had begun just as I had described it to her, but by the time she wrote me I was aware that he wanted more from me than friendship. It was obvious that he had bed on his mind. His overtures to me were not physical, but intellectual. The heart of his argument was that I had nothing to lose; if I didn't enjoy myself, he wouldn't insist. Why not give it a try? We liked each other, I had told him I didn't find him physically repulsive, and I didn't have to do anything I didn't want to do; he'd respect my desires or lack of them.

At first I said no. I told him I wasn't that way, that I was attracted only to the female body, and that although I valued his friendship, my feelings for him went no further than that. Corrado listened sympathetically, smiled, and did not insist. He continued to invite me to go along with him, and introduced me into his world of established working artists and performers, a world I longed to be a part of. The opening of an exhibition at an uptown gallery of his remarkable drawings of concentration camp scenes attracted a lot of attention, and I was flattered to be included in his brilliant circle of friends.

Finally, a night came when he did at last talk me into bed with him. We had been out to dinner with a party of musicians and ballet dancers, after which Corrado invited me up to his place to spend the night. He lived in a cold-water railroad apartment on Second Avenue in midtown. We had several glasses of wine together and then he again suggested I give sex with him a try. At first I refused, but after twenty minutes or so of discussion I decided what the hell, why not? I wasn't getting laid anywhere else then, and I had always envied the gay world because everyone in it seemed to be constantly in bed with everyone else. I took off my clothes and lay down beside him, having no idea what he expected of me.

Looking back on this experience, I realize that Cagli must not have been a very expert lover. There was some clumsy groping about and an only partially successful attempt to get me erect, after which he made it clear that what he wanted was penetration. I told him that definitely was not my scene and retreated across the room to a single guest bed, where, fairly drunk on the wine I'd consumed, I soon fell asleep. In the morning, we had a cup of coffee together, after which I went home. We never discussed what had happened and he made only one more unsuccessful attempt to seduce me. But he continued to invite me along to rehearsals, art openings, and parties, for which I remained grateful to him. He made me feel I belonged in this adult world of artists working hard and well at their professions.

Two days after my one overt brush with homosexual love, I received another letter from my mother. The tone of this one was quite different from all the others I had been getting. My aunt Franca had taken her to see a celebrated *mago*, a wizard who foretold the future and who had acquired a large following among middle-class housewives in Rome. He had predicted that I would have a brilliant career, perhaps not in music, and that my mother was to stop worrying about me. He had been so amazing about his knowledge of me and what I was about that she had instantly felt reassured. I was to go on studying and practicing hard and everything would be all right. What was the matter with her? I wrote her back indignantly. Of course I was going to be all right, but not because some *mago* had gazed into a crystal ball. No, no, she answered, the *mago* read cards and he was truly extraordinary. Yes, it was silly, she agreed, but life was a mystery, wasn't it, and *non si sa mai*, one never knows. At least she hadn't consulted a priest on my behalf.

I was enjoying my time in New York, but I was also becoming increasingly frustrated by my lack of vocal progress. I could sing all right up through an F sharp, but I couldn't seem to hit any of the tenor high notes. I realized much later that this was because no one had ever spoken to me about such crucial matters as passage notes, head tones, and, above all, sustaining a vocal line on a firmly supported column of air. All I knew was that I was working hard at all of my exercises, but that for some reason I wasn't learning how to sing properly. My teachers assured me that eventually I would begin to sing like a god, but I was beginning to have my doubts.

My mother sensed my frustration. Her solution was to suggest I join her in the spring of 1947 in Italy and spend the summer there. For my twenty-first-birthday present, she would pay for my ticket and all my expenses. Then, in the fall, I could come back to New York and start again, perhaps with a different teacher. I could see Mammina Ester and my aunts again and also meet the rest of my Italian family, none of whom had set eyes on me since I had left as a small boy of eight. Just breathing Italian air might be good for my singing, she suggested. After all, Italy was the cradle of opera; spending time in the country was sure to open up my throat and improve my whole outlook on song.

I jumped at the opportunity. Suddenly my head was full of the fragmented memories of my childhood, snapshots of myself on the pebbly beaches of Capri and in the streets and piazzas of Rome, with a warm sun overhead and a clamor of voices and church bells in the distance. I had shut all these sights and sounds out of my consciousness for so long that now, as they came flooding back on me, I felt a tremendous pull toward this world I had denied for so long. I wanted to throw my arms around Mammina Ester again, to bask in the delicately perfumed warmth of her embrace and uncritical approval. I wanted to eat the favored dishes she would cook for me, *pomodori al riso* and *mozzarelle in carrozza;* listen to the tales of her younger years, when she had been at the center of the nation's cultural events. The whole prospect became bathed in a warm glow of anticipation, as if I were a prodigal son returning at last to the scene of some former, long-lost triumph.

I sailed in early June on the *Saturnia,* an aging Italian liner that during the war had been converted into a hospital ship. Most of the passengers occupied large open spaces between decks and slept in double bunks. I had managed to wangle myself into one of the few cabins, up under the bow. We were eight in the room, but compared to the chaos elsewhere, with children running up and down the passageways and half the passengers seeming to suffer from seasickness as they lay moaning on their mattresses, the accommodations were luxurious. I made friends with an old man from the Abruzzi, who slept in the bunk below mine and who was going home to his ancestral village in the mountains to spend his last days with a brother he hadn't seen in forty-seven years. Although he kept to himself and hardly ever spoke, for some reason he took a fancy to me and we spent some time in each other's company. He became the central character in a short story I wrote a decade later, my first appearance in *The New Yorker*. I remember being enormously grateful to him, because in this unfamiliar complement of mostly immigrants going home for the first time in many years I felt like a stranger, almost an intruder.

For one thing, I discovered I couldn't speak Italian anymore. Apart from the bits of family chatter that had survived over the years, I had shut myself off from the language and, though I could understand it, I had lost the practice of daily communication. Alarmed and embarrassed, I paced the upper decks of the ship trying to summon it back by constructing sentences and conjugating verbs. Worse from my point of view was my inability as a singer to hit high notes. I was one of seven tenors on board, including Giovanni Martinelli, a lion from the golden age of the Met, and I was the only one who couldn't sing in public, at least not in my proper range. Nobody wanted to hear Gilbert and Sullivan or the *arie antiche* I had been practicing for months. The other tenors, except for Martinelli (who whisperingly referred to all of them as "dogs and goats"), would give spontaneous concerts in the lounge every night, bracing themselves against the movement of the ship while belting high notes off the walls. I had told everyone that I, too, was

a singer, but I couldn't compete. I remained off to one side, cha-
grined and envious.

The old man consoled me by telling me that I was right not to
sing. These other tenors on board were indeed all dogs and goats;
just being able to hit high notes did not make them singers. One
day, after I had studied enough, I would show them all how to do
it. He also helped me with my Italian, although he himself, I realized, was barely literate; he was much more at home in a dialect I
couldn't understand at all. I was grateful to him. I had begun to be
afraid of what would happen on my arrival, that instead of returning to a home I had left as a child, I would walk down the gangplank as a stranger. I seemed not to be connected anymore to my
Italian background, whereas this old peasant from the Abruzzi still,
after all these years of exile, had his feet planted firmly in the rocky
soil of his native mountains. "No, no, you will see," he said to me
one afternoon, as we sat in deck chairs staring out over the sea, "it
will all come back to you. You do not forget your past. It is in your
bones."

Very early on the morning of our arrival, just after dawn, I went
up on deck. We were about to enter the Bay of Naples after ten
days at sea, and the old ship had slowed down. In the dim light we
glided noiselessly through a fog that tucked us in like a soft blanket,
with an occasional blast from the ship's horn to announce our impending arrival. Suddenly, the fog began to lift as the sun rose, and
a rocky hillside dotted with whitewashed houses appeared off the
starboard side. The sight stunned me, as if I had turned a corner
and come unexpectedly face to face with an old friend I had
thought had vanished forever. I was gazing at Capri, which now
looked as familiar to me as the streets of New York. As the old man
had predicted, I still had the place in my bones.

ELEVEN

TRANSITIONS

The summer of 1947 changed my life. I had been worried that I would find myself a stranger in Italy, but from that first glimpse of Capri from the deck of the *Saturnia* I knew that I was coming home. The chaos of the arrival in Naples, where the ship was met by a huge unruly crowd of relatives and friends searching for passengers whom some of them had not seen for decades, with porters and officials of one sort or another swarming aboard as the passengers struggled to disembark down the gangplanks, seemed perfectly normal to me, and hilariously delightful. I had a large steamer trunk full of necessities my mother had asked me to bring—sugar, chocolate, nylons, soap, Kleenex, even toilet paper— unavailable in Italy except on the black market. Had I been told to open it going through customs it would have immediately been confiscated, but instinctively, as if born to the job, I had known what to do. I had grabbed one of the porters coming on board, a wiry citizen with the shrewd, acquisitive face of a pawnbroker, and promised him ten dollars, a small fortune to him, if he could get my things through without being opened. "Don't worry about it," he said, maneuvering my huge trunk onto his dolly. We swept past the customs officers on the pier, pausing only long enough for my man to whisper in the ear of one of them. When I tipped him another five dollars, he wanted to know if I needed a good hotel, a taxi, a virgin. I said no, thanked him, and waved goodbye as he rushed back toward the ship to seek out another client.

My second cousin Franco came to meet me. He and his family lived in Naples, where his father, a civil servant in charge of awarding building permits, was soon to become very rich. Franco was almost exactly my age. He had blue eyes, a full head of curly blonde hair, and spoke Italian like a Frenchman, rolling his r's at the back of his throat. He threw his arms around me, kissed me on both cheeks, and whisked me off to the American Express office, where I checked my luggage before going off to lunch with him at an outdoor restaurant along the waterfront. I had several hours to kill before my train left for Rome. It was a bright sunny day, the whole city basking beneath a blue sky with Vesuvius, a wisp of smoke curling out of its crater, lurking in the background. As we ate an incredibly good dish of pasta and drank glasses of pale white wine, Franco filled me in on the family news, peppered with names I dimly recalled but whose exact relationship to me remained a mystery. I listened with half an ear while my eyes scanned the waterfront, seeing the ruined buildings from the wartime air raids, the carcasses of ships half sunk in the harbor, the hordes of people passing by our table who seemed to be dressed mostly in rags, but finding the whole scene inexplicably cheery. As Franco rambled on, all I could think about was how happy I felt, how excited at just being there.

It was a feeling of exhilaration I couldn't banish, even after lunch when Franco gave me a quick tour of the area. He was full of concern for the desperate situation most of the local citizens were in. He had a head full of statistics about the unemployed, the homeless, the orphans, prostitution, the ruined infrastructure, the seeming inability of the government, both local and national, to do anything about all the problems burdening the society. As we strolled through narrow streets crowded with poor people, with ragged children scampering underfoot, he continued to pour out his litany of woe. I gathered that crime and the corruption of the people in charge of the city government were among the major issues that had to be dealt with forcefully and immediately. I listened attentively now, but still I couldn't respond to his catalogue of despair. The city was too alive, these streets too full of the clamor of activity, these children too mischievous and energetic, these older people too full of their own gossipy affairs to seem as defeated and desperate as Franco made them out to be. When he spoke of the need to construct a new society, a socialist one founded on justice and public works, I nodded in agreement, but in my heart I denied the message he was spouting. Naples had always been poor, I knew that, ever since the demise of the Bourbon monarchy and the unification of the country under the Piedmontese, but somehow it had survived. "It's enough we have this sun, it's enough we have this sea," was a line from one of the Neapolitan songs I sang; and now, as I walked along beside Franco, I understood its exact meaning.

When I expressed a doubt or two to Franco about the need or even the possibility of such northern solutions for such a people, he shook his head vigorously and told me I didn't understand. Once I had spent some time in Italy, he said, I would begin to see he was right. A new society, a new Italy would have to arise now out of the ashes of the old one, founded on the true democratic socialism Karl Marx had envisaged when he wrote *Das Kapital*. Yes, yes, he was right, I told him as I allowed myself to be led this way and that through the narrow alleys and refuse-strewn streets of Naples, but maybe tomorrow or the day after that or the day after that. But not today, not under this sun, not in this hubbub of conviviality, not with the sounds of mandolins in the air. As we emerged suddenly from a side street and I found myself again confronted by a view of the whole magnificent harbor, with the ancient city sprawled around its sweeping curved shoreline in the shadow of the volcano, it seemed to me I could hear singing, as if I had unwittingly strolled into a scene from a romantic opera.

Rome was even more of a revelation. I stepped off the train to find myself immediately at home. Not that I recognized the Stazione Termini, a vast white structure partly shattered by bombs. No, it was the smell of the city that hit me first, an odor of old marble and ancient subterranean passages, of dusty cobblestones and grass and packed earth baking in hard sunlight. No other place in the world smells quite like it. I sniffed the air and walked out into the street as if into the courtyard of an old, familiar palazzo whose crumbling stairways and musty old rooms I had lived in all of my life. "Rome was a shock to me when I first came here in 1921, as Paris was not," Janet wrote about the city in a journal she began to keep in 1947. "There was a strong smell, which was of old human usage, which offended me and added what was the barbaric quality of antiquity to its buildings and palaces, a red and yellow antiquity and still lived in. I had accepted the ruined antiquities of Greece, which are white and in which no one lived. Paris was like a dream of acceptable loveliness. There is a savage quality in Rome which frightened me then, which I now accept and am stimulated by. . . ."

My mother and a friend came to meet me at the station in the friend's car, an ancient Fiat sedan, as taxis were still scarce. We had another of our grand reunions, this one in Italian. No sooner had I landed than I had begun to speak the language again, full of grammatical errors and curious omissions and hybrid words I adapted from English, but with the élan of a returning native and a sudden lack of self-consciousness that within weeks had me chattering away like a citizen. The American years peeled away from me like the outer layers of skin from a snake and I plunged back into my Italian background as easily as if I had never left it.

My mother's apartment consisted of a large fourth-floor studio room overlooking the street, with a small bedroom, bath, and kitchen tucked in behind it. The bathroom fixtures were black, in keeping with the previous occupant's career as a Gestapo agent. From there it was a short walk to the Via Veneto with its sidewalk cafés, or up into the park of the Villa Borghese, where I had played as a child and roamed about under the trees to search for pine cones out of which I would dig the tasty white nuts. With my mother I revisited many of my old childhood haunts, and in her company I also became reacquainted with some of my relatives. Mammina Ester lived in an apartment only a few blocks away with Franca and her young son, Federico. During the war Franca had had an affair with the painter Emmanuele Cavalli, then had left her husband to go and live with Cavalli and his wife in Florence. This untenable domestic arrangement had not lasted very long, and Ester had had to go to Florence to rescue her. This family drama had consumed Ester's attention and, to a lesser extent my mother's, for several months.

Lea and Akos and their daughter Flavia lived in a luxurious penthouse overlooking the Corso. Akos was busy writing screenplays and trying to organize various movie productions, while Lea complained constantly about him and disparaged him openly as a failure despite the fact that he seemed to be doing very well. I became very fond of both of them, but almost every visit to their house degenerated into explosive scenes of accusation and recrimination. And all our other relatives, of whom there seemed to be dozens, were involved in tangled intrigues and disasters large and small that apparently had no end. My mother kept up with all of them and couldn't seem to keep from becoming involved, if only as an opinionated spectator. After several weeks, it was a relief to get out of Rome to spend a month on Capri, where my mother had rented a small house halfway up the slopes of Monte Solaro overlooking the harbor.

We saw very little of each other the rest of that summer. The morning after our arrival, while sipping a cappuccino and reading a

Neapolitan newspaper in the tiny central piazza, I fell into conversation with a large, cheerful group of young Italians at the adjoining tables. They invited me to a party that evening at somebody's villa up the slope of the hill leading to the ruins of the Emperor Tiberius's palace. It turned out to be a terrific party, packed with guests of all ages from all over the world, among them Sinclair Lewis. The novelist, whom I had admired as a writer since my early teens, when I had first read *Babbitt* and *Main Street*, was too drunk to carry on a conversation, but stood in a corner of the room, his back against the wall, staring dumbly at the goings-on. The hostess was a loud American woman married to a wealthy Egyptian and neither she nor her husband seemed to know any of their guests. Later that night, hopelessly drunk herself and cackling like a terrified hen, she suddenly toppled backwards from an outside terrace into the garden two stories below, where she lay on her back until one of her servants propped her up on her feet again. Few people even noticed the incident, and no one seemed even mildly concerned about her.

I fell in with the group of young Italians I had met earlier in the piazza. Among them was a beautiful red-haired woman in her midthirties whom I'll call Daria. She was a Florentine princess, rich and long-separated from her husband. She was spending the summer with her younger brother Guido in a small house they had rented on the other side of the island toward the Piccola Marina. He was gay and living with his older lover, Willy, who had just opened a dress shop off the Piazza di Spagna in Rome. Daria liked me, I liked Daria. She and Guido and Willy and I all left the party together and walked down to their villa in the early hours of the morning. I was invited to spend the night, which I did, mostly in Daria's arms. We made love till dawn, then slept till noon, when we arose, drank a caffè latte together and strolled back up toward the piazza. I finally got back to my mother's house around dinner time to find her sitting out on the terrace, a glass of wine in hand and looking out at the sunset. "I imagined you were having an adventure," she said,

with a laugh. "Did you have a good time?" The best, I assured her.
Italy obviously had a lot more to offer a young man than New
York. I hadn't been to bed with a woman since my last few weeks
at Harvard months before.

I spent most of my time on Capri with Daria, Guido, and Willy.
I came home every night, so that my mother wouldn't worry
about me, but in the morning, after breakfast and with a tooth-
brush tucked into my breast pocket, I would walk down to the piazza to meet my new friends. After a cappuccino together, we'd go
off for a day of swimming and boating. They had rented a motor
launch that would take us to any of the dozens of secluded little
coves that dotted the shoreline or in and out of the island's many
caves. We would swim ashore on some empty beach or disembark
on a rocky outcropping to eat a picnic lunch, washed down with
orange juice and champagne, then spend most of the afternoon
basking in the sun, with occasional plunges into the cool, clear water. Sometimes we'd hike over the hills toward the main town of
Anacapri and climb up to various spots from where we could look
out over the whole bay toward Naples and Sorrento. Before dinner
we'd go back to their villa and rest, though much of our siesta time
was taken up with making love. Daria was an experienced and vo-
racious sensualist who taught me more about the pleasures of the
flesh than I had ever imagined as a feckless teenager. We'd doze off
eventually in each other's arms, then get up around seven or seven-
thirty for drinks before venturing out into the night for dinner and
dancing until the early-morning hours. By the time my month on
the island was over, I looked the picture of health, brown as a wal-
nut from the midsummer sun, but I was actually bone tired from
not enough sleep. Daria and I parted amicably, without tears or
sentimentalities, in the piazza one morning, as if we had been no
more than casual friends. They were leaving two days later, Daria
to go home to her palazzo in Florence, Guido and Willy to Rome
to reopen their dress shop after the summer vacation. I never saw
any of them again.

●

My mother did not seem to be working very hard at her new career as a freelance writer that summer. She had begun to research
her possible book on the House of Savoy, but her efforts in that direction seemed halfhearted to me, as if she lacked confidence in
the project. Nor did she seem very intent on gathering material for
magazine articles. For one thing, she was too caught up in the family dramas, which to me seemed unending and so convoluted that
no solution to any of them was even faintly possible. The most serious of them was the one raging on the Corso. Lea, constantly at
war with Akos, seemed to be slipping permanently into madness.
Doctors were being consulted and various medications tried out,
but without much success. Her rages, delusions, and severe bouts
of depression became more frequent, drawing my mother, Mammina Ester, and others into the whirlpool of emotions that afflicted
her household.

In the middle of all this I became ill with a spontaneous pneu-
mothorax, a sudden partial deflation of my upper right lung, that
was at first misdiagnosed as tuberculosis. For the first few hours of
my attack I sat in my mother's apartment pinned to my armchair,
fighting for air. It was several hours before I could move and a couple
of weeks before I could walk more than a few yards without having
to rest. Alarmed, Janet wrote from California, where she was helping
to care for her sick mother: "I am speechless. I have nothing to answer back to the impersonal entities primitive civilizations used to
call *fate, destiny,* providence or even God and Devil." She wondered
whether I had a congenital weakness that might have been behind
my inability to produce much operatic volume as a singer. My
mother, however, was convinced I was paying now for what she
viewed as my summer of self-indulgent debauchery. Because she
was never ill herself, for several days she couldn't make herself believe that I had anything more than a cold. When she became aware
that I couldn't even walk across the room without being stopped in

my tracks by the pain, like an iron hand clamped around the upper lobe of my lung, she finally took me to a doctor, a well-regarded lung specialist. He diagnosed consumption and recommended a complete deflation of the lung and six months in bed. Luckily, we ignored him. Every day I improved a little, and by the time we left for Paris in late September on our way back to New York, I was able to walk almost normally, though I didn't dare open my mouth in song. For some unknown reason a bubble of tissue had burst inside my lung, for which the only cure is time; the organ slowly reinflates itself. After six months, I was back to normal and singing again, an American doctor having assured me that the ailment was unlikely to recur.

I was going back to New York to resume my vocal training, while my mother's plans were to spend the next six to eight months there working on her book. Janet would come to New York to spend the winter with her, after which they would return to Europe. Janet, however, had to rush again to California that fall to spend several more weeks in her sister's house in Altadena helping to care for their dying eighty-four-year-old mother. Hildegarde, on whom had fallen the entire burden of her mother's illness, was exhausted. She had a small son of her own to take care of, and a husband, the architect Eric Monhoff, who was too busy working and teaching to be of any practical help around the house. Janet found their living conditions filthy and their marriage in danger of breaking up from the strain.

"H is absolutely exhausted by a quarter century of umbilical cord service to mother," she wrote Natalia. "If mother doesn't leave life soon, H's will be dangerously shortened." Janet, who hated all forms of housework, spent her days cleaning up, doing laundry, and helping to give her mother the shots of vitamins and painkillers that were prolonging her life. Mary had stomach cancer, but her doctor thought her heart would fail long before the cancer killed her. She lingered on drugs, however, for weeks, sleeping twelve hours a day and needing constant attention when awake. Finally, during the night of December 3, as Janet sat beside her with the family cat on her lap, she died peacefully in her sleep. "She had finally laid down her years," Janet wrote. "Now she is ashes, like all fires that are burned out."

When Janet returned to New York after her mother's funeral, life resumed on the rooftop chickencoop much as it had been during the early war years. My mother worked on her book on the House of Savoy and Janet began to work on another book project of her own, this one a history of the Paris Commune of 1871. She didn't seem to be making much progress on it and worried whether she had the staying power to turn out a full-length manuscript. "Pretending that I am trying to work and not really working," she confided to her journal. "This does not fool me, as a result, but it does at least pro- duce another result. I am irritable, vexed and vexing. This state, these three states, this nasty and vicious poisoned trio of states will continue until I do work. I am nearly fifty-six years old and have known this condition, this set of conditions, to operate for at least thirty years of my fifty-five." She never did finish the book.

She was happier putting together for *The New Yorker* a Profile of her friend Cheryl Crawford, a Broadway producer and one of the founders of the original Group Theatre and later the Actors Stu- dio. She knew she was working well when she could be unaware of the passage of time, look up from her desk to find that the hours had passed in seconds.

For my mother it was a happy winter. Despite her financial wor- ries about the future, she had Janet back to herself and away from what she called "the sinister Paris influence," by which she meant Janet's deep attachments to old relationships and an independent way of life in which my mother could never play a significant part. Intellectually, she understood Janet's position, but emotionally she couldn't accept it. She longed for a permanent arrangement that would enable Janet to be with her all of the time; she wanted a marriage. But Janet could not and would not let go of her past or turn her back on the old lovers and friends who had enriched her life. "I have told you that twenty years habit of life plus, even more moulding, my habit of work here had made my ties, which are painful to loose," she had written Natalia earlier in the year.

You know that. My feelings and attitude toward Noel have not changed except that I try to be less irritable, a bad habit I have been growing into with everybody but you. Our relations have not changed since the first minute I saw her. My sadness in her regard has been dual. One is for her, as a person, because it must always surely occur to the mind of the one who has fallen out [of] love how painful it must be to the other who still loves; and second and even more destructive is the evidence of not only the ephemeral quality of love itself, where I am concerned, but the curious violence of my physical repugnance, almost, once the earlier relation is finished. To dislike the touch even of the hand of someone one has deeply loved is so unpleasant, so mean a mystery. Do you feel that way? It makes every organic emotion seem so insecure. Do you feel that way about Joan [du Guerny.]? Tell me or am I only a monster? On the other hand, the sociable relation with those I have loved—that hangover which you loathe—seems to me, on the other hand, only admirable and consoling, as natural as the revulsion seems unnatural.

I was not a part of their household that winter. I had resumed my vocal studies at the Manhattan School of Music, but I had moved to the Village to share a twenty-two-dollar-a-month cold-water flat on Tenth and Hudson with my oldest friend from Dalton, George de Kay, who had embarked on a career in publishing as an editor at Doubleday. We lived in bohemian squalor, relieved occasionally by the weekend appearances of girlfriends whose major contributions to our lives were to clean up our messes. Tim Seldes, another Dalton pal, also working at Doubleday, practically moved in with us, and we spent many of our nights in Village bars, mostly in pursuit of girls. My Italian summer seemed like a dream. And as I continued to fail at making much progress with my singing, I began to scheme about returning to Italy, a prospect that I became convinced was essential to my future. Through a connection of my mother's, I had gone to sing for Giuseppe De Luca, a great baritone from the glory years of the old Met. "Yes, I hear a voice there," he had said, after I had run through a couple of my Italian songs, "but it is blocked in the throat. You must study." I was studying, but I was getting nowhere. Italy became identified in my head with everything I now most wanted in my life—not only an ability to sing like a god, but also with living well. How could I adjust to poverty in New York, when I had just had a taste of Rome and Capri?

TWELVE

ROADS
TO
ROME

On March 3, 1948, Janet sailed back to France. "We left with the band playing 'God Bless America' and 'Happy Days' and I crying," she wrote to Natalia from her cabin on board the *America*. "I love you and my heart, so often wounded, with cracks in it like cracks in a Roman glaze, suffered another permanent injury to leave you. I am going to earn like any man and will *help you* to come over to Rome, if circumstances permit." She was approaching her fifty-sixth birthday and full of doubts and misgivings about herself and her ability to write anything worthwhile. She had made little progress on her book about the Paris Commune and blamed the failure partly on her age. "I hope this is my last birthday," she noted despairingly in her journal. "I have never loved myself nor respected me strongly, but I was able to be tolerant of me. Now no more. I find no excuse. My body feels old, I lack muscular control and I think my mind is definitely failing. The difference between fifty-four and fifty-six is, in my life, fatal. It is a ten-year stretch."

Janet had hoped that the book project would engage her attention completely and make a break from *The New Yorker* possible, so she and Natalia could be together permanently. She had already hinted to both Shawn and Ross that she would like to withdraw as a regular contributor from her Paris post in order to spend more time on other work, though the real reason was obviously a desire not to lose Natalia. They had had a happy winter together in New York, but neither of them had succeeded in solving the permanent puzzle, which was how they would manage to support themselves. The small advance Natalia had received for her book on the Italian monarchy would not keep her solvent and she was actively looking about for a job, possibly again with NBC. If she were to remain in New York, what would Janet do? The solution Janet hoped for was Natalia's return to Rome. Perhaps next year they could be together in New York again, if nothing materialized to keep Natalia in Italy.

The pressure my mother applied on Janet for some sort of permanent arrangement was unrelenting. In her own uncertainty and her unhappiness at seeing Janet go back to Paris, Noel, and her old circle of friends, she never allowed Janet to ignore how much suffering she was causing by insisting on her independence. I caught whiffs and glimpses of this aspect of their relationship in New York, when my mother would hint darkly in Janet's presence at her selfishness or casually drop some small but devastating observation about Janet's avoidance of responsibilities, her distaste for the routines of human life, as if nothing mattered but her precious work. Janet, still riddled with guilt over Hildegarde's self-sacrifice on behalf of their mother, had no defense against Natalia's passionate feelings. "I have used myself and people who loved me like victims of a series of emotional accidents," she wrote in her journal. "There has been blood, pain and groaning." She thought she had arrived on the downhill slope of life, with nothing before her but old age and failing creative powers; she would never be the person she had dreamed of becoming, but remain "desperate and homeless because I have no place to go, to remove me from myself." She was happiest with Natalia and was now determined to bring about a working and living arrangement that would unite them, even if it meant breaking with *The New Yorker*, the one relationship in her life that had provided not only a living for her but a regular and now prestigious outlet for her best work.

My mother spent most of that spring and summer trying to figure out a way to make her return to Italy possible. She hoped, among other ventures, to become a regular contributor to *Flair*, a new magazine being launched in New York by Fleur Cowles, the wife of the publisher of *Look*. Cowles was young, aggressively ambitious, and had hired as her editor-in-chief George Davis, who was a friend of ours and who at *Mademoiselle* had published one of my mother's pieces from Italy. *Flair* was to be modelled on the old *Vanity Fair*, a slick, elegant magazine aimed at an upper-middle-class market. Natalia suggested a number of story ideas, and Davis introduced her to Cowles. It looked promising, but how many articles a year would any American magazine be able to publish out of Italy? Surely not more than two or three. Still, the assignments might be enough to take my mother back to Rome for a few months at least, after which, she thought, she and Janet could return to New York.

In Paris, Janet had quickly resumed her work for *The New Yorker*, even as she had notified Shawn and Ross that she would soon be giving it up. She rushed off to Königstein in Germany, not far from Frankfurt, to do a story on the trial of Fritz Thyssen, an industrialist who had cooperated with the Nazis, and went on to tackle another piece about a camp for displaced persons, refugees awaiting asylum somewhere. She was full of projects and working hard. It seems unlikely to me even now that she ever really meant to leave the magazine, but she had to go through the motions of a separation, if only to ease her conscience. She felt a tremendous sense of obligation to Natalia, while at the same time she was clearly exas-

perated not only by the compromises love imposed, but also by the
basic needs of the flesh. "There are moments, Natalia, when the
very thought of a sexual organ, with its opening and rosiness and
strange ill-organized shape, its peculiar cleft trident, fills me with
real shock and horror," she wrote to her.

So much done for that which is strangely small. Life. Another version of it, even if unfertile. That is the idea which often so con-
stricts me with my love for you—you know that; the idea that at
my age my machinery of activity is *that,* seems both improper and
inactivating; it almost makes me impotent. At this time I should be
motivated by another organ, the brain. . . . You have given me
more interest, solidarity in ideas and better conversation than any
other lover, my darling. The real regret is that I did not meet you so
early that I knew nothing else and that you are not a Roman man,
for I should have changed and been yours, a masculine wife but
adoring. My admiration for you is as high as my contempt for the
sex relation which moves us all our lives till we die in that organ.

Back in Paris and at work on her Letters, she received what she
thought was a strange communication from Ross—strange because
she had lost confidence in her ability to write anything worthwhile.
"I think of writing you every time I read a Paris Letter, but then I
grow depressed, wondering what we are going to do when and if
you pull out of Paris and that discourages me and I fall to brooding,"
Ross told her. "I realize each time that we aren't going to replace
you, baby, and that we'll have to arrange for something else from
out of there. Maybe we'll be able to do something good and maybe
not. God will decide. You have been writing with more authority
than ever this year and it seems to me that you have been really ex-
celling yourself, which is a feat." Though Janet kept insisting that she
was doing poor work and writing well below her potential, it seems
clear that she also wanted Natalia to know the extent of the sacrifice
she was prepared to make for her.

That spring, Italy was in the throes of a major election upon which the attention of the Western Allies was closely focused. The Italian Communist Party, the largest in Western Europe, was threatening to acquire enough votes to take over the government, a prospect that especially alarmed the U.S. Ross and Shawn wanted Janet to go to Rome to cover the election, but Janet was afraid Natalia would object. She had always relied on Natalia to help her with her research in Italy, especially as she didn't speak the language, and she was afraid of angering Natalia by writing trivially or incorrectly about her beloved's home country. She would have Franca to help her this time, however, and Natalia grudgingly allowed her to proceed.

What Janet found in Italy that spring was not a country about to be taken over by a Communist regime, but an ancient civilization in jeopardy because it still could not provide enough employment for its people. "In two thousand years it has not conquered poverty," she noted in her journal. "Poverty is what has helped cause the necessary political invention of Communism. Italy is thus an object of conquest now by a going political concern which is only thirty-one years old. The Italians resent American imperialism as they did English imperialism and the French empire." She also observed that Italians should be the last to criticize the U.S. "Rome was great only as head of an empire. It first patented the idea in Western Europe."

Her reports from Italy were not as authoritative as her Paris Letters, but she predicted correctly that Italy would not go Communist and explained why. She also enjoyed herself with Franca, Mammina Ester, and a number of my mother's friends. Franca, especially, was a delight. Not only was she helpful to Janet as an interpreter and expert on Italian affairs, but she had a lively, enthusiastic personality and a wide circle of friends and acquaintances in the arts. She could make Janet laugh and she whisked her around the city in her tiny Fiat with the reckless panache of a race-car driver. Janet was very fond of her and admitted she could not have written so authoritatively from Italy without her help. She also acquired a renewed appreciation of the ancient capital she had come to admire. "Rome is the other handsomest city in Europe," she wrote. "And it is still peopled by the handsomest race painted." Her only unpleasant experiences were limited to the city's bathrooms. "The toilets and plumbing of Rome never work properly," she complained. "It may be that the cloaca maxima of antique Rome functioned because it probably ran downhill. But no other cloacal plumbing has operated well in the last two thousand years, I wager. I fly into a dainty feminine rage when faced again and again in life with man's virile indifference to human excrement and what to do with it, nicely. He builds palaces and flying machines and invents philosophy and baroque and is perfectly indifferent to a bowl of turds around his own house."

While my mother was struggling that winter and spring to put her own professional life in order, I was becoming increasingly dissatisfied with my own situation. I was having a pretty good time frequenting Village bars and chasing girls, but my career was going nowhere. I wasn't learning how to sing properly, and was becoming frustrated. All I could think about was getting back to Italy, where I had convinced myself I'd finally learn how to sing. The only problem I had was how to support myself over there. My mother gave me a thousand dollars, all she could afford, and I would still have some money from the government, under the G.I. Bill of Rights, to pay for my singing lessons, but I needed to find another source of income.

My father suggested I might be able to earn some money by becoming a stringer for *Variety* and *Billboard*, the two entertainment weeklies. He set up appointments for me with the editors there, and I was taken on as a part-time correspondent, to be paid a few dollars per column inch for whatever material I'd be able to get into print. The money was insignificant, but the connections would enable me to join the Stampa Estera, the foreign press club in Rome, where I might be able to land other writing, reporting, or translation jobs. I had never considered becoming a journalist or a writer, but I felt confident I'd be able at least to earn enough money to keep afloat until I could launch myself into the world of opera.

Then word came from Rome that Mammina Ester had been hired to be the editor of a new Italian encyclopedia aimed at the American reader. It would publish articles in English by well-known Italian authors and experts on every aspect of Italian life. Most of these pieces would have to be translated from the original Italian. Mammina Ester would commission the articles and I would be in charge of the translations, with a small staff working under our supervision. The salary was low, but enough to enable me to live reasonably well. I wrote back to Mammina Ester, accepting the offer, and booked a cheap passage for myself in mid-May to Genoa on a Greek freighter sailing out of Hoboken, New Jersey. Janet knew my departure would upset my mother and wrote to console her, but she also told her I should be encouraged to go, that getting back to Italy would be "a sweet relief, surely, for his young spirit."

By this time my father had given up his attempts to keep me in college or influence me in any way. He had recently remarried, to a brilliant young woman from Brooklyn named Florence Smolen, and seemed happier than I had seen him in years. The final parting from Ilka had been bitter, and he had been wounded by rumors circulating around New York that she had left him because he had been unable to function sexually anymore. When Florence gave birth to twin boys in the fall of 1947, I had been at his apartment to greet him coming home from the hospital. As he emerged from the elevator and I shook his hand, he said, "That'll show her," meaning Ilka. I thought it was an odd thing for him to say on such an occasion, but I hadn't realized how deeply he had been humiliated.

I saw little of him that last winter in New York, but he was working very hard, still smoking heavily and drinking a lot. Television was beginning to take over the world of radio, and the transition from one medium to another was monopolizing most of his time. Not since the advent of sound in movies had there been such an upheaval in the entertainment industry, and my father was totally enmeshed in it, with all of the William Morris Agency's many clients involved. Surveys had shown that the minute people acquired television sets they stopped listening to radio. The trick was to move the Morris clients into the new medium without endangering their careers, but already it was becoming obvious that not everybody was going to make it. My father was putting in long working days and coming home to an apartment full of the clatter and confusion of child-rearing.

I was reading voraciously, although I didn't know why. I had always read, even as a child, but that year I began to read as if my life depended on it. I would find an author whom I liked and go through his whole output. I had long ago worked through Hemingway, Fitzgerald, and Sinclair Lewis, and in school I had read much of Dickens and Hardy. Now I discovered Dostoyevski, Turgenev, Chekhov, Anatole France, Stendhal, Maupassant, H. G. Wells, Samuel Butler, Galsworthy, Maugham, Waugh, Dos Passos, Dreiser, a host of others. I had no fixed program, no particular goal in mind. I seemed to be impelled toward literature like a desert traveler toward water. My gods were George Orwell and Bernard Shaw, whose rational, cool voices spoke more clearly than anyone else to me. Especially Shaw. I revelled not only in his plays, but especially in his prefaces and his two long essays on Ibsen and Wagner. Like Janet, I had resisted all forms of organized religion and called myself an agnostic, but I embraced Shaw's theory of creative evolution.

When I boarded my Greek freighter that spring I took along thirty books, including *War and Peace*. There were no distractions on board. I was one of seven passengers, the only one who spoke English, and the trip to Genoa took nineteen days. I went through

War and Peace in three and a half days and thought it was the greatest novel I had ever read. (I still think so.) By the time we docked in Genoa, I had finished all of my books and reread my favorite sections of Tolstoy's masterpiece. I had spent the entire trip reading fourteen hours a day, so that I was exhausted by my first hours ashore and literally unsteady on my feet. Franca, who came to meet me at the Stazione Termini in Rome, couldn't believe I had actually lugged thirty hardcover books across the ocean with me, but in her cheerful laughter I sensed a new respect for this peculiar American nephew of hers. She was the first of my relatives to suspect that I might become a writer.

I knew after the first few days I spent with Mammina Ester on the encyclopedia project that it was a doomed venture. The publisher was a distant Italian cousin of ours who, I soon found out, had a long history of failures behind him. The articles we were commissioning were mostly by undistinguished academic hacks and pedants, difficult to translate because they were so poorly written. Mammina Ester presided over our efforts with enormous elegance and grace, sitting at her desk attired as if for a fashionable soirée, but she, too, was aware that the venture was headed nowhere. Her main task was having to defend me and the other translators from the fury of the authors, who were often outraged by our efforts to untangle their cumbersome prose and make sense in English of what they were trying to say. In a matter of a few weeks the whole project collapsed like a deflated balloon, with our cousin in full flight from creditors and the unpaid contributors. He apparently had counted on selling the scheme to an American publishing house, but no one even so much as nibbled at his prospectus. I figured I was lucky to escape with my last week's pay, in the form of a handful of ten-thousand-lire notes stuffed into an envelope and handed to me on my last day by the harried administrator.

Everything else in my life, however, seemed to be working out splendidly. I had begun taking singing lessons every day at a studio just off the Corso run by an elderly couple named Calcagni. She had been a distinguished lyric soprano, who had among her pupils Caterina Mancini, a dramatic soprano soon to make her operatic debut at the Rome Opera before going on to sing at La Scala. The men were taught by her husband, who hadn't a clue about the training of the human voice. Nevertheless, I flourished. The lessons cost me the equivalent of about fifty cents a day, and just being around a group of other young singers soon freed me from my inhibitions. Nobody minded if you broke a top note or ran out of breath; you simply kept trying until you got it right. I hung around the studio for several hours every day and filled in on duets and ensembles whenever needed. I also observed my fellow students and imitated the better ones, going over and over phrases and passages I found difficult to master. Soon I discovered I could actually sing, and I tackled arias with top notes that had been forbidden to me in New York and that I hadn't dreamed I could take on. I became solid up through a high A, then a B-flat, and learned on my own how to support the tone on a cushion of air controlled by my stomach muscles. My only worry was that my voice was small (a true *tenore leggero,* the Calcagnis informed me), but I felt sure it would grow in time. I was deliriously happy with my progress.

I joined the Stampa Estera and wrote some stories, primarily for *Variety.* Rome was becoming a movie capital, not only for Italian productions but also for the American industry. It was cheap to shoot in Italy in those days and several Hollywood studios had scheduled big-budget ventures, such as *Quo Vadis* and *The Prince of Foxes,* the latter starring Tyrone Power, for filming at Cinecittà, the major studio facility on the southern outskirts of the city. The *Rome Daily American,* the newspaper founded after the war by Americans who had fought in the Italian campaign, had taken to referring to Rome as Hollywood-on-the-Tiber. This development enabled me to write enough news to fill a few columns and led to me frequenting the press club to pick up enough gossipy tidbits to keep myself going.

One afternoon, at the press club bar, I heard from a friend of mine, Reynolds Packard, the correspondent for the New York *Daily News*, that the local bureau of Time-Life was looking for a stringer, someone who spoke Italian fluently and who knew how to research a story. I had no idea how to research a story, but I did speak the language, so I went to see the bureau chief, an affable soul named George Jones, and was hired. I was to be paid twenty-five dollars a day plus expenses and was guaranteed a minimum of eight days of work a month. It was a small fortune to me at the time and would make my life in Rome easy. I lived rent-free in my mother's apartment and mostly ate out. On this income I could pay Pierina, my mother's maid and a terrific cook, and live like an established bourgeois.

At first the bureau used me only as a translator and interpreter, but after the only staff member who spoke Italian took a leave of absence, I was given a chance to do some reporting of my own. Jones told me to go into the old Jewish quarter of the city, on the banks of the Tiber behind the ancient Teatro Marcello (also known as the Palazzo Orsini), to find out what the reaction of the locals was to the possible return to the quarter of a woman named Celeste Di Porto. According to stories in the Italian newspapers, Di Porto, a beautiful Jewish girl who had grown up in the area, had saved herself from arrest and deportation to a concentration camp by turning in to the Fascists other Jews, including several members of her own family. Most of them had died either in the camps or in the massacre at the Ardeatine Caves, where the Germans had slaughtered 335 people, 73 of them Jews, in retaliation for a Partisan ambush that had killed thirty-three German soldiers. Nicknamed Pantera Nera, Black Panther, Di Porto had become the mistress of a Fascist officer and had reportedly been paid five thousand lire a head for every person she turned in. Arrested in the north by the Allies after the liberation of Italy, Di Porto had spent several years in prison, but had been released and was reportedly planning to come back home, as if all had been forgiven. Two thousand ninety-one Roman Jews had perished in the Nazi extermination camps, and the inhabitants of the quarter were apparently up in arms over the prospect of her return, which some locals predicted would end in her murder.

My journalistic efforts up to this point had been limited to the show biz gossip I had picked up in the press club bar. I didn't even own a notepad. I grabbed some sheets of paper, folded them into squares, stuck a pencil into my pocket, and walked into the quarter, which consisted mostly of ancient houses constructed partly out of the fragments of Roman ruins that had once littered the area. The buildings lined up along the Via Portico d'Ottavia and several narrow, crooked alleyways off it in which the sun never shined. I had no idea how to find out anything, but as soon as I mentioned to a group of men chatting in the street that I was a reporter for an American news magazine, I was whisked into a local trattoria named Gigetto and regaled with tales about the infamous Black Panther and what life in the ghetto had been like during the war years. After several hours of making notes and walking around the quarter, the second-oldest ghetto in the world (after the one in Venice), I went back to my desk at *Time* and wrote a nine-thousand-word epic that was cabled to New York.

My story about the Black Panther appeared in the next issue of *Time*. It had been cut down to a few hundred words by some rewrite man in the home office and was unsigned, which was the custom at the magazine in those days. The style was pure *Time*-ese, punchy and terse, but several of my better quotes had made it into print. I felt immediately proud of myself and asked in one of my letters to my father if he had happened to read my story. He wrote me back immediately to say that he had, not realizing that I had been responsible for it, and found it "a damn good job." They were the first words of praise I had ever received from him and, as it turned out, the last. Two months later he died suddenly of a massive heart attack, at the age of fifty-nine. I didn't go home for the funeral because I couldn't afford the airfare. Ilka was the only person from my father's world to write to me, describing to me a service at Trinity Church in downtown Manhattan full of flowers and music, his first love.

Janet's reaction to my father's death was stern and unforgiving. "Bill displeases me and disappoints me, dead, as much as he did in the little I knew him in life," she wrote to Natalia from Paris. "He forbade to others, like his son, the intellectuality amidst which he posed when old and which had given him pleasure and strength when young; and on the money side, to which he had sacrificed his mentality, he did not even function with efficient fidelity to Mammon; he left neither life insurance, like a good American tycoon, nor did he remember his firstborn son, if only as a form of snobbery among his millionaire class of friends who usually imitate that aristocratic consideration for primogeniture. . . . I am glad that Ilka, at least, had a mind warm enough to write to Billy and present the last picture. . . ."

My mother came back to Rome in the fall of 1948. She had several magazine assignments and hoped to pick up more work on the spot, but her future remained uncertain. Janet, however, was ecstatic and soon hurried to Rome to be with her. She also cabled Ross and Shawn that she had changed her mind about leaving *The New Yorker.* She would remain at her post in Paris, with frequent trips to Italy and elsewhere in Europe to report on events. "Am overjoyed at news that you will stay on in Paris," Shawn cabled her. "I had naturally hoped that one way or another you could without personal sacrifice reach that very decision. I am glad we realized that there is only one of you in this world."

Janet moved into my mother's apartment on the Via Piemonte, after which they went on to Capri and Naples, with Janet turning out Letters for the magazine. I had moved into a smaller flat of my own, or rather a series of flats, since I couldn't seem to find a place

*F*rank Flanner, Janet's father, was a prosperous undertaker who dabbled in real estate. *(Author's collection)*

*G*iulio Danesi, Natalia's father, was a painter, lithographer, and printer who ran a studio and printing plant in Rome. He was charming and handsome, but his poor business sense put the family into financial peril. *(Author's collection)*

*M*ary Ellen Flanner, Janet's mother, was a beautiful woman with theatrical aspirations who encouraged her three daughters to pursue their interests in the arts. *(Author's collection)*

Two formidable women: Natalia with her mother, Ester Traversari. After the death of her husband, Ester managed not only to support her family but to become a successful writer and editor, and an influence on the Italian cultural scene. (Author's collection)

Mammina Ester, the first Italian female war correspondent ever to visit a front, stands where Italian troops faced Austrian lines during World War I. (Author's collection)

*M*y father, William Murray, with my mother and me in New York, 1929. At first Natalia was dazzled by my father, who was older and very well connected in the artistic circles of New York. But the marriage was not a success, and Natalia fled back to Italy. (Author's collection)

*N*atalia with Joan du Guerny in Italy, 1932. My mother met Joan on the French Riv-ieria, and she came to live with us on Capri. English-born and formerly married to a French count, Joan was bright, funny, and outspoken. My mother's relationship with her would last several years.
(Author's collection)

*M*ammina Ester, my second mother and the no-
blest Roman of them all. Intelligence, a strong will,
and a fierce sense of independence were the traits she
passed on to her daughters. *(Author's collection)*

*N*oel Murphy around the time she first met Janet.
An aristocratic New Yorker, she and Janet met in
1932. After the death of her husband, Noel bought
a house in the village of Orgeval, northeast of Paris,
which was to become Janet's second home. Like all
of Janet's deepest attachments, their friendship
would last even after their love affair was over.
(Author's collection)

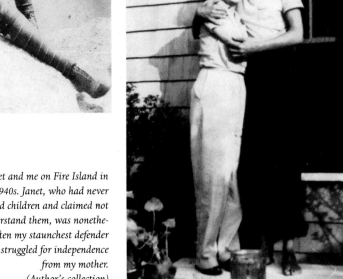

*J*anet and me on Fire Island in
the 1940s. Janet, who had never
wanted children and claimed not
to understand them, was nonethe-
less often my staunchest defender
as I struggled for independence
from my mother.
(Author's collection)

N*atalia broadcasting* The Italian Hour *in the 1940s. The NBC-produced news and talk program was intended to introduce an American voice into Fascist Italy; I jokingly referred to my mother as "Tokyo Rosa." (Author's collection)*

W*ith my mother on Capri, summer 1947. (Author's collection)*

Back in Italy, 1948, where I pursued my ambition to become a professional opera singer. To earn a living, I became a stringer for Time magazine, thus unwittingly beginning my career in journalism. *(Author's collection)*

Janet and Natalia on the Spanish Steps in Rome, early 1950s. In the early years their careers kept them on separate continents, and their relationship would go through periods of turmoil. Eventually they were able to spend longer, and happier, periods of time together. *(Author's collection)*

Me at the time my first novel, The Fugitive Romans, *was published. It was Janet who inspired me to become a writer; she was often my toughest and most honest critic. (Barbara Sutro)*

J anet and Natalia in Natalia's New York apartment in 1977, shortly before Janet's death. *(Author's collection)*

N atalia reading from Darlinghissima *at the Manhattan Theater Club, 1986. In editing this volume of the correspondence between herself and Janet, my mother worried about how much she should reveal of their relationship.* (Daniel Root)

O*n the roof of the grandstand at Del Mar, California, keeping an eye on the horses. (Boardman Photography)*

T*he last photo of the three Danesi sisters: Lea, Natalia, and Franca. (Alice Murray)*

W*ith legendary* New Yorker *editor William Shawn, who was Janet's life-long friend and editor, and who eventually gave me my first job at* The New Yorker *as a fiction editor. (Author's collection)*

to live that didn't have some crippling drawback. Eventually, I settled into a two-room apartment on the Via Flaminia that I shared
with a colleague from the Stampa Estera who worked for a news
agency and the *Rome Daily American*.

I saw a lot of my mother and Janet that fall and also of the
group of artists including several American painters and sculptors
who had settled in the city and who had become friends of theirs.
We met often in the evenings at a café in the Piazza del Popolo,
where we sat out in the open and talked for hours, after which I
would walk home in the cool night air through the empty, silent
streets and piazzas, devoid in those days of the automobile. My life
had a rhythm to it and a purpose it had lacked in New York, and I
was certain I had made the right decision to come back. I felt no
compulsion to be immediately successful, and the future seemed
assured and bright. As for my mother and Janet, they seemed happier in their relationship than I had ever seen them. I was completely unaware at the time of what it had cost both of them to
stay together, and of a crisis in their relationship that had taken
many weeks to overcome.

THIRTEEN

A PORTRAIT
OF THE
HEART

It's hard for me to imagine now that I could have been so ignorant of the turmoil in my mother's and Janet's lives during this period. I was always aware that there had been difficulties, but I had assumed that they would overcome them, that they were destined for each other and would always remain together. Not until after my mother's death in June 1994, did I fully grasp what they had gone through, a crisis that had brought them to the brink of separation and wounded both of them deeply. I had been insulated from this turmoil by my self-absorbed concentration on my own life. In my early twenties I had evolved into a typically ambitious young American male around whom the universe revolved, uninterested in anything or anyone but himself. That I could be so unaware of the suffering and anguish of the two people I most loved and valued in my life and for so long is proof that I existed at the time in a self-contained world in which, like Wagner's Siegfried, I believed only in the sanctity of myself and my naive aspirations.

My mother was a magpie. Unlike Janet, who lived most of her adult life in hotels and was uninterested in possessions or in preserving mementoes of the past, my mother collected and stored away the bits and pieces of her days, including almost every letter ever written to her by anyone who counted in her life. Thus it was that, after her death, I found myself in her New York apartment painstakingly going through for many hours the stacks of files and boxes stored away in various corners of her rooms. Under the windows in her bedroom was a heavy, dark antique wooden chest full of papers, photographs, and objects from her past, the most intimate and guarded items that she had not wanted revealed during her lifetime. Often, as I was growing up, when I'd ask her about past events she did not want to talk about, such as the extent of her relationship with Gabriele D'Annunzio, she'd say, "Ah, you will have to wait till I am gone to find out about that." And once, toward the end of her life, she had looked at me and said, "Poor Bill, you will have so much to go through after I am gone."

Most of what she had kept secret about herself I found in that chest, most significantly the notes from D'Annunzio and a packet of letters from Janet. In 1985 my mother published a selection of Janet's letters written to her over the course of their long relationship, framed by my mother's own narrative recollecting the course of their "loving friendship." In the book, called *Darlinghissima: Letters to a Friend*, the years from 1947 to 1949 are quickly glossed over, with only a few excerpts from the correspondence to illustrate the chronicle of events. This, as I discovered while reading through the letters salvaged from the antique chest, was because my mother did not want either the full extent of her love affair with Janet or the personal difficulties they had overcome to be known during her lifetime. After her death, she had made it clear, it wouldn't matter; she wanted me then to write about her and Janet and the family. If she hadn't wanted this, she would have destroyed the letters or made me promise not to reveal their contents and I would have honored her wishes.

Even as she had been putting together *Darlinghissima,* she had agonized over how much to reveal. She had been fearful that her grandchildren, my two daughters and my son, might be shocked or might disapprove of what they read about her. She discussed this with me; and if I had told her I thought they might disapprove, she would have dropped the project entirely. She had led a free and adventurous life, but at heart and in her soul she remained a firmly middle-class Roman woman. "I hope that my grandchildren, and other young women like them, born in a freer, more liberated society, more knowledgeable about relationships between the sexes and without the inhibitions or taboos of an earlier era, will understand and value our experiences and efforts to be, above all, decent human beings," she wrote in her introduction to *Darlinghissima.* "That is the intention of this book. The letters speak for themselves." As do the ones I discovered after her death, tributes to the strength of a love and a commitment ferocious in its intensity.

My mother's unhappiness with the long separations from Janet worsened in 1946, when she was stuck in New York and Janet was back in Paris, working hard for *The New Yorker.* When it became evident that the State Department would not send Natalia back to Italy and she became increasingly frustrated in her attempts to return there, she began to write the sort of letters to Janet that not only conveyed unhappiness but were intended to get Janet to do something about it, to acknowledge the extent of their commitment to one another. One of her tactics, all too familiar to me, was to retreat into a cold, rational shell from which, with often devastating logic, she would state her position and point out the failures and omissions in the behavior of others. One such letter, obviously complaining about Janet's disinclination to assume the practical responsibilities of a long-term relationship, reached Janet in late March 1947. Janet immediately replied, dealing first with Natalia's complaint that Janet had allowed her to take on all the financial burden of maintaining and running the New York apartment. "Darling, your troubled, detailed and dry letter has just arrived," Janet wrote back. "Certainly I have made destruction in your pattern of life, in your freedom to manipulate your life. You have made the same in mine and certainly only our consolidation can relieve either of us from the breakdowns and the tension."

Janet proceeds to discuss practical matters concerning money, promising to contribute her full share to all expenses, then assuring Natalia that she will come back to New York with her in September. "I know I have been a burden to you; I know you have been a burden to me," she continued. "I never heard of any relation which did not include the gestures of carrying, of weight and often fatigues; I've met the same situation, more or less, all my adult life and know you have, too. Some situations bring less burden than others, especially if they occur when one is young and one's shoulders are free from past efforts and connections. One of the burdens is the character of the other individual in the love relation; there you are certainly superior to me. Superiority is lighter as a burden than inferiority of character; there certainly I weigh you down more than you weigh me."

Janet thanks Natalia for having nourished her by her illuminating conversation, but can't recall her lover ever having thanked her for her own personal contribution, apart from her writings:

For heaven's sake, take SOME of the good which my love, my efforts, my loyalties, my willingness and volition offer you; and see also whether they have human values or not in your estimation; and if not, then say so and admit that I am not good enough for you and throw me out. But don't continue making me feel that I am nothing but a destruction and burden in your life. Both our lives were far simpler if emptier before we met than after. Your problem in relation to me, since the war, has been one of trying to shape a new life and jobs; mine has been the effort of deciding to tear down an old life and job and also create a new one. As you said here in Paris, mine was in many ways the more masculine element in our relation because I had worked longer, at the same task and because a heavier investment of time and responsibility, such as usually come to the male and breadwinner, were involved. That is true, it was something I could never bring myself to point out bluntly because it would have been an indelicacy coming from my side and because you still think me conceited about my work. Twice I have asked you to remit that early unfair critique you made and you assented but not quite believing and only to please or quiet me. . . . I am very upset at the hopeless tone of your letter. I have waited so long to hear from you. The letter which came the other day was also almost devoid of emotion. . . . I shall go out to New York with you in September; I shall come to Rome in June. If I remain only a burden, we shall then have found it out. I love you and I am very upset. Half of my nervousness is the world, half is you and over both is also the burden I bear, which each bears, at being himself or herself. I have never been in love with myself, my dear, no matter what you may mistakenly think. I have suffered most of my life, and not with morbidity or melodrama alone, at being me. For Christ's sake don't always add to the epitaph of the unheavenly which is always like a script in the back of my mind. *Je t'aime.*

On June 27, after my mother's return to Italy, Janet wrote to tell her that Ross had finally given her permission to take two months off from her Paris Letters, "accorded, typically, in a scrawled blue pencil postscript to a paean of admiration about Rebecca West and her Greenville piece." A. J. Liebling, who was supposed to substitute for her in Paris, was suffering from a bad case of bursitis and was unavailable, but she would be coming to Italy anyway. She went into detail about all the practical matters concerning herself and the magazine that she felt Natalia ought to know about:

I have the feeling that this all will seem to you an American businessman's report which he reads aloud to woo his bride. I MUST develop the habit of speaking freely because otherwise I develop the habit of secrecy which enlarges into lies, which you loathe and I despise. Part of my timidity is my own weak character and part is grown through fear of displeasing you and your romantic tenderness and of seeming unaware of your sacrifices and your long period of waiting which in themselves all constitute a gift of soul. These last weeks of thinking that I may never work for the magazine again in this particular choice capacity has been a great depressant; you complain that I have three wives and the truth is, as you know, that I also have a husband, *The New Yorker.* . . . This is a hell of a letter. I am so tired and driven and worried that when I think of Capri and you and Teresina's cottage terrace it is like a remembered dream of unreality. I feel a foreigner everywhere in life, unsatisfying, polygamous, neither Christian nor pagan, neither good friend nor loyal lover, neither bold enough for my desires nor harsh enough to be responsible for my acts which I slip into like chasms. I am sure only that I have loved and that I do love. I have been what is called abnormal so long, organically though that is a commonplace exception in nature which Papal civilization has made a ridiculous and unscientific lot of fuss about, that I now accept the fact that I am also far more abnormal in my ability to love not too little but too long, that it may be a burden which drives me crazy to love without stopping, even after sex stops, but that I do so continue to love those I have loved and I do love you. . . . I hope I make you happier than I am in this world. I hope our work will sustain our minds and spirits and that we will be contented to try, at any rate, to leave a small record. I should think that all your hopes now are in Billy; until he has made all his life quota of errors you can hope, as I do for Jan, my nephew. . . . You are a wonderful woman, Natalia, and I love you with my pain as well as my pleasure, my weakness as well as what is my windy strength. God bless you, my sweet. We shall walk up to Teresina's terrace together and lie down in the night and the sun.

After their two months together in Italy and their time in New York the following winter, their relationship seemed once again solidly established. But when Janet went back to France in the spring of 1947, leaving my mother alone in New York and scrambling for work, her future insecure and nothing definitive having yet been decided, the strain reached a breaking point. Finally, in May, after Janet had gone back to Paris after covering the Italian elections, Natalia wrote asking for a definitive commitment in the form of concrete answers to several important questions. Unfortunately, this letter, like most of my mother's correspondence to Janet, does not survive, but it's easy to imagine what her demands were. She wanted Janet to agree to spending more time with her, even if this meant having to leave her Paris job and live in New York most of the year; she wanted Janet to assume her share of the practical considerations of their relationship, which meant some of the expenses of the New York apartment and the Fire Island house; and she wanted Janet to be less evasive and more truthful with her about her other relationships. Even I had heard rumors of a recent purported outside affair with another woman in Paris, but Janet had assured my mother that it had never occurred and blamed the story on a vicious falsehood perpetrated by one of their acquaintances, a well-known seducer with a reputation for scandalmongering.

Janet had apparently replied immediately to my mother's demands and also sent along a check for a hundred and fifty dollars to help with expenses. Somehow this letter went astray. When Natalia received no reply to what amounted to her ultimatum, she sat down at her desk in Fire Island and wrote Janet a calm, rational letter of farewell; since Janet could not commit herself to the conditions my mother deemed essential to their life as a couple, there was nothing left to do but say goodbye. As she saw it, she was setting Janet free.

Janet wrote back on June 2:

My darling, your letter of May 28 arrived late last night from Fire Island, a miracle of rapidity and despairing news for me. I have been in so insane a fit of tears since its arrival that my mind makes little clarity, as objects under water are also unclear and slightly distorted. I shall try to write you later today, tonight even, it is now six P.M. and I have been crying for several hours but without any sort of relief or goal. I have not been able to shed tears except two days after my mother died; this is also a kind of death to the love part of my life which is you. I think that I seem to have felt you ebbing away in the past two months because my contact with reality has been slipping away; it is more difficult each day for me to know who or what I am. I do not know, this minute, what to say or think because there is no sort of precision in my utter distress; it is general, like a landslide, like an earthquake or like being drowned. I think there is too little hope in my future ability to work to make your decision to free me worth the decision, but if I am not alive enough to work I am not alive enough to love or be loved. I read and appreciate your calm in your words if I cannot meet it. In trying to think I can only suppose that disorder in general has undone me and now I cannot stand it, after many years. With the pain you have had in knowing of your sister's illness [Lea had had a mental breakdown] I could almost wish that there was some similar precision in my case of feeling helplessly slipping away from connection with this room, this hotel, this street, this machine that I write to you upon and the scene of you in my mind's eye, with . . . the bay or sea behind you. Your decision does not free me from mine. I do not think I will be able even to work for the magazine till the year's end; with each Letter I expect to be told it must be the last. I do not know what to do, Natalia, or where to find any respite. I feel beyond salvage.

By now you must have received my letter answering your six questions. It was sent and why did you not have it? What has happened to it? Why did it not arrive, or do you mean it arrived but was no answer? This is Wednesday and Friday you wrote me and there is only a difference of five days. The freshness of your letter only adds to my grief, it makes it seem tangible and close. I will try to look out of the window and look around my room and make contact with this day, this place and reality and write you from it later. You are my last attachment to my imagination and now I have nothing to look forward to but only myself to look back on. Maybe everybody suffers like this in youth, I did not, but the pain is more unbearable now because this love-pain involves my entire life to be and will not stop because nothing will take its place. When young something can take its place but nothing will take your place because you are my last horizon, your figure, your shoulders, your straight waist, your shapely legs, all of you standing against a scene and that is the last thing my eyes in love will ever see. You are my last portrait of the heart.

When Janet's earlier letter answering all my mother's questions never arrived, Natalia repeated them. Janet answered on June 9:

Darling, darling, yes, I did indeed answer your questions and my answers indeed were Yes, yes and yes. Perhaps they are floating in the Great South Bay or blowing around Greenwich Village. I do not remember where I sent that letter because it was the period of not knowing precisely where you were. . . . I am too stupefied by your recent decision to know anything that I did not know before; that I love you, that I am probably declining in all variants of my working power so that this decision, which costs you such blood and me such anguish, no more frames the tableau than an infinitely costly vast golden frame could hold in place a small printed epitaph. To the very center of my brain I understand the futility of this decision which operates in the heart and should remain in its own region, my darling one. By worry, confusion and my own psychic weaknesses I have worn my thinking apparatus to a point of despair and in which I have no control over the *planning* of what I do, until after it is done. So after each piece of work I regret with a feeling of bewilderment and utter confusion what I have just written and wonder why I was not able to see I should have written something different. . . .

Already burdened by guilt over her mother and Hildegarde and under constant pressure to resolve her situation with Natalia, Janet during this period of her life seemed to have lost confidence not only in herself as a human being but in her ability to write well. She even thought that her preference for women might have contributed to her decline. In her letter of June 9 she raised that possibility with Natalia:

Do you think that being a woman loving women has also helped tear me and my life and my brain to bits? Tell me. You have stronger resources in your nature and past lives through centuries. I wish I did not remember what mother said, almost the last thing, to me: "Oh, my darling, protect yourself, even late in life, from all that which can destroy you, your precious talent. . . ." She always knew, of course, what my life was, though only once did she ever mention it years ago, as a result of a letter sent by a jealous maniacal woman whose younger sweetheart was in love with me as deeply as I was horrified by them both. When I made a wholesale denial of any such passion—true and a lie at the same time—mother dropped to her knees and kissed my hand and begged my forgiveness. There are perhaps only a dozen clear memory scenes in my life with her, most of them minor and inexplicable; that one scene, of course, is so anguishingly clear that just as I remember precisely her face, then bent head and body at my knees and touch of her mouth on my lips, so do I even remember the room it occurred in and where the chairs stood and which pictures were upon the wall and the time of day, noon, summer, hot. I swear I would rather see a young girl dead than go through the struggles against society, for self-control, for peace and for the mad kindly tender joy only such love brings; it is a love which truly understands the beloved because there is no different ratio of reaction or character as between men and women. I feel it is the most equal and therefore the most powerful in its imaginative bliss and pain; each truly shares. I share, you share, I pay, you pay, my body is yours in our struggle for survival, at a distance for a few more months, as it is in love when we are alone. For all that science or biology or doctors know, write, tell, plan or counsel, the motor power of sex is still unique in whatever knowledge it gives each individual. . . . I love you. I slept one hour last night. I feel shaken, ill, an old frame of nerves, trembling with decisions, hopes, experiences, patterns and delicacies.

She signed that letter with a kiss in bright red lipstick. And so the biggest crisis of their relationship passed. There would be others, but none so close to a final parting as this one. At the time I knew nothing about it. Surely, however, no one could have resisted the outpouring of love and grief Janet spilled onto the pages of her reply to Natalia's letter of renunciation. To be able to love with such intensity is a great gift, and writers are lucky to be able to experience it, because they have been blessed with the talent to express it.

FOURTEEN

DEBUTS
AND
DEPARTURES

Janet always suspected I might become a writer. After all, it was in the blood, given my family's long history in the arts and journalism. Even before I had taken on the job at *Time*, she had written to Natalia about the possibility. "I have always said Billy could write as a career," she observed, "if he would work at it, train and start in some sort of small job on *The New Yorker*." She never spoke or wrote directly to me about it, because she had never interfered in my life in any way—partly, I'm sure, so as not to arouse my mother's proprietary instincts, but also because she knew me well. At this delicate, insecure stage of my life, with all my hopes centered on an operatic career, I tended to resist fiercely any attempt to dissuade me from my goal.

Meanwhile, during the two years I worked for the Rome bureau of *Time*, I was learning the journalist's trade and having a splendid time doing it. With each story I filed I became increasingly irritated with the high-handed way the rewrite men in New York were adapting my copy to their own views of the events I was reporting, but I hadn't yet developed enough of a writer's ego, to say nothing of a style of my own, to object to what in later years I would have considered a mangling of my texts. Mainly I concentrated on learning how to research a story and interview my subjects; then I'd structure my copy so as to tell that story without leaving anything out. What part of it the magazine would use was a decision made in New York. When I mentioned to bureau chief George Jones that I thought New York tended to overedit and rewrite to the point of actually sometimes altering the meaning of the piece, he agreed, but added that nothing much could be done about it. "Someday somebody is going to go into the *Time* morgue and dig out the original stories filed by our reporters," he said. "They'll find some of the best unused material ever written."

Jones was a first-rate bureau chief. During my years with him we filed proportionately more stories than any other foreign bureau. At one point we were asked to relax a little, because the staff in Paris, a bureau three times our size, had complained that we were getting too much reportage into the magazine. But at the time, Italy was proving to be a rich source of stories. The Italians, energetically and chaotically rebuilding their society after the cataclysm of the war years, were a reporter's delight, always deeply involved in whatever dramas engaged them and never reluctant to air their views on events.

At first I covered everything, from politics and crime to the arts. I went to the huge Communist Party rallies in the Piazza del Popolo and watched from the safety of a doorway as the government's riot police, the dreaded Celere created by the defense minister, Mario Scelba, broke them up, sending jeeps packed with club-swinging thugs spinning through the ranks of demonstrators, who fled shrieking toward the safety of side streets and buildings. I attended religious ceremonies in St. Peter's Square, jammed in among thousands of worshippers to listen to the homilies and anti-Communist exhortations of the Pope, a tiny white figure high up on his balcony on the façade of the great cathedral, the distant voice of the status quo. I covered art and museum openings, concerts, opera galas; interviewed politicians, celebrities, cultural prime movers, criminals, and cops. Some of these pieces never appeared in print—but what a training writing them was for a neophyte. And whenever I wasn't sure how to handle a particular story, I had George Jones there to clue me in, a never-failing source of support and counsel.

I spent ten days in Sicily reporting on the attempts by the Italian government to capture a celebrated bandit named Salvatore Giuliano. Handsome and charismatic, he had become an international celebrity and a national scandal. Nicknamed Turiddu, after the leading character in Mascagni's opera *Cavalleria Rusticana,* he made his living by kidnapping the rich and holding them for ransom. He was regarded by many Sicilians as a local Robin Hood. From his various lairs in the mountains around Palermo he issued proclamations and often granted interviews to visiting foreign journalists, who seemed to be able to get to him even as the police searched everywhere in vain. A beautiful blonde Swedish reporter had even spent a few days with him and had her photograph taken arm-in-arm with him outside a cave, a picture that made front pages all over the world. Finally, after an uproar in Parliament and dozens of mocking editorials in the Italian press, the central government in Rome had dispatched a special unit of carabinieri to track him down. This force, under the command of a tall, forceful professional soldier named Colonel Ugo Luca, had set up headquarters outside the town of Partinico and begun a meticulous search for the bandit. By the time I showed up, they had been on the scene for several weeks but had had no more success tracking him down than the local cops.

The trouble was, Colonel Luca informed me, that the Sicilians regarded Luca and his men as *sbirri,* spies, foreign agents sent in to meddle in local affairs. Sicily, repeatedly invaded and exploited for

centuries by foreign governments and occupying armies, treated the
colonel and his men exactly as it had other invaders, with contemptuous silence. No one would speak to them, no one had heard or
seen anything, no one knew what they meant when they asked
about Giuliano. A few days before my arrival, a band of assassins had
shot up the marketplace in Partinico, killing several people. No one
had heard the shots, no one, not even the relatives of the victims, had
any idea who might have been responsible. *Omertà,* a conspiracy of
silence, was the time-honored way Sicilians dealt with outsiders.

I passed a fascinating week driving around the barren countryside, talking to anyone in the dusty villages who would talk to me,
and making notes about a way of life that seemed arcane and mys-
teriously ominous. I also researched Giuliano's background and
discovered that he had been a landless young hood and drifter, who
during the war had been a hired gun for a Sicilian separatist movement that had petitioned the United States, after the liberation of
the island, to become an independent nation. Giuliano and his rag-
tag army of Sicilian patriots had had the backing of a number of
rich landowning nobles, who had long dreamed of freeing Sicily
from the clutches of the "mainlanders" and of reestablishing a feu-
dal form of government controlled by themselves. When this effort collapsed, after the newly formed postwar Italian government
had sent troops to the island to crush it, Giuliano and a few of his
friends had taken to the hills and embarked on their new profession. Because of the bandit's good looks and his ability to charm
the press, he had so far made a raging success of it.

My story was not only about Giuliano, but also about the society that had created and nurtured him. I thought I had written a
good piece, even though very little of what I'd reported appeared
in the magazine, just a few hundred words about the operations of
Colonel Luca's force in the climate of hostility that surrounded it.
About two weeks after my story appeared, Giuliano's body, riddled
with bullets, was found in the street of one of the villages I had visited. The official version of events was that he had been betrayed

to the local police by his chief lieutenant, Gaspare Pisciotta, who had been arrested and jailed but was to be leniently treated for his cooperation. Unfortunately, Pisciotta was murdered in prison by drinking an espresso laced with arsenic. Nobody knew who could have been responsible, and it was years before a plausible account of the events appeared in the Italian press. The Mafia had taken care of Giuliano. At first it had ignored him, then it had supported and protected him, because he had, by the flamboyance of his behavior, diverted the attention of the authorities from the Mafia's own operations as it reestablished itself locally and internationally after the end of the war. When the Italian government dispatched Luca and his *sbirri* to the island, however, their presence had begun to interfere with the Mafia's affairs. Also, the attendant publicity had cast too much light on criminal activities in general. So it had been the Mafia, acting through Pisciotta, who had betrayed and killed Giuliano. They had left his dead body in the street and tipped off the police, who had arrived in time to pump their own bullets into the corpse in order to claim credit for the coup. Pisciotta had quickly been silenced in his turn, because the Mafia couldn't risk what he might have to say in court about the case. The Mafia, like any responsible business organization, has little room in it for the romantic aspirations of a Robin Hood figure.

The Giuliano story made an impression on my editors in New York. A couple of months after I'd filed it, George Jones informed me that one of the heads of the foreign news bureaus would be coming through Rome and wanted to meet me. "I think they're going to offer you a staff job," he said. If I accepted, I'd be sent back to New York to work out of the home office for a few months to familiarize myself with the magazine's operations in general, then be assigned to a foreign bureau, probably not in Italy. After two or three years in the post, I'd be sent to another one. *Time's* correspondents never remained in one place for more than a few years; the magazine's policy was not to let anyone get too entrenched in any one post, but always to have a fresh pair of eyes covering the scene. I thought this was a dumb policy and said so, pointing out to Jones that a writer's familiarity and feel for his milieu was essential to writing well about it. I cited Janet's presence in Paris for *The New Yorker* as a prime example. "We're a news magazine," Jones replied, "not a cultural one." Anyway, he added with a shrug, that was the policy and they weren't going to alter it for me.

I was tempted, but I realized, of course, that accepting the offer meant putting an end to my singing career. And this was happening just as I was beginning to acquire confidence in myself. I had recently sung for the first time in public, as one of six Calcagni pupils in a concert given in a church on the outskirts of the city. Nearly paralyzed by stage fright, I had cracked my very first high note in an aria from *Mignon,* but I had managed to recover and get through the rest of the program of arias and duets without trouble. In fact, the hit of the afternoon had been the love duet from *Madama Butterfly,* which I had sung with Caterina Mancini. At the end of the piece, I had opted to go with the soprano for the high C, rather than the more conservative line Puccini had composed for the tenor, and I think I must have hit it, though I'll never know for sure. This was because Caterina, who had a voice like a fire siren, was bellowing her high note in my ear and I couldn't hear a thing. All I know was that my mouth was open, my diaphragm was tensed, and I was trembling from the effort. The audience responded with applause and bravos and I was dazed with happiness.

When *Time's* foreign editor, a small, trim middle-aged woman with cold dark eyes, met me for drinks at the Hotel Excelsior bar on the Via Veneto a few days later and did indeed offer me a staff job, I asked her if I could have a year to give my answer. I had told her I was studying music and that I felt I owed it to myself at least to find out if I could have an operatic career. I was planning to move to Milan, the country's operatic capital, in the fall and begin to audition for the impresarios up there. Meanwhile, I hoped I'd be able to go on working for *Time* as a stringer.

The woman looked at me in amazement. I don't think anyone

had ever turned her down before and I think, if it had been up to her, she'd have fired me on the spot. But George Jones came to my rescue. He persuaded her to let me have my way and arranged for me to become *Time's* North Italy correspondent, though I could also cover stories elsewhere in the country, if I wanted to. At the end of no more than a year, if I desired then to accept the magazine's offer, I would contact the home office and perhaps the position would still be open, though there was no guarantee it would be.

I moved to Milan in the fall of 1950, settling into a small apartment a couple of blocks behind the city's famous cathedral, which looked to me like a great white wedding cake. I found a coach with whom to keep on working on my voice and studying scores and I began to audition for the independent impresarios who haunted the cafés of the Galleria between the Piazza del Duomo and La Scala, the opera house generally regarded as the most famous in the world. I planned one day to sing there, but in the meantime I needed to get some experience in the provinces. This was an era in which nearly every town in Italy still had an opera season. Most of the singers for these seasons were recruited by independent entrepreneurs based in Milan. By this time I had mastered two roles, Almaviva in Rossini's *Barber of Seville* and Alfredo in *La Traviata*, and I began to audition for anyone who might engage me to sing. One elderly ruffian, who operated out of a small office in the Galleria itself, offered me a chance to do Alfredo in a company he was putting together to tour down south, but informed me I would have to pay him the equivalent of about a thousand dollars to get the part. I refused on general principle, even if I could have afforded it, and went on studying and auditioning, but without success.

Meanwhile I continued working for *Time.* My first assignment from Milan, oddly enough, took me back south to Naples, where I covered the Piedigrotta, the famous annual Neapolitan song festival that had launched into the repertory such classics as "O Sole

Mio" and "Torna a Sorrento." The local composers were still churning out these romantic ditties as if the pop musical scene had been frozen in a time warp somewhere around the turn of the century. The lyrics all toasted the beauties of Naples and bemoaned the inconstancies of love, usually frustrated or betrayed.

While there, I ran across another story I've always thought of as typical of Naples. A famous local nicknamed Giovanni the Immortal had just perished, run down by a speeding taxi, and the whole city had turned out for his funeral. Giovanni was a middle-aged man who had lived his whole life in a one-room hovel on a fetid narrow alley in one of the city's poorest districts. For years he had supported not only his family but several of his neighbors by stepping in front of moving vehicles. After every such event, witnesses would testify to the fact that Giovanni had been innocently crossing the street when hit, and the insurance companies would have to cough up some money to compensate him. Giovanni always made sure that the car, truck, or bus that laid him low belonged to a company rich enough to carry insurance. Although hospitalized a number of times and badly injured on a few occasions, he had survived every accident and become a legend in his own time, as well as a hero to the intimates who benefitted from his sacrifices. Unfortunately, this time Giovanni had miscalculated and stepped in front of a taxi that was going a little too fast. He died on his way to the hospital. At the funeral procession, which wound its way on foot through the teeming quarter where Giovanni had lived, his casket mounted on a black coach drawn by black-plumed horses, thousands of mourners lined the streets. An Italian reporter caught up to one of the old men who had acted as a witness for Giovanni on every occasion. "Obviously this is a very tragic event," the reporter said. "What do you think of the death of your friend Giovanni?" The old man shook his head sadly. "This time he exaggerated," he answered.

Neither of my stories from Naples made it into print, but I had loved writing them, just as I had always loved the old city, an area that had been a part of my childhood. The Neapolitans, it seemed to me, were wiser in their poverty and understood more about life than most other Italians, especially in the industrialized north, where everyone seemed to be obsessed with the pursuit of money. On my last day in the city I sat at a café table along the waterfront, sipping an espresso and reading an Italian newspaper. I remember thinking, as I sat there in the sunlight and gazed out over the bright blue water of the gulf, how much I loved Italy and how I planned to spend the rest of my life there. I wanted to be Italian, and everything I had on that day, from my shoes to my necktie, was Italian. During the hour or so I sat there, ten or twelve people came up to me to sell me something—a fountain pen, a watch, American cigarettes, a bolt of cloth, Scotch whisky, a virgin. Not one of them addressed me in Italian. "Hey, Joe, you wanna see this?" or, "Paisà, look, I sell this to you cheap!" were the usual approaches. It served to remind me that I was indeed an American and that Naples was the most sophisticated city I had ever been in.

Soon after my Neapolitan adventure, *Time* sent me off to do a story in Genoa. This one had been dreamed up in New York, where somebody had been struck by the fact that Genoa celebrated Christopher Columbus's birthday despite the fact that the city had a newly elected Communist government. George Jones informed me that New York expected a tale full of incongruous and funny tidbits about the festivities, with lots of good quotes from the participants. I thought this was a lousy idea for a story, especially after I arrived in Genoa and discovered there wasn't much humor in the situation. The city had been badly bombed during the war. The harbor was still partly clogged with sunken ships; the fishing industry was in crisis; and the Breda steel mill, one of the largest in the country, had been demolished, throwing thousands of people out of work. A quarter of the city's workers were unemployed, and there were beggars on every street. This was what I wrote about, a serious piece ironically contrasting the elaborate celebration under way with the cold misery of much of the population. I also pointed out that the municipal administration had so far proved itself to be efficient and honest, devoid of the corruption of such cities as Rome and Naples where the Christian Democrats and other conservative parties were in charge.

This piece was not a success. Jones was instructed by New York to send another correspondent to the scene, which he did. He used part of my story as background for his own, a remarkable invention depicting exactly the scene New York had envisaged, teeming with pompously comical Communists jovially celebrating the birthday of the local hero who had discovered America, the home of capitalism. I thought the piece was dishonest and told Jones I would no longer write political stories for the magazine but would concentrate instead on back-of-the-book pieces on the arts and cultural affairs.

As it turned out, my career at *Time* was over. Soon after getting back to Milan, I heard from a friend, a local baritone, that a big musical show with an international cast was auditioning talent. It had never occured to me to sing in a musical, but I was getting nowhere with the opera impresarios and I wanted to sing in front of a public somewhere. I auditioned for the producer, the director, and the musical director with a song from *Brigadoon* and a spiritual, "Go Down, Moses." To my surprise, I was hired at the less than munificent salary of about twenty dollars a day. The next morning, with rehearsals only a week away, I gave up my job with *Time*.

The show was an old-fashioned musical revue called *Black and White.* The plan was that it would open in Milan, play there a couple of months, then go on the road for an additional six to eight months, depending on how successful it was. In addition to its Italian cast of actors, comedians, and nearly naked showgirls, it featured a French ventriloquist named Robert Lamouret, the four African-American tap-dancing Step Brothers, a hula dancer named Louisa Reyes, and Leo Coleman, an African-American ballet dancer who had created the part of the mute Toby in Menotti's *The Medium.* There was also an all-English chorus line identified in the

program as Les Bluebell Follies. I was the boy singer, with two so-
los of my own, including "Go Down, Moses," and I also sang in
every big ensemble number, including both finales. The curtain
went up a little after nine o'clock and came down well after one,
nine performances a week with matinées on the weekends. It was
an exhausting schedule, but I was happy to be singing profession-
ally at last, even though it wasn't in an opera house.

Opening night at the brand new Teatro Manzoni, in the heart of
the city a few blocks from La Scala, was a near catastrophe. None
of the stage machinery worked, forcing the stagehands to emerge
from the wings to change the sets; the sketches were not very
funny; the Bluebell girls were out of step with one another most of
the evening; the Hungarian soubrette fell off the ramp in front of
the orchestra pit into the string section; and I had to sing "Go
Down, Moses" while Louisa and Leo danced the hula in back of
me. The reviews the next morning were savage, but it made no difference: The public came anyway and we were a hit at the box office. The Step Brothers were sensational, Lamouret was very
funny, and the Italian audience had never seen a show like ours,
with so many foreign performers.

I was vastly disillusioned. Not only that, I wasn't very good. I
had had no training for the musical stage. I didn't know how to
move, how to dance, or how to sell a song. All of my numbers fell
flat, except for the spiritual, which I could really sing and which always went over well. I also caught a bad cold; but, since I had no
understudy, I had to go on performing every day. After a couple of
weeks, I completely lost my voice and had to leave the show, re-
placed by an Italian pop singer whom the audience loved.

I lingered in Milan for another month, not knowing what to do
with myself, then moved back to Rome. George Jones had been
called back to New York and I couldn't go to work for *Time* again. I
tried my hand at writing some articles for Italian magazines and I
picked up some movie script translations, but otherwise my life
seemed to have come to a standstill. I couldn't even sing anymore. I

had been told by a doctor that I would have to keep quiet and use my voice as little as possible for at least the next six to eight months.

Back in Rome, I became aware that my mother was also unhappy and in trouble. Her attempt to make a new career for herself in Italy had begun well enough in the spring of 1949, when she had been hired to handle publicity for an Italian and British film to be shot that summer in Bordighera, on the Italian Riviera. Produced by Alexander Korda, the movie was called *My Daughter Joy;* it was directed by Gregory Ratoff and starred Edward G. Robinson, Peggy Cummins, and Richard Greene. Janet was working hard on a profile of Léon Blum, the French Socialist leader and a politician she admired, and was able to bring her research to Bordighera to stay with Natalia. Although the work was demanding and tiring, Janet's presence during those summer months made Natalia happy. "At the end of the day we would be together," she wrote, "sharing our daily experiences, enjoying the peaceful surroundings and each other's company." When it was over, however, Janet moved back to Paris and Natalia found herself alone again.

The movie job didn't lead to anything else. And no sooner had she returned to Rome than she found herself plunged into a family crisis. Lea had suffered a nervous breakdown and had been hospitalized, where she was to undergo electric-shock treatments. This had come as no surprise to me, as I had seen a good deal of Lea and Akos since my return to Italy. They still lived in the penthouse above the Corso and I had spent time there, especially early on, when I had yet to establish myself and make new friends. I loved them both, but Lea had always struck me as unbalanced. She was brilliant, witty, deeply cultured, and stimulating to be around, but also unhappy and troubled by demons that caused her to explode into terrible rages. These seemed to be directed mainly at Akos, who would put up with them for a while and then react fiercely in self-defense. Their arguments eventually drove me away from their house, even though

I became increasingly fond of Akos, who was charming and unfailingly kind. A Hungarian aristocrat, he was my idea of a truly civilized man, and I continued to see him alone. We would meet for lunch in a small trattoria near his apartment and he ultimately became my point of reference in Rome, invariably for the rest of his life the first person I would contact whenever I came back to the city after being away. When I heard that Lea had apparently gone mad, I thought mainly about him and my cousin Flavia, whose childhood had been scarred by the furies unleashed around her. Eventually, Lea recovered, though she and Akos separated.

As if their troubles weren't bad enough, Mammina Ester had been made an outcast by her adopted country. A naturalized American citizen, she had had her American passport revoked because she had failed to return to the States within the three-year period the naturalization law provided, even though she had asked for an extension on emergency grounds. This discriminatory provision was eventually abolished, but at that time my grandmother suddenly found herself a stateless person. Her citizenship was restored months later only after my mother was able to get someone in Washington to intervene on her behalf. Sick with worry, my mother spent weeks in Rome rushing between the American Embassy and the hospital, dealing with these family problems.

In December she went to Sicily to do a long article on the island for *Flair* and returned to Rome to find that Lea was on the mend and that things had calmed down a bit. Then Janet, still hard at work on the Blum profile, came to Rome for a stay of two months, which helped to keep them both happy. After Janet returned to Paris again, however, life seemed to close in on my mother. She had lost her apartment in New York, there were rumors that *Flair* was in financial difficulties and about to fail, and no other job offers were coming her way. She had also dropped her book project on the House of Savoy. "Everything I had attempted to do since the end of the war seemed either to have failed or was going to, like *Flair,* on which I had based so much hope," she wrote. Even when she went to consult her favorite wizard, she was told she was going through a seven-year cycle of misfortune. By the fall of 1950, when Janet sailed off to New York to see Ross, who had summoned her to come and witness what was going on with the magazine, and to visit Hildegarde in California, Natalia had come to the unhappy realization that it would be impossible for her to remain in Italy.

She decided to go back to New York the following spring, after a visit to Janet in Paris. On her way she stopped off in Milan to see Arnoldo Mondadori, who had rebuilt his badly bombed printing plant in Verona and quickly reestablished himself as Italy's most important and largest publisher of books and magazines. Her timing was excellent. Mondadori had decided to open an office in New York, and my mother was obviously the most qualified person to run it. Her job would be dual: to represent Mondadori's authors and books for the American market and to acquire the Italian rights to American publications. Before agreeing to take the job, she discussed it with Janet. It would once again mean long periods of separation between them, broken only by Janet's visits to New York and my mother's trips to Italy, as well as month-long vacations. They both anguished over the prospect, but Natalia really had no choice. The opportunity was too good to pass up. Besides, she wouldn't be so alone in New York. I had already gone back, my hopes of an opera career pretty much abandoned and the job at *Time* no longer open to me.

Janet knew that Natalia would accept the Mondadori offer and conveyed her feelings in a letter on April 2, 1951. The Mondadori job was indeed the obvious answer to her problem, "more of your mind and level and would give you physical, spiritual independence," she wrote, but added that she was heartsick at the forthcoming separation. "Our hearts will be cut off."

When my mother arrived in New York early that summer, I was once again on the pier to meet her. This time there was not much joy in either of our hearts.

FIFTEEN

THE
GENERAL'S
BLESSING

It was during this unsettled period of their lives that Janet recorded in her journal a paragraph from one of Natalia's letters to her that was characteristic of my mother's view of the human condition. "Nothing that has not been paid for by suffering is worthwhile," Natalia wrote. "Nothing. The reason why America produces so many unbalanced people, alcoholics or neurotics, is because Americans have not known real misery through history. The magnificent phrase in your Constitution, 'the pursuit of happiness,' has been interpreted as if happiness could indeed be pursued. When this proves not to be true, certain Americans are astonished and broken into small pieces. They do nothing to learn that happiness, first of all in the pure sense, does not exist and, second, that all must be paid with real blood. In other words, happiness is a kind of maturity reached through suffering and experience, not a gift due to us because a Constitution promised it, or God. The Catholic Church, which is wise and old, does not promise happiness on this earth. It promises it in heaven as compensation for suffering here on earth. It is the church's greatest investment and invention." To which Janet added, on another page of her journal, "Italians know that the only way not to die is to be immortal."

I was always astonished at such manifestations of hard-nosed ancient pessimism on the part of my mother, because in her personal life she was such a positive driving force, and her own pursuit of happiness was so relentless. No sooner had she arrived in New York than she rented a small apartment on upper Madison Avenue and plunged with enthusiasm into the Mondadori job. Her office was located in the Scribner Building at Forty-eighth Street and Fifth Avenue, a few floors above the celebrated old bookstore and in the heart of the publishing industry, then centered in midtown Manhattan. Her arrival on the scene was announced in *Publishers Weekly* and she soon made her presence felt by contacting the foreign rights departments of every major publisher in town, with business luncheons and meetings taking up most of her days.

Janet, working hard now on a profile of Matisse, wrote encouragingly from Paris: "I can almost see your office by your description, darling. The handsome huge Italian furniture will give you an ambiance of familiar line and volume that should aid your imagination and even resistance; like eating in an Italian or French restaurant in New York to pretend one is in Italy or France." She promised to come to New York for Christmas, but didn't, putting off her visit until February.

In early December 1951, Harold Ross died. He had been suffering from lung cancer and expired soon after exploratory surgery. Natalia cabled condolences to Janet, who replied that she had known of Ross's illness and so was not entirely unprepared for the loss. Still, it was a grievous one. "The question is not where do the dead disappear but how extraordinary the shock is, each time, that anyone CAN die; friends look so immortal, we all feel so ageless. . . . I have really been so shaken with sadness that I could hardly write with a pen or pencil, my hand shook so. It was like a sickness, feeling so sad, feeling such a loss, as if the landscape had dropped away around me, all being now unfamiliar. . . ." She decided not to rush to New York for the funeral, but to remain at work in Paris on the Matisse essay and the other assignments okayed by Ross and Shawn.

For once in their relationship, Natalia did not press Janet to come as early as she had promised to. She had now embarked on her own road, committed to a career that would occupy her for the rest of her life. She had temporarily resigned herself to a permanent separation from Janet, to be broken only by the two or three months a year they would be together. She didn't much like her new apartment, which fronted on Madison Avenue and was noisy, but she clearly relished her new job and the prestige of her office arrangement. Janet, in the meantime, had moved in late October to the elegant Hotel Continentale, where she settled, surrounded by her newspapers and books, into a mansard room with a magnificent view over the Tuilleries, with the Eiffel Tower in the background. Their correspondence continued to flow back and forth, full of personal news and their usual speculations and observations on current events and historical tides, but for once free of recriminations and complaints. Natalia was so wrapped up in her new career that even Janet's prolonged absence failed to trouble her, though she was clearly worried about me.

The fact is, I was having a difficult time. I had come back to New York in the spring and hated every moment of it. The noise of daily life in the city was deafening and television had invaded the landscape, including most of the bars and restaurants where I met my old friends and tried to catch up with what they'd been up to in my absence. Not much, in my judgment. They all seemed to have settled quickly into the careers and jobs their backgrounds and education had prepared them for. Most of them had already married, and it seemed to me that their lives had become predictable and empty of adventure. Still, I had to admit to myself that they, at least, had a future, whereas I seemed to be trapped between two careers and not succeeding at either.

One of my first moves had been to look up my old boss, George Jones. He was glad to hear from me and invited me over to see him at *Time*'s home base in Rockefeller Center. Instead of in an office of his own, however, I found him sitting in a cubicle lost in a sea of mostly empty desks, a far cry from the grandeur of his digs in Rome. "What's going on?" I asked him, as he shook my hand and gazed sheepishly up at me.

He said that his situation at the magazine had become untenable. He had made the mistake of getting into a territorial war with a senior editor who had more clout and direct access to Henry Luce's ear. He had been recalled to New York, but instead of being given another foreign assignment he had been outcast to this slough of despond and given essentially nothing to do. Periodically someone would ask him to write an essay or rewrite somebody else's copy, but mostly he was allowed to sit at his desk in this empty room. They obviously wanted him to resign. "The accepted technique around here for getting rid of people is either to give them nothing to do," he explained, "or assign them to some doomed project, after which they can saw the limb off behind them. No one above a certain level is ever just fired." He had become a victim of the former tactic. When I asked him what he was going to do, he shrugged and smiled wanly.

I urged him to stick it out. He had always wanted to write a book, I reminded him, and here was the perfect chance. He had a desk, a typewriter, a phone, and unlimited office supplies. No one was going to bother him for a while. He could spend the next few months writing his book at *Time*'s expense while on full salary, then move on. He laughed and said he had considered doing just that, but wasn't sure he could stomach his situation much longer; it was embarrassing to bump into people every day in corridors and elevators who had been his colleagues and who now shunned him as if he were a leper with a bell around his neck. He asked me what I was up to.

Over lunch I regaled him with an account of my misadventures in Milan and told him I had now come back to New York to pursue my journalistic career. I gathered that I had little chance now of catching on at *Time.* He agreed with me, but suggested I contact the editor I'd met in Rome and tell her I was now available. I took his advice, but she wouldn't even see me. A month or so after our meeting, Jones left *Time* and went on to a successful career at *U.S. News & World Report.*

I also tried *The New Yorker,* though without enlisting Janet's or anyone else's help. I didn't feel I could put her in that position; and on what basis could she recommend me, apart from the opinion that I had talent? I foolishly hadn't saved any of my copy from the articles I had written for *Time,* and so I had nothing to show the very nice man who answered my letter of inquiry by telling me there were no jobs then open at the magazine but asking me to submit some samples of my work. I could have done that, I suppose, by collecting some clips from the *Time* morgue, but I felt oddly reluctant to pursue it. I was awed by *The New Yorker* and really didn't feel I had accomplished enough to merit being hired there.

My mother came to my rescue. I had very little money, so while I was floundering around she was able to pay me to help her at Mondadori. I worked the telephone for her and scouted books and magazines for possible publication in Italy. We worked surprisingly well together, with no major blowups, considering how often in the past I had rebelled against her dominating presence in my life. She knew I was in trouble and, as always in such circumstances, she became a small army of support rather than The General in command of her troops. "I am sorry Bill didn't get the *New Yorker* job, sorrier he didn't get the *Time* one as yet," Janet wrote from Paris, "for that is his special problem and he can work it out there better than elsewhere. That is where his first comprehensible revolt started, that is where he can best find out what revolt costs and also what it is worth."

Until then I had been spending most of my afternoons at the racetrack. I was living in a tiny walk-up apartment loaned to me by Gilbert Seldes, from where I sallied forth to the track by subway. I'd sit out there in the stands every day, rain or shine, to make one or two sizeable show bets on horses that couldn't lose. I had managed, after several weeks, to save two hundred and fifty dollars, which I kept in a cardboard shoebox marked Back to Italy Fund. My mother found out about it when I came down with a bad cold and she came to see me, lying exhausted and feverish on my sweaty sheets. I quickly recovered, but a few days later a thief broke into the flat and made off with my fund. "Money earned by gambling is never kept," The General pronounced, in her least attractive voice of doom. But I was not in a position to argue with her.

I also answered the cattle calls for chorus jobs in several Broadway shows, but, as I was not a member of Equity, the actors' union, I had little chance of getting hired, even though I thought I sang well enough at my auditions. I was offered one job, the tiny part of Hortensio, in a bus-and-truck touring company of Cole Porter's *Kiss Me, Kate* that was about to ramble through the Midwest. After my audition number, the song from *Brigadoon* I had sung in Milan, the producer, a corpulent bearded man in a food-stained gray suit, asked me if I could sing high. I told him I could. "Show me," he said. I sang the aria "Questa o Quella" from Verdi's *Rigoletto*. "Can you sing higher?" the producer asked. How high would I have to sing, I wondered. I had just hit all sorts of operatic high notes, including B-flats. "Yeah?" the producer said. "They don't sound that high." He went on to explain that in the small company I would have to fill in in all the chorus ensembles. He'd pay me a hundred and fifty dollars a week, out of which I'd have to take care of all my expenses. And I would have to help move the scenery and props on and off the truck. I decided that this offer was one notch above working in a circus cleaning out the animal cages and that I didn't love show business enough to accept it.

Toward the end of the summer, through my mother's connections in New York's Italian colony, I got a job at ANSA, the Italian news agency. I was hired to put out a daily news bulletin in English on events and happenings in Italy that might be of interest to the American press. I culled my items off the wire service from Italy and typed up a mimeographed bulletin that went off daily to the *New York Times* and a dozen or so other ANSA clients. It was hard and unrewarding work, but at least it paid me a living wage. I also began to contribute freelance articles to several small magazines, most notably the *Nation,* for which I wrote a first piece about the Mafia's operations on the Hoboken, New Jersey, waterfront.

In addition to my unglamorous journalistic career, I persisted with my singing and landed the tenor role of Cyril in *Princess Ida* with a Gilbert and Sullivan opera company that played a repertory of weekend performances in the basement of a church in the East Seventies. I also appeared as Luiz in *The Gondoliers,* a high baritone role, but left the company after two months because my schedule was threatening to put me in the hospital. During the week I would go straight from my office at ANSA in Times Square to evening rehearsals, snatching a bite to eat on the way, then play four performances on the weekends. Needless to say, the singing job paid me nothing, though I enjoyed it until my stamina gave out.

Somehow I also found time to fall in love that autumn and winter with the younger sister of an old classmate and friend from Exeter. Her name was Doris Rogers and I had known her since she was fourteen, even then a treat for the eyes and soul. She was living with her widowed mother and working at *Architectural Forum,* a slick, very elegant monthly. We decided to get married, the only trouble being that at the time I didn't seem to have much of a future. I was also pining to get back to Italy. When a newly formed outfit called Italian Films Export offered me a job that would return me to Rome, I immediately accepted. Financed by the Italian movie industry, IFE was set up to promote and publicize Italian films in the U.S. The main part of my job would be to keep a constant stream of stories, photos, interviews, and gossip flowing from Italy to the American media. I would also be expected to take care of the American entertainment press when any of its representatives showed up in Rome. That part of the job appealed to me less, but I didn't anticipate that I might not have the right temperament for that kind of public relations. I had begun to think about writing a novel, even though I had no idea yet what to write about, and I reasoned I'd be able to find enough time in this job to do so. After I accepted the IFE offer, Doris and I decided to get married on April Fool's Day, just in case, we laughingly told each other, we decided to call it off at the last minute.

Janet had arrived in New York in early February 1952, and she and Natalia had spent a happy, active winter together. Immersed in her new job, my mother found herself psychologically better able to adjust to the long separations, during which they were linked only by their letters and occasional phone calls to one another. They had both met Doris and approved of my choice; in fact, I think they both worried about whether I could make her happy, a legitimate concern given my poor track record as a careerist. I would have to become a serious person now, The General persistently admonished me as the date of our wedding neared. I would have to become responsible for my actions. I couldn't go on throwing away opportunities, as I had so often in the past.

For once, I didn't argue with her or bristle at her criticisms. I had always known she loved me and that she had always supported me in every crisis. And I agreed with her that Doris was a find, a beautiful, warm, witty, and intelligent partner who deserved the very best I could give her. So I was startled when, less than a week before our wedding, my mother told me one night that a woman named Berit had been trying to reach me from Chicago and that my mother had assured her I would call her.

"Berit? You told her I would call her?" I asked, amazed.

"She still loves you," my mother said. "Don't you want to see her?" She made it clear she thought I should get in touch with her.

I had had several love affairs in Italy, not unusual for an unattached male in his early twenties. The last one had been with Berit, a Swedish soprano I had met in Siena and with whom I had carried on a tempestuous affair that lasted through the summer of 1950, until she had gone back to her husband and two children in Stockholm. For months we had written each other passionate letters promising to wait until we could at last be together at some future date. The correspondence had eventually petered out, and it had been more than a year since I had heard from her. Now here she was, singing in Chicago. After her engagement there she wanted to come to New York to see me.

My mother had never met Berit, but she had known about her and I'm sure did not approve. She was older than I was, married, with children. Impossible. Unthinkable. We had never discussed the matter. But now? "I'm getting married next week, remember?" I said. "To Doris. Remember Doris? Remember what I told you? If I don't marry Doris, I'll never marry."

She stared at me, a curiously mischievous expression on her face, her eyes bright with excitement. "I think you must call her," she said. "She loves you."

"No, she doesn't," I said. "It's over. And I love Doris."

That was the end of the conversation. I never did call Chicago or hear from Berit again. Nor did my mother ever mention the incident again, though it made me regard her forever after in a slightly different light. She had never before so nakedly revealed the extent of her possessiveness.

Janet left in late March to visit Hildegarde and Eric in California, as planned, but wanted to fly back for my wedding. "I should be standing with you at your son's wedding day," she wrote Natalia. "Too many omissions are mine, and many are exterior to me. I am eager to fly to be with you if you will let me. I feel a personal connection with your events. I feel a vital personal connection with you because what touches you touches me."

Natalia told her not to come, as she knew it would cut short her California visit; air travel was still an expensive luxury then. Doris and I were married in a modest ceremony in the side chapel of the Madison Avenue Presbyterian Church, with only family members and old friends present, George de Kay acting as my best man. A few days later I left for Rome to take up my assignment for IFE, with Doris scheduled to join me in two months.

The day before I left I received a long letter from my mother that amazed me. "In the hectic hours of these last days and in the excitement of the events which are shaping your new life," it began, "we had hardly any time to give words and form to the feelings and thoughts crowding the heart. Perhaps it has been a good thing, a kind of shield against the flow of the emotions. I do not know why I should feel so emotional at this point. Except perhaps because I realize that finally my job is done. You are spreading your wings for the full flight." For three more pages she poured out her feelings of love and pride in me, telling me in detail what she had never told me before and concluding, "I am glad that you are going to be in Rome, in my lovely city, near Ester and the family and that you are going to live in my little flat with faithful Pierina as a guardian angel. . . . Bless you, my Bill. I did not realize how much you were a part of me until this moment!"

I didn't consider myself worthy of such praise. I was twenty-six and had accomplished very little. I had failed at what I loved most, my singing career, and now I was going back to Rome to become a flack for the Italian movie industry. What I suddenly realized, as I held this letter in my hands, stunned by the extent and power of the maternal love contained in it, was that the one person who had believed in, trusted, and supported me in everything I had ever tried to do was the one I had struggled hardest to free myself from. Perhaps, I thought, by always withholding her deepest feelings from me she had granted me the freedom I had needed to become a man, however flawed and insecure.

SIXTEEN

STEPPING
INTO
THE PROGRAM

I hadn't been back in Italy long before I realized I wasn't going to make a success of my new job. I could handle the routine of it all right—the interviews, the photo shoots, the news bulletins, the compiling of industry gossip—but the personal element would inevitably do me in. I wasn't temperamentally cut out to handle the demands of the touring American entertainment press. These people expected me to provide them and their wives and escorts with cars and drivers, throw parties for them, take them out to lunches and dinners, and provide free passes to everything. Leonard Lyons, then a powerful syndicated newspaper columnist, was among the worst. When I told him I couldn't provide a car and driver to take his wife shopping and then on to Naples for a weekend tour of Vesuvius and Pompeii, he said he wouldn't run a single item in his column about Italian movies. I said to him, very politely, that my job was simply to provide contacts and information; what he did with the material I gave him was entirely up to him. Because he had to fill his columns with something, he wound up using quite a lot of the items I provided, but he later complained about me to my boss in New York and almost succeeded in getting me fired. I didn't care. I had a one-year contract, with a renewal option three months before its expiration. I intended to quit at the end of the year.

I made one friend from the visiting press, a most unlikely one. This was Irving Hoffman, a columnist from the *Hollywood Reporter* and freelance contributor to a number of general-circulation magazines. He telephoned my office from his hotel one morning and told me to come over and see him. I had prepared a packet of stuff for him, press releases and glossies from various movies then in production, but I wasn't looking forward to meeting him; his voice on the phone had sounded harsh and humorless, hostile to the very idea of having to deal with me.

He was staying in the penthouse suite of an expensive but ugly modern hotel in an unfashionable part of town, near the railroad station. When he opened the door for me, he was dressed only in pyjama bottoms and slippers. Without bothering to shake my hand, he ushered me inside, then shuffled down a long corridor ahead of me. "This way," was all he said. A tough-looking young woman in her mid-twenties with dyed blonde hair suddenly emerged from a bedroom and walked swiftly past us, her high heels clacking loudly on the uncarpeted marble floor. "See ya, honey," Hoffman said, as she left.

He led me out onto a terrace overlooking the street, sat down in a chair next to a table covered with magazines and newspapers, and gazed at me over a pair of thick horn-rimmed glasses. He was nearly bald, in his middle or late forties, and had a soft white body covered by masses of curly dark hair. "What have you got for me?" he asked. I handed him the packet. Without opening it, he dropped it on the table. "I'm not going to use any of that shit," he said.

"I don't care what you use or don't use," I said. "My job is to give it to you. The rest is up to you." I turned to go.

"Sit down," he said, peering through his glasses at his wristwatch. "I got nearly an hour. Want some coffee? It's still hot."

I sat and he poured me a caffè latte from a serving tray next to his chair, then stretched in the warm morning sunlight. "I love this fucking place," he said. "Great city, great broads."

I told him I had expected to find him ensconced in the Excelsior or one of the other luxurious hostelries along the Via Veneto, where most of the other visiting journalists stayed. "Nah," he said, "too rich for my blood. I like this place. It's central and I can do what I want."

What he wanted, I found out, was to run hookers in and out of his suite several times a day. In fancier hotels he'd have had a harder time, whereas in this one no one stopped the girls or asked them any questions on their way in and out. "Where do you find them?" I asked.

"Anywhere," he answered. He only liked prostitutes, and he would pick them up off the sidewalks or from the cafés they haunted. He had to have two or three women a day, every day, and Rome was one of his favorite cities because these working girls, as he called them, were so readily available there. As we talked, he leaned over the pile of newspapers and magazines in front of him and began laboriously to clip out articles and items that interested him, not all of them having to do with show business. He used a long pair of shears, peering closely at each page, his eyes in their thick glasses no more than a few inches above the text. He was nearly blind. "So," he said, after we had finished on the subject of women, "what's a nice kid like you doing in a rotten business like this?"

I told him I was trying to become a writer, but that I had to earn a living. "Yeah? Why?" he asked. "You'll never become a writer if you stay in publicity too long. What writers do you like?"

I told him, and for the next hour or so we talked books and authors. He had read everything and had strong opinions on literary matters. We both admired the same writers and believed that writing beneath one's true abilities simply to make a buck was a form of betrayal, almost a mortal sin. "The only pure writer I know," I said, "is Janet Flanner, *The New Yorker*'s correspondent in Paris."

"I know who Janet Flanner is," he said indignantly. "She writes great stuff. I read everything she writes. She must be a tough old broad."

I laughed and told him she wasn't, that she was one of the kindest, gentlest people I knew. His doorbell rang and Hoffman stood up and headed for the front door. "You'll have to excuse me, kid," he said. "I got a date. Give me a call tomorrow, will you?"

I followed him out and said goodbye just as he opened the door to admit a tall, lanky brunette in a low-cut blouse that revealed most of an enormous bosom. "Ah, Marcia," Hoffman said. "*Avanti, avanti.*" He put an arm around her waist and swept her inside, then shut the door behind me as I left.

I saw Hoffman every day of the week he spent in Rome. I got him a car and driver and made sure he received all the press releases and gossip items I could scrape up. We never talked about the movies or show business at all, but only about literature and good journalism. He had high standards that obviously didn't apply to his own work, but he never discussed what he wrote for a living. He persistently urged me to get on with my own writing and get out of the public relations game before it ruined me. He never made any demands on me and wound up using everything I brought him in his columns. The last time I saw him that spring was the day before he left. I was sitting with a friend at a sidewalk table on the Via Veneto at about noon when I saw Hoffman shuffling slowly toward me between the parallel rows of tables and peering closely from side to side. He was dressed in pants, a jacket thrown over his pyjama top, and slippers. "Irving," I said, as he reached my table, "what's going on?"

"Ah, she stood me up," he answered. "I met her here yesterday afternoon and she said she'd come to the hotel this morning. So I came looking for her. Her name's Laura. She's short, stacked, a lot of curls. You seen her, maybe?" I told him I hadn't and he moved on, his bald head swivelling from side to side as he searched for Laura.

I only saw Irving Hoffman one more time and that was back in New York well over a year later. Since then, however, I had heard a number of stories about him, many of them having to do with how he had befriended the working girls of New York. He could always be counted upon to put up bail for them when they were arrested or find them a good doctor when they were sick. He knew the exact weights and measurements of all the girls and their particular sexual specialties, and he graded them on their performances. They apparently regarded him as a sort of patron saint. When I saw him in New York, he was sitting at a desk he rented next to a window in an open area of one of the upper floors of the old *Times* tower in Times Square. He worked there, he told me, because it was cheap, central, and the light was good. An enormous circular file in front of him contained hundreds of names, most of them of working girls. "Hiya, kid," he said, as I announced myself. "Sit down. I've been reading your stuff. You're a good writer. I told you to get out of that shit job."

I had gone up to see him mainly to thank him, but also because I thought he'd be a great subject for a magazine piece. I had been hearing from him regularly. Every time an article, an essay, or a review of mine had appeared in one of the small, mostly obscure publications I worked for, I would receive a communication from Hoffman, always in the form of a printed sheet listing various sorts of encomiums or condemnations, such as "Nice job" or "Great article" or "You stink" or "You ought to be burned at the stake." Next to the appropriate line he would paste a gold star or a soaring rocket or a huge exclamation point. Once, across the bottom of the page, he had scrawled in his own hand, "So what about the novel?"

Hoffman shrugged off my thanks with an embarrassed mumble I couldn't decipher, but quickly disabused me of any hope of writing a piece about him. "Are you kidding?" he asked. "Joe Mitchell at *The New Yorker* wants to write about me, too, but what's he going to say? That I run hookers and procure for the stars? Forget about it, kid. Nobody's gonna write about me."

I've always wanted to use Hoffman as a character in a novel, but never have. A few years later, I talked about him with Joe Mitchell, but Mitchell agreed that Hoffman probably couldn't be written about, certainly not in *The New Yorker* in those days. Mitchell also told me what I now consider to be a classic Hoffman tale. It seems that some years earlier Hoffman had been writing disparagingly in his column about a Hollywood studio mogul who was celebrated for his dismal taste and the terrible movies he had been producing, all of which Hoffman had panned scathingly in his column. The exasperated mogul had called a meeting of his publicity heads to discuss the situation. "This guy Hoffman," he commanded, "put him on the payroll." This exhortation had been succeeded by a moment of embarrassed silence, after which one of the publicity staff finally spoke up. "Chief," he said, "he *is* on the payroll."

Hoffman may not have been the most admirable character in the world, but he taught me a lesson about integrity; he couldn't be bought. For years I continued to hear from him, always after some article or story or book of mine appeared in print, and always with words of praise and encouragement.

The low point of that year as a publicity flack came a few months before the end of my contract. I was invited to sit in as an interpreter at a meeting between the Italian heads of IFE and a representative from the American Legion of Decency, an American monsignor who had been sent to Rome to do something about the content of Italian films. He and his colleagues were upset that the movies Italy was producing were not suitable for American audiences. Too much sex, too much free thinking. He wanted the Italian movie industry to conform to the standards of the Legion of

Decency and its Production Code. He suggested that the country's moviemakers should submit their scripts to the Legion for approval before putting them into production. Perhaps IFE could send someone to New York, who could familiarize himself with the Production Code. If that didn't work out, perhaps someone from the Legion could be permanently stationed in Italy to apply the code. The two representatives of IFE at this meeting agreed that the suggestions had merit and promised to act on the Legion's proposals. After this encounter I made notes of what had transpired and later, back in New York, I wrote a pseudonymous article for the *Nation* about the Legion's attempt to pre-censor Italian movies. I was no longer under contract to IFE and had embarked on a full-time career as a freelance writer. The piece for the *Nation* garnered my first encomium from Hoffman in the form of one of his printed sheets with a positive comment accentuated by a fistful of gold stars and eight exclamation points.

Apart from my job, Doris and I had had a good year in Italy. We were happy in our marriage, and we had friends and family, as well as an active social life, to keep us contented. But I now had a novel I wanted to write, about American expatriates living in Italy and supporting themselves by working on the fringes of the movie industry during the production of an American epic called *Ave Caesar*, based on the filming in Rome of *Quo Vadis*. I had been thinking for several months about using the making of a movie as background for a novel, but I hadn't focused on a theme; I wasn't sure what my novel would be about. After my week with Irving Hoffman, I had begun to think of it as a story about maintaining one's integrity in a world full of temptations and easy compromises. I even had a title for it, *The Phantom Caravan*, which reflected an image I had of life as a sort of touring circus full of animal acts and spectacular deeds of daring. I had enough money to keep us alive and well for six months or so, but we both wanted to go home, where I could also start earning a little money with freelance magazine pieces. Back in New York Doris could go back to work, perhaps as an editor in magazines. I was no longer a singer and I knew now I would never become an Italian, although leaving Italy again was like leaving a second home. I told myself that I would always come back to Italy, but that I had no choice. If I wanted to make a living as a writer, I would have to pay my dues in New York. "You can write and will hit your mark, be patient," Janet wrote from Paris.

It had been a good year for Janet and Natalia as well, with both of them happy in their circumstances and their work. Janet's pieces in *The New Yorker* were dazzling. I read her religiously and continued to admire her enormously; she was living, in my opinion, the ideal writer's life in her Paris hotel room. She had no responsibilities, no distractions to contend with. Although she complained constantly about being unable to work or finding it very difficult to do so, her daily routine struck me as ideal for a writer. Breakfast was served to her in her room and she had no household chores to pull her away from her desk; the hotel staff catered to her every need. She could sit quietly and peruse the French newspapers for story ideas and to test the pulse of the city and the nation as a whole, after which she would make her appointments to go out into the world to find out for herself what was really going on or to interview the people who most interested her. She avoided politicians, whom she considered to be congenital liars, but could always get a sense of what they were really about by talking to their cronies and enemies. She sifted tirelessly through masses of information before settling down to her task of getting it on paper, which, though often very difficult for her, was also a source of deep satisfaction, even rapture. She worked for hours at a stretch, sometimes not leaving her room for days, except to descend to the bar for a cocktail in the late afternoons. "I love to look up at the clock over my bedroom door," she noted, "and discover that an hour and forty minutes have gone by unobserved since I last looked because I was working and time didn't count." She described this act of creation as "the most satisfying oblivion."

Sometimes physical ailments, not all of them minor, made it difficult for her to get her copy in on time. She smoked heavily, she drank too much, and she suffered from attacks of rheumatism, especially in her back and shoulders. Periodically, she would abstain from tobacco and alcohol, take hot baths and medications for her pains. But always she went on working, alone in her room, hour after hour, day after day, and the amount of copy she produced was sizeable. She thought much of it not very good and told her editors at *The New Yorker* that she was failing. Shawn, however, was always there to comfort, reassure, and praise her; he was the ideal editor for her. And always, no matter what the difficulties and insecurities she encountered, the quality of her writing inspired me. Over and over I was struck by the beauty and precision of her descriptions of people and events. "In his eighty-second year, three years before his death, Matisse was still an impressive figure," she wrote in her profile of the painter. "When he stood by his easel or rose from his easy chair to greet a visitor, he looked like a massive, well-preserved ruin, like an important structure that had been undermined mostly by the weight of time, but the upper and lower stories—his heavy torso, his dwindling limbs—maintained a precarious, majestic balance, with some inner girders of will power holding the whole together."

I despaired of ever being able to write that well, but Janet's work also inspired me to try. She was the one, not my mother, to whom I confided my deepest aspirations as a writer and who never failed to support and encourage me, but always with a certain diffidence, as if by championing me too openly she might encroach on maternal territory. Shortly after our return to New York, when I wrote a "Letter from Rome" for a small magazine called *UN World,* it was to Natalia that Janet gave her opinion: "I think Bill's UN Letter from Rome was very, very good. Talented writing, facts well assembled, very amusing, developed critical faculty, *bref,* very good indeed. Since *The New Yorker* developed this type of foreign letter (or actually I did), I took a modest pride in a second-generation correspondent, like our Bill, stepping into the program."

Once settled back in New York into a one-bedroom apartment in the East Seventies, I plunged immediately into my new career as a freelance writer. In addition to my "Letter from Rome" and my pseudonymous piece for the *Nation,* I hustled up whatever assignments I could get, all of them from small magazines. The pay was atrocious, never more than a hundred dollars for even a full-length article, but my main concern was to get myself published and establish a recognizable byline. I wasn't even thinking about *The New Yorker,* although Janet never abandoned hope that someday I would wind up there. "I wish I could see Bill's Italian literature piece," she wrote to Natalia. "He is such a good reporter and critic that he will surely find openings on *The New Yorker* soon." She had urged me to send samples of my work regularly to Mr. Shawn, but I never did, mainly because I didn't think anything I was writing in those early days was good enough. I allowed Janet to believe I was doing so, however, because I didn't want her to think I didn't take her advice or her interest in me seriously. She was horrified by what I was being paid for my work and continued to worry about me. "That is horrible pay for an article that Bill got," she told Natalia. "I feel that if he continues sending stuff to Bill Shawn he will get his chance, if only for writing some Reporter or something which would anyhow pay well. I enormously admire his rectitude and purity and determination. I wish there was anything I could do." My mother never passed on any of Janet's favorable comments to me, except for also urging me to keep Shawn up to date on my efforts. She was afraid, I think, that too much praise would weaken my resolve.

In between magazine pieces I went to work on my novel, using a first-person narrator named Tom Gallagher to tell the story. Like me, Gallagher was a young American at loose ends in Italy who was working in public relations. He didn't believe in anything in particular and was drifting into a messy love affair with the English wife of an ex-RAF pilot who had settled in Rome. Gallagher's friends were rather typical expatriates, who were lingering in Europe passing themselves off as would-be artists and writers. The central figure in Gallagher's narrative was Allan Reade, an aging, amoral ex-star of a series of B-pictures who had come to Rome to salvage his career by getting himself employed in a huge spectacle production about to start shooting at Cinecittà, the Italian film industry's major studio on the outskirts of the city toward the Alban Hills. What happened to Reade and how he reacted to the persistent persecution of him by the film's director, a man Reade had once humiliated and denounced as a fraud, was the raison d'être for the novel. At the end of it Tom Gallagher presumably would have learned something about himself and his own talents and aspirations.

In the roughly three months during 1953 that I'd been working on the book I had managed to write fifty or sixty pages in rough draft, but I needed a long uninterrupted period to write the bulk of the manuscript. Doris had not yet gone back to work, so we took the summer off and drove out to Neenah, Wisconsin, Doris's hometown, where I'd be able to devote myself totally to the book. We stayed as guests in a large lakefront mansion belonging to the widowed mother of Doris's best friend and sister-in-law. Every morning by nine o'clock I was at my typewriter in the dining room, from which I would not emerge until I had typed at least fifteen hundred words. I had decided that I needed to tell the story first, no matter how clumsily; I would worry about rewriting and polishing later. By the time we came back to New York in the early fall, I had a completed first draft of about three hundred and fifty pages.

I've always loved rewriting, polishing, and editing; the hard part is to write the rough first draft. The secret, I discovered, is to set yourself a goal, so many words or so many pages a day, every day, with no deviations or procrastinations. Even at the modest rate of only a few hundred words a day, it's astonishing how fast a manuscript will grow over a period of only a few months. No sooner was I back in New York and once again trying to hustle up magazine assignments than I began to revise, cut, add, restructure, and polish, a much slower procedure but to me an enormously satisfying one. To help keep us alive, and also because she wanted to get back to work, Doris landed a job in the publicity department of the Museum of Non-Objective Art, soon to become the Guggenheim and move to a new building designed by Frank Lloyd Wright, one of Doris's heroes.

At this point I had shown the rough manuscript only to a couple of friends in publishing, mainly to get some feedback and benefit from any suggestions or criticisms they might make. One of them, on holiday in Paris, looked up Janet and told her I had written the book too hurriedly for it to succeed. Janet was appalled and immediately communicated her disapproval to Natalia. "Bill's novel was about the filming of *Quo Vadis,* so I suppose it is more a satire book than a novel, after all?" she wrote.

> [His friend] said the idea was good and could have been handled but that Bill had written it in six weeks. This shocked me. I hope he is not going to take into his writing that fatal juvenile idea he previously had in Rome about everything—that he will not do anything he does not want to do, such as really working, exhaustingly as is often necessary, over one's writing, to make it good, to make it better and above all to learn what it is one wants to say and how best to say it. If he is going to belong to the school that says, "It doesn't interest me to work over my writing, it has to stand the way it comes out in the first draft," then he is only an amateur writer with talent and will never be a professional and will never run the course, never last to the end. However I cannot believe he will take this attitude—except that he already demonstrated it in submitting a six-week manuscript.

My mother didn't show me Janet's letter, but told me what had happened and what her reaction was. I was stunned and also furious, not only at the friend who had, I felt, betrayed me, but also at Janet for believing him. I wrote her an indignant letter that I had indeed done much of my work on the first draft of the novel during the two months (not six weeks) we had stayed in Wisconsin, but that I had worked on it earlier, was still working on it, and had no intention of submitting it anywhere until I felt sure I had the manuscript in final shape. When Janet didn't answer my letter right away, I fired off another one and received a placating note from her. "I had another note from your Bill," she also wrote to Natalia, "still pretty cross that anybody could dare think he was not serious about writing. Nobody does, I imagine. I merely thought few serious writers can write their best in a two-month novel; and few ever have either. But DON'T repeat this, please, my beloved. Enough is enough."

It was. I went back to work on the book, having learned one valuable lesson from the experience, which was never to show an unfinished manuscript to anyone. And it was several years before I forgave the friend who had caused this mischief between us.

SEVENTEEN

STENDHAL'S PROTÉGÉ

"My darling, I have been in bed with a tonsil. Everyone in Paris has been in bed with a tonsil and with each other also, I suppose," Janet wrote to Natalia in the fall of 1953. "Beautiful bright Indian summer weather with nature looking healthy and an epidemic of colds, mostly tonsolitic [sic], that must come from the extra long season the flowers in the gardens are enjoying and by which they are discharging heavy old pollen. My theory. I was in bed off and on a week, working just the same or mostly, though it took all I had of determination." She proceeded to assure Natalia that she was planning to come to New York for Christmas and to remain for at least several months. She had been working very hard on her profile of André Malraux and was tired of grinding out her Paris Letters every two weeks; she thought they had become slick and stale. Most of all, she worried about the continuing sacrifice she had made of her personal relationships in order to keep on working. "What am I doing with my life?" she had asked herself earlier in the year. "So far from you and how will I stop living in today's terms of work and start living in terms of what is the residue of love?" She wished to God she had been born "a roaring Irish Catholic from Indiana so as to be better equipped to have a natural place for the senses in my life. . . ."

Natalia had been putting renewed pressure on Janet to make a more active commitment to her, in the form at least of devoting more time to their relationship. She had been in her Mondadori job long enough by then to have had a strong whiff of office politics back in Milan and to have seen some of her best recommendations and projects sabotaged or denied by her bosses. She had lost some of her interest and pride in the job, which caused her once again to look to Janet for comfort and a solution. Janet sympathized, but told her to hang on, that "work itself has meaning and it cannot lightly be devalued of it despite the disgusting fleshly relations that stand behind, the people behind who have disappointed so horribly that they become different people, not the same as when they seemed paternal, kind, logical, safe." She still derived much satisfaction from her own work. "Not as much, but it still keeps me alive, keeps me breathing even when I work so much slower but with desperate devotion, as on the Malraux. . . ."

Natalia now had an additional card to play in her long campaign to capture Janet. In New York she had met a middle-aged Austrian psychiatrist who had fallen in love with her and proposed marriage. He was intelligent, charming, kind, and amazingly tolerant. He knew about Natalia's involvement with Janet, but was undeterred by it. He was apparently even willing to allow her to go on seeing Janet from time to time, if only she would marry him. Natalia passed this news on to Paris, but also assured Janet that she had just broken off with him. She wanted Janet to know the full extent of the sacrifices she was prepared to make on her behalf.

Janet continued to promise that she would spend more time in

New York, even if it meant leaving *The New Yorker*. "Yes, darling, we will pursue the plan we made this summer in Rome, solidifying its outlines and aiming completely at the security you feel your due and which love gives," she wrote on October 9.

Knowing you, you will not regret in principle your discarding of the doctor, because you were not in love with him; and two marriages without being in love are too many, for in this case there would not be the child to attach you. I know you well enough now, in recollection especially, to realize there will always be small angry spasms of grief for you that you did not make the life, years ago, where the male element *naturally* takes over, protects and supplies, freeing the female from fears and anguishes of self-support. I cannot feel that way, I always retracted away from it, so I substitute for it less naturally than some lady lovers do. But I swear I shall do all in my power to make you not regret your late decision, to make you happy, to make a home for you.

She returned to this theme again in another long letter the following day.

I am at work on my Paris Letter for next week, but my thoughts are more with you than on it. I hope we can found the plans at Christmas which will settle the single element of concern to you, my darling, and will include also the means for me not to do more destruction of all and sundry, including my Quakerisms, than are encumbent upon one so old as I and so little wise. I cannot even look back with clarity for I realize I was never clear enough to furnish a picture of my actions, which were always based upon my dominant characteristic, a romantic sensuality and secondly a real fondness, a tenderness for those I had loved.

Natalia was not entirely reassured by Janet's protestations and expressions of love; she did not entirely trust in her promises anymore. Janet, however, persisted. "It is true I do not want to live in New York," she wrote on November 14,

> because I have made half of my life here. It seems true to you now that you do not want to live in Italy, being too Manhattanized, being as you say part of the American continent. (Far more than I am part of France. A foreigner does become an American, it is a legal metaphysical act of transmutation and change, but an American remains an American, especially if dealing with America as a topic or business, even after living half a life here. There is observation, alteration, identification which I have known here, but no feeling of national intimacy or even responsibility, either I toward France or it toward me. This is one of the elements, I think, which has strengthened in me my sense of a peculiar celibacy.) I have all along thought that you would not be contented being idle nor would you be anything but vexed with a *quelquonque* job. That is as much a problem for me to think of in terms of you, darling, with your alert sagacious mentality which has so enriched me as for you to think of me in terms of these last remaining years—how long?—on my job. You *must* have a domestic life. It is your classic need, too long denied you by me, by my character, habits and work. We have gone over this so often, my beloved, that I do not know a new exit for thought; there is no sortie except by sacrifice on one side or the other, we know that. . . . I am certainly growing old rather rapidly, my darling. Except in your presence I never feel a touch of Venus and at Christmas, when you were here, we three—you, Venus, and I—were rarely all of us together. I, too, am utterly worn out with the sense of guilt, of struggle, the self-contempt for not making you happy, for not destroying my life as it is, for not cracking it asunder and putting you in what is left of its epicenter, in the domesticity you long for. . . . Our love is not the same today as it was when we were younger, not so impetuous, so heated, so filled with acute suffering. I often feel almost paralyzed, cut off even

from myself and my own heart and soul. I have been more destructive in your life than you in mine because I have sacrificed
you, my beloved handsome one. I must stop thinking of it for a
little now. . . .

She was finishing up the Malraux profile and about to get it off
to Shawn at the magazine, who had already told her that what he
had read so far was perhaps the best work she had ever done. She
was also still worried about my outraged reaction to what she had
said about my novel and didn't blame me for being angry with the
friend who had spoken to her about it. But she still thought I
hadn't spent enough time on my book, "such a possible weakness
in it, *entre nous,* that Bill is touchy about it, I feel."

It was lucky for me that my mother didn't pass on this after-
thought to me either, because I was having a very difficult and
troubled time in New York trying to make a living while still working on the manuscript. Janet's loss of faith in me would have been
a blow from which I might not have recovered.

Doris had a modest income from her father's estate and was working at the museum, but we were making barely enough to survive
in New York. The small magazines I contributed to paid
wretchedly and I spent much of my time scrambling about for
money. I wrote liner notes and translated libretti for LP opera
recordings; I bought encyclopedias on credit and sold them to second-hand bookstores; I even went to work for a while as a copywriter in a book-advertising agency, but couldn't stomach it and
quit after three months. I walked out, I remember, without giving
notice or picking up my final paycheck. I even applied for grants,
but soon discovered that I lacked the academic credentials to qualify for them. I felt like a tightrope walker balanced high above an
arena lined by pitiless spectators and with no net to catch me if I
fell. The only thing that kept me going was the hope I had invested

in my novel, which by then I felt was ready to be submitted somewhere. I even had an agent, an old friend from Exeter named John
Cushman, who had gone to work for the large firm of Curtis
Brown. He loved my book, he told me, but warned me that it
would not be easy to sell a first novel by an unknown writer. I already knew this but still had high hopes, even after the book had
been turned down by the first two publishers to whom John had
shown it.

Once again it was my mother who came to my rescue, although
inadvertently this time. Sometime during the late fall of 1953, she
gave a cocktail party. I don't remember the occasion, but, as usual
with her parties, she made no attempt to ensure that her guests
would all come from roughly the same backgrounds and would all
get along together; she simply invited anyone she liked, trusting in
her instincts about people finding one another interesting to talk
to. Nor did she pay much attention to the number of people her
premises could comfortably accommodate. She lived at the time in
a modest two-bedroom apartment on East Eighty-first Street.
When I arrived shortly after six o'clock the place was packed with
guests, most of them forced to stand for lack of seating and talking
animatedly with one another. The roar of conversation could be
heard in the elevator as I approached the landing. My mother's parties were always triumphant occasions, as if she had carefully
screened all her guests beforehand. People who had never met before became lifelong friends at them.

One of her guests that evening was the novelist James T. Farrell,
whose trilogy on the adventures of Studs Lonigan, his Chicago
Huck Finn, had delighted me while I was still in prep school. I had
no idea my mother had ever met him, nor why she had invited him
to her party. I spent most of the evening talking to him about
books and authors, and he took a liking to me. Toward the end of
the party, as the guests began to wander away to dinner, he asked
me what I did for a living. I told him I was working as a copywriter
in an ad agency, but that I hated it. "Yeah," he said, "so that's what

you do with your left hand. What do you do with your right one?"
I confessed I had written a novel. "Send it to me," he said, scribbling his address on a piece of paper and handing it to me. "If I like it, I'll give it to my editor at Vanguard."

The next day I took Farrell a copy of my manuscript. Four or five days later he called to tell me he thought it was pretty good and would pass it on to his editor, Julian Muller. A week or so later, I received a phone call from Muller and was invited to lunch. The editor was an affable, solidly built man with slicked-back brown hair, dark-brown eyes, an open, confident manner, and a ready laugh. "I like your novel," he said, as we sat down in a crowded restaurant off Madison Avenue a couple of blocks from the Vanguard Press offices. "It needs some work and maybe a better title." He then outlined for me what he thought I needed to do to strengthen the story and my characters.

I quit my job as a copywriter and went back to work on my book. Most of Julian Muller's suggestions turned out to be enormously helpful. He had done for me what any good editor is supposed to do for a writer, which is to point out structural weaknesses in the story, question the characters' motivations, force the author to reach deep inside himself to improve and clarify exactly what he is trying to say. By the time I had finished my revisions, a couple of months later, he had even come up with a good title, *The Fugitive Romans,* an allusion to T. S. Eliot's play *The Family Reunion:* "In a world of fugitives / The person taking the opposite direction / Will appear to run away."

By this time I had sent Janet a copy of the manuscript, even though I worried that she might not like it. I had tried to keep the writing lean and spare, much influenced by Hemingway, with none of the reaching for apt metaphors and similes of the sort that graced Janet's work. My narrator, Tom Gallagher, and his friends were also not the sort of people I thought Janet would feel any sympathy for; they were young, wisecracking, cynical, directionless, and macho, with contemptuous attitudes toward homosexuals. My heroine, Pamela, was an amoral, self-indulgent English-woman who was ready to sacrifice her marriage and her lover to the pleasures of the moment. Nevertheless, I now felt confident enough in the novel to let her have a look at it. And I was proud of the book; I thought I had finally accomplished what I set out to do, which was to write a novel about a segment of my generation and its disillusionment with the American scene and its commitment to self-indulgent materialism. That these young men and women drifting through an expatriate life abroad, while living well off the strength of the dollar in the war-shattered economies of Europe, had failed and were failing to commit themselves to anything or anyone was not a hopeful message; but it was not far, I felt, from Janet's own view of Americans in the world at large.

She wrote me a long, thoughtful, detailed critique from which I realized that she hadn't liked the novel, though she did her best to disguise that fact by lavishing praise on what she did like: my portrayal of the old B-movie star down on his luck, the relationship between my narrator and his English lover. I wrote her back, thanking her and trying to explain to her what I had tried to do, comparing myself, I'm afraid, to Stendhal, whose great novel, *The Red and the Black,* had become one of the beacons for my own literary aspirations. Janet wrote Natalia that I had taken her criticism "amiably," but soon revealed in two later letters to her exactly what her real feelings were about the book.

"I wrote very carefully in my report on his book," she confided to Natalia,

> knowing how ill he supports criticism. But truly how can he hope to interest sentient readers in characters content to talk in hard-boiled lingo from which every idea but mere revolt—how elemental—is as absent as it would be in bar-bouncers in the Klondike or in East side Bowery slums? *Only to you can I say this.* It is not mere revolt against ignoble means of earning money that will reach any ideal of intelligence or literary style. He talks of

Stendhal's simplicity. I wish he would note how different it is from Murray's monosyllabics. *He has organizing talent for novel writing* indubitably. When he stops thinking himself called to *épater le bourgeois* and starts giving reasons why the bourgeois are as they are he can be a bigger novelist provided he wants to learn to *write* as well and fluently and with as much education as he talks. If you tell him this, I *shall never forgive you,* please. It would be a betrayal—not only of how I feel, but of how you really feel, I know. . . ."

In this letter Janet had confessed to Natalia that she was suffering from a deep depression, and a day or two later she wrote again:

I have been nowhere but in my room and a fine journey that has been, in the inside of my head. It is ironic that the climax of physical bile and my bilious depressed outlook on life finally reached its outburst in a letter to you, sent to your flat in New York, where . . . I sent it and where I wish you to destroy it without reading, please. It was my second reaction to Bill's novel, a reaction to it after receiving his letter in answer to mine. In it he made so much clearer his juvenility, if I may say so, in the American line of satisfaction in "jerking those self-satisfied bourgeois out of their seats" that it summed up, at that moment, my whole grief and despair at the plight of the American writer and his imagination and problem, without education as a rule, and in his case using an education, as an Italo-American, principally to compare the simplicity he aims for to that of Stendhal—yes, yes, can it be believed?—and it seems to me speaking with a pomposity about the problem of the artist . . . which could only seem to me to show that he had not the faintest idea of what he was talking about to me. In any case his letter filled me with a really despairing grief at the plight of the USA, reinforcing that despair you so often feel along with me, that my letter to you was almost as illegible as it was crazy. I regretted it the moment I sent it; it will only wound you unnecessarily and is a hideous welcoming home missive. I ask you to destroy it unread. The mystery about Bill is to me how he can talk in conversation with such maturity yet when it comes to writing write in so callow a manner of thinking and vocabulary; doesn't he see that such a limited set of words—he called them "key words" in his letter to me, I gather they are key words such as might be found in one million Western Union telegrams—there can be no ideas formulated? . . . There is exactly ONE thing in his book which I truly admire and where I base my hopes; his real novelist's handling of the relation between Tom and Pamela; there he worked as a novelist; that I made quite clear in my letter to him . . .

It was during this time, as the book was going to press, that Julian Muller suggested I ask Janet for a quote that Vanguard Press could use to publicize it, perhaps also on the jacket. I balked. I knew in my heart that Janet disliked the novel and I did not want to put her in the difficult position of having to refuse me. I loved her and I knew that that love was reciprocated. "He is partly like a son to me, too," she had told Natalia in that same anguished letter. I informed Julian that Janet would almost certainly not give me a quote and that I wouldn't ask her for one. Julian insisted, because he knew that a favorable quote from Janet would help enormously, especially with critics. Against my better judgment, I allowed him to write to her directly, which he did, pointing out that "few young authors get a hearing unless special favors are accorded them." Janet replied in a letter to Natalia that she thought I was "a born novelist because of his treatment of the young man and his English mistress," but said of herself, "I had never been associated with the hardboiled-egg writing school, being another softer-egg school of style myself, and so any statement from me would be beside the point and without authority; also . . . one should stick to one's own line of country and mine was not that of knowing about novels. . . . Muller of Vanguard seemed an exceptional nice and intelligently-minded man for a publisher."

Janet was so worried that I might find out how much she disliked my novel that two weeks after her first letter she wrote yet again to Natalia about her initial reaction. "I am reminded of that brutal depressed letter I wrote which I wish you not to read, to destroy, about Bill's book and my anguish in general about young Americans, suffering as I was at that moment from a kind of national *empoisenement de la foi;* it is written by hand, in ink, and even the writing looks rather mad. You can tell by its opening tone in any case that you are to go no further, darling. Please forgive and favor me, as I ask."

The Fugitive Romans was published in March 1955, and received on the whole excellent reviews, especially where they counted the most—in the daily and Sunday *New York Times, Time,* and *The New Yorker.* No one acclaimed it as a Stendhalian masterpiece, but the consensus was that I had written a satiric, understated, often sharply funny book. I *was* compared to Evelyn Waugh, another of my heroes, and the reviewer in the daily *Times* described the novel as "a provocative, exasperating and thoroughly readable example of a sad young man in action—a virtuoso performance that reveals the species at his best and worst."

Natalia sent on clips and quotes from the major reviews to Janet in Paris. "*Mia amore,* what quantities of good news for Bill," she replied, with characteristic generosity of spirit, "for you as military commander and general. I saw the review in *The New Yorker* and thought it highly useful, also just, as to me also the best character was the drunken actor; but had not yet seen the *Times* which you quoted; excellent. Well, there it is; he was right and we were wrong; what he had to say served as a vehicle for his protests, of which latter you and I certainly approved, and if there seemed lack of logic and maturity to us, it did not seem so to others. I shall write him a note."

She did so, but I subsequently lost it. It was full of praise and en-

couragement, I remember, and it made me proud, more than any
of the favorable reviews I had received.

As I began to write this account of a life in the company and
nurturing of these two extraordinary women, I went back to *The
Fugitive Romans* and reread it, more than forty years after its publication, an event which had given me more happiness and satisfaction than anything else I had ever done in my short life to that
point. I was surprised to discover that it wasn't a disaster, that it actually held up quite well and was indeed funny in spots. It was a
young man's novel, full of male posturing and often absurd attitu-
dinizing, but, as Janet had said, the relationship between Tom and
Pamela and the portrait of the actor were its main strengths and
helped compensate for its major flaws. The "hard-boiled" writing
Janet had objected to seems very tame now, after two generations
of fiction in which nothing obscene or merely unsavory is with-
held from the reader and vulgarity has been enshrined as the ulti-
mate literary accomplishment. Henry James I was not. Nor
Stendhal. As a writer I was still finding my own voice in the kindly
shadow of the love of these women.

EIGHTEEN

THE STRAIN
OF TENDER
FEELINGS

It seems to me in retrospect that these middle years of the nine-teen-fifties were crucial ones for me in my development as a writer and to Janet and Natalia as a period of confirmation in their rela-tionship. The tension between them, largely provoked by my mother's need to have a domestic life and Janet's slippery evasions in defense of her freedom, once again reached a near breaking point. I sensed it and it troubled me, but there was little I could do about it but express my love and support to both of them. In *Dar-linghissima* my mother refused to acknowledge this struggle and decided to ignore much of the correspondence that dealt with it, choosing to record from that period only their views on events in the world at large.

On New Year's Day, 1954, Janet wrote Natalia a letter summing up their relationship and reminiscing about an episode in her childhood at the turn of the century that, she felt, had helped define her outlook on life and her feelings about her background. It is worth reproducing nearly in full:

> Beloved Natalia, another year has turned over on the calendar paper. When this year's summer comes in with June it will be fourteen years since we met and fell in love. We have had our long and intense floral season. Nothing can replace it, nothing mow it down in memory and value of harvest. I feel you have changed more than I in that time; you retained your classic essentials and their knowledge that led to judgment on values of meanings, on what was still valuable after centuries in conduct because it had been used in that way, was still true, still represented a basis for relations between human beings. These things you had possessed when I first knew you and were part of your structure that caused my admiration, then as now. Your change came in something else which was the individual side of life and conduct; in something which was perhaps an Italianate emotional version of the classic Roman philosophy that outlined the first part of your stability I mentioned; in the second realm you became less conventionalized by the dramas of jealousy and orchidaceous feminine growth which was a standard, I realize, in Italian existence, giving it its vital fiction quality that animates ordinary lives, making them bearable—if noisy, you always point out; though God knows you never raised your voice except to sing, even there too softly for me as I have had more pleasure from your singing than from any other private person in my recollection. For that I shall never forget the night at Bordighera when you sang like a human lyre. . . .
>
> I seem to have changed not at all but to have dilapidated, like a plaster statue. I have made you pay the highest human price for my work which cannot have been worth flesh, blood and hope. It has been worth merely a good career and some money of late, I think as I look back. It has not developed me because I was not energetic enough nor had enough intellectual curiosity to grow,

myself, by constant replanting, constant new planting. I learned to work on picking, choosing, redoing, borrowing, never on learning. All these years in Paris, I do not know French history even of the nineteenth century to pull it from my head onto my pen, without assistance. I who see history as the image of personalities and their events, I whose only minuscule gift was its surface interpretations, sometimes with the sense of a bone showing through.

These are my thoughts as the old year disappears behind me and the new one rises. I can remember the beginning of this century. We lived in the country in a hideous pretentious house my father had built and could not afford; his notion seemed emptied of reality; he saw the house as a large structure but had no sense of filling its future with the lack of financial strain which is a home's only furnishing for a peaceful family life. He had promised to wake us three daughters just before midnight; I was aged seven, Maria aged twelve, Hildegarde aged two, an extremely pretty black-haired baby, solemn, intelligent, considerate. The family clustered in my room because it faced south toward the city; the room was cold, I recall, uglier by the chill and my feeling that beauty should be part of importance, that events that lacked beauty, like scenes or landscapes or clothes or sentiments, were frustrating, almost maddening, that importance was denied to what was not beautiful, a surety already that the old was beautiful, that the new, in Indiana anyhow, was unbearably ugly, that tears were a kind of rain that had a natural climate, tears in disappointment at the hideous in life, the sadness, yes, always the ugliness which came from a sparsity of imagination. So as midnight drew near, father, who had a strong historical sense, even an intelligent one, who had preserved intact from boyhood a worship of Lincoln as a great humanist and American, mentioned Lincoln, said the century that had known him and his works was coming to an end in a few minutes and we could faintly hear the whistles from the city, a few miles away. I was comforted by my father's identification with Lincoln, whom I thought handsome like a tree in winter. Then faint lights began rising in the sky, rockets and fireworks, set off in the city centers. The new century was in, seen by us young girls at a distance, in various sensitivities to disappointment and the strains of tender feelings which never could find expression, even with a new century arriving like an epoch in the keeping of time, by calendars and clocks. . . .

I had not thought of this incident in years. It can mean little to anyone else, anyone born in the beauty of Italy, of Rome. You have been as beautiful as a monument or painting to me. I have never not looked at you with a connoisseur's appreciative eye. You have represented the perfect lack of answer which is the true description of true love. Beneath your charms, your qualities, you still represent the question which has no answer yet whose answer is the fact itself; your inspired love in me; why; not why did you inspire it in me, why is it inspired in anyone by anyone else? Affinity must be the answer; identification; chemistry; choice. Yes, it is choice, of the unconscious imagination. Love is an occurrence. It comes to pass. It took place between us two. For it all I thank you, as changed and bettered and ameliorated as I could become, you made the changings and had I been less a resistant egotist, you could have done the perfect wonder. You have been the perfect romantic love and mate, on our strange sorority side of life. I embrace you, sitting by my window, in imagination and look forward with tense expectation to seeing you and kissing you on the riverside. That tense look for the waiting face and body on land. Yours . . .

What kept them united and enabled them to maintain the intensity of their relationship was the longer periods of time they were now able to spend together. Janet came to New York that winter and stayed for several months, interrupted by a visit of a few weeks to Hildegarde in California. Natalia went to Europe in the summer, stopping off in Paris to spend time with Janet, who then followed her to Italy for a few weeks. This was the pattern they now adhered to, especially throughout the nineteen-sixties. In 1955, Natalia bought a small property in the ancient fishing village of Sperlonga on the coast halfway between Rome and Naples. It was merely a ruin once used as a pigsty, but was converted into a tiny jewel of a house with picture windows and an open rooftop terrace overlooking the sea. She and Janet were to spend several weeks of the year there nearly every spring and/or fall all through the fifties and sixties. They managed thus to be together an average of about four months a year, with occasional long breaks in between, usually due to Janet's work commitments that would force her from time to time to cancel departures from her Paris hotel room for weeks, occasionally for months. These interruptions of their plans to see each other were galling to both, more so to Natalia, with her fierce possessive instincts and longings for a more settled life.

Their letters to one another also continued to be full of indignant and despairing comments on the American scene. Janet, ever disturbed by the absence of grace and civilized discourse in art as in daily life, put much of the blame for this dismal state of affairs on American marketing techniques. She thought the hysteria of the McCarthy era, with its paranoid view of Communist spies infiltrating and corrupting American society, was due to "our national suggestibility to advertizing, to publicity." We had lost our critical faculties, also partly because we spent so much time reading comic strips, "with Boom, Bing, Bump as language for thought and drama and our craze for detective fiction." These aspects of American life had so deadened our critical faculties that they had "taken the place in the country of philosophy, religion, thought, opinion and even investment." She thought the Russians, "as serious and illogical as the Catholic Church," were better organized than we were, better equipped to make their system work, and that Communism would eventually supplant Christianity by promising everyone a heaven here on earth instead of one "the other side of the unpleasant grave."

With her Profiles and the pressure of a biweekly deadline for her Letters, Janet often worked twelve to sixteen hours a day, sometimes all night. She would have her meals sent up by room service and emerge only when she had finished one of her pieces. She also found time, even during these most intense periods of concentration, to write Natalia every two or three days and keep up a lively correspondence with Hildegarde, friends, and ex-lovers. Unless she was absolutely swamped at her desk, however, she always found time for a late-afternoon cocktail or two in the downstairs bar, where she became famous for holding court. In fact, she became such an established figure there that sometimes complete strangers would pop in on her, introduce themselves and find themselves included in what amounted to impromptu cocktail parties. "Courtiers' patience and reverences are always the height of human consolations," Janet informed Natalia, "and are consolations for the desperate loneliness of the royalty who have deserved it." Whenever the writer Niccolò Tucci was in town, these sessions became boisterous semipublic events. Tucci had become famous at *The New Yorker* for dropping in unannounced, using other people's offices and telephones, and collaring employees to request favors or money or sometimes merely to engage them in time-consuming conversations. Katharine White once wrote a poem in rhyming couplets about the effect of his forays onto the premises. "Nothing could be horrider / Than meeting Tucci in the corridor," it began.

In Paris, Tucci made Janet a frequent target of his impromptu visits. On one such occasion the conversation strayed into the area of genius. "Suddenly he and Edgar Varese, the modernist musician, began talking about geniuses they had met and loathed," Janet recalled.

Tucci told of Rachmaninoff who though rich was so mean that he let his sister sell milk in Russia to the neighboring gentry to which they belonged; a horrible man, Tucci snarled, adding more details of disapproval and hate. Then Varese started on Toscanini, a beastly man, he said, a foul selfish brute, insensitive, tyrannical, greedy for money, harsh to those beneath him, etc. (He added that the maestro had refused a composition of his, which of course explained part of his fury and also his typical naiveté, of the talented minor men. Tucci interrupted and stood up for Toscanini politely but sincerely.) I stood as much as I could, then said that I had known few geniuses or men or women of important talent; but my impression was that they had bad characters and characteristics like anybody else, like untalented people, like dull people, but thank God their talent was something extra, that alone made their bad characters relatively unimportant; that we had to live with each other, we non-geniuses, with our bad characters unrelieved by the genius quality, which if it doesn't make Rachmaninoff's avarice more attractive, does not permit his music to be less musical. I said to them you are both talented, you both have foul characters, I am sure of it. I have a bad character and I am talented; the important thing to us three is our talent. Our characters can be found anywhere unrelieved by our gifts. I finished off by telling them they talked like bourgeois moralists who seemed to think talent or genius should be a moral refinement, when morals are the last thing that talent is based on or has to do with and once more I cited them, these two men facing me, this time as proof. That settled that idea, but they appeared so cast down I had to order them new sets of drinks. Not being an avaricious Rachmaninoff that was what I did . . .

That fall Natalia went to Los Angeles for three months to work with Anna Magnani on the filming of Tennessee Williams's *The Rose Tattoo*. She took a leave of absence from her job, which enabled me to fill in for her in the Mondadori office and so earn some decent money while waiting for my novel to be published. Before she left, she entertained Anna Magnani in New York for a few days, while her boss, Arnoldo Mondadori, and his wife were also in town. Mondadori had not wanted her to go to California, but he was flattered to find himself in the company of the famous actress and included briefly in the world she inhabited, full of meals and parties attended by celebrities. Usually at such luncheons, cocktails, or dinners, he would be expected to pick up the check, which he always did uncomplainingly. I remember one such evening when we went in a large group to see Mae West perform at the Latin Quarter. Also in the party were Williams and Judy Garland, with her husband, Sid Luft. When West appeared in her opening number surrounded, as usual, by a half-naked muscular male chorus line, Magnani looked disgusted. "Always the usual faggots," she growled, in her husky Roman voice.

Mondadori allowed my mother to take off for this period partly because he was reassured by my presence in the New York office. I knew my way around the New York publishing scene by this time and my fluent Italian reassured him. In fact, he favored me so much that Janet became alarmed. She thought, knowing how the male chauvinistic Italian mind worked, that the Italian publisher might offer me Natalia's job or at least persuade me to come to work for him in a position that would sooner or later undermine her. She needn't have worried. I now thought of myself only as a full-time working writer and I had no intention of launching myself on a new career, especially one that might endanger my mother's own. Some months later, Mondadori did offer me the job of advising him editorially on how to make his new weekly picture magazine, *Epoca*, as much like the American *Life* as possible. With Henry Luce's okay, I was allowed to infiltrate the home offices of Time, Inc., where I spent six weeks studying their editorial procedures and interviewing department heads and staff members on the criteria and methods used to put *Life* together every week. I then went to Milan, where I was installed in the editorial offices of *Epoca* and given a free hand to remake the magazine. It was an ab-

surd task, if only because I found that the staff of *Epoca* consisted
of about twenty people, who were putting out a magazine that in
New York would have employed several hundred. To the staff's
vast relief, and, I suspect, old Mondadori's as well, I contented myself by typing up a long, detailed report outlining how *Life* operated, after which I turned it in, thanked everybody profusely, and
flew back to New York to resume my literary career. *Epoca* continued to be put out every week by its tiny editorial crew. The magazine looked every bit as good to me as its much larger and richer
American counterpart.

Natalia had an agitated and adventurous time in L.A., staying
with Anna Magnani in a bungalow at the Beverly Hills Hotel. The
actress complained about the food, her neighbors, the hotel staff
and services, and the working hours; she was used to the far more
leisurely pace of Italian filmmaking, which usually got under way
around noon. My poor mother had to handle her outbursts of
protest and convey her frequent complaints to the hotel management as well as to the movie company. My mother, whose own
personality was nearly as dominant as Magnani's, turned out to be
the perfect duenna, though she made it clear that she would not repeat the experience. What she hated most was the smog, which
had become ferocious. Hildegarde had already written about it to
Janet. Oil, Janet informed them both, was far more important to
the American way of life than breathing.

As the filming was winding down in early February 1955, Natalia told Janet that Magnani was lingering on in California, even
though principal photography had been completed. "Is she so mad
on the USA that she is going to remain forever?" Janet asked. "How
about her fond electrician in Rome?" When Natalia called her in
Paris, Janet noted that her voice "sounded absolutely manly . . . and
wonderful. You are tired and that always gives your voice a deepened register. Even the phone girl here asked me if I had been able
to hear Monsieur clearly. I had been, thank God. I would have liked
you even if you *had* been a man, I am sure of it; I would have made

a strange undersized neurotic *New Yorker* staff writer, in small-cut Brooks Brothers suits and pink ties, probably, living with another fairy, I dare say. But sex is so clear in you, had you been a man you would have been a proper Don Juan and had my heart, too, with many others. . . ."

No sooner had Natalia's stint in moviemaking ended and she was back in New York than she began again to press Janet into giving more time to her. Through a string of letters written in the spring of 1955 she continued to urge Janet to give up *The New Yorker*, at least as a full-time occupation, and think about retiring. They would then be able to divide their time together between Europe and New York. "Yes, we'll see what must be given and proved in the autumn and it may not be so difficult as appears," Janet assured her. "I am tired. The Malraux tired me because I overworked here, not in New York where going home to you was a check on my abuses at night. So giving up my work may be less alarming than you fear and I might fear, too. It is certainly a description of me as an American businessman that retiring might be thought to empty my life; nothing in it but work is inferred. Not even golf to fall back on! Of all the onanistic games on earth, that seems to me the strangest. Alone with one's ball. . . ."

NINETEEN

THE
RAT PILE

By the early summer of 1956 I was again nearly broke, and we
were living hand to mouth. In mid-June Doris had given birth to
our first child, a girl we named Natalia in honor of her grandmother. We had rented a small cottage for the summer in Amagansett, on the southern shore of Long Island a few miles beyond
East Hampton. Doris's widowed mother, a gentle loving woman
with an independent income, had moved in with us to help pay the
summer rental and take care of the baby. I spent the weekdays in
Manhattan scrambling about for freelance work and dreaming up
money-making schemes, most of which failed. I was contributing
regularly to the *Saturday Review of Literature*, as it was then called,
but the magazine paid only about a hundred dollars for a feature
article and fifteen dollars for a five-hundred-word book review.
(The low point came when a review I had written was cut by about

a third and I was sent a check for ten dollars.) During all of 1955 I had managed to earn $5,275 from my writings, and so far in 1956 I was earning at about the same rate. The difference was that Doris had had to leave her job and the arrival of the baby had effectively impoverished us.

I was working on my second novel, *Best Seller*, an Evelyn Waughish (I hoped) satire on the book publishing industry and had sold it to Harcourt, Brace and Company, where Julian Muller had moved from Vanguard. I had also dashed off a thriller, written in six weeks for a quick thousand dollars, for publication as a paperback original by Popular Library. This novel, originally entitled *Affair in Rome*, was launched onto the reading public as *Passport to Terror*. When my editor at Popular Library had suggested I come up with a sexier title to match their cover illustration, which featured a postcoital naked blonde draped in a sheet, I suggested *Crime and Punishment*. I had discovered that you couldn't copyright titles. "Be serious," my editor, a young man with a terminal case of acne, informed me over the phone. "We're not peddling the classics here." I came up with *For Whom the Belles Toil, Oliver's Twist, War and Piece*, and several other absurdities he dismissed out of hand. "We'll think of something," he finally said. I didn't care. I had written this potboiler quickly for the money to pay our medical bills, and my name wasn't on it.

Max Daniels, the putative author, was the central character in *Best Seller*, who writes a book plagiarized from a story by Edgar Allan Poe in the style of Mickey Spillane, then at the height of his success. The project wound up delighting me because it fitted perfectly into the ethos of the world I was depicting in *Best Seller; Passport to Terror* was exactly the sort of project Max Daniels would have involved himself in. After the book came out, I dropped the editor a note suggesting that Popular Library ought to title all of its publications after famous classics. The sexy covers would help to sell them and they would never go out of print. For some reason he never answered me.

Apart from my literary work, I had no respectable sources of income, but I was determined not to yield to advertising again or try for an editorial job, even though most of my friends had gone into publishing and I might have been able to land a position somewhere. I continued to buy encyclopedias on time payments and sell them to second-hand bookstores, and occasionally I'd sneak out to the racetrack to make a sizeable show bet on some horse that couldn't lose. I even made a last try at a grant. That spring, in the classified ad section of the *Saturday Review,* I had come across a notice from the Andrew Carnegie Foundation to the effect that it had a program to dole out funds to writers in need. No one, I thought, was more in need than I was, so I wrote to the foundation outlining my situation and explaining that I needed enough money to stay alive so I could finish my second novel. I received no acknowledgment of my letter and forgot all about it, though I did mention it to some colleagues of mine at the *Village Voice,* where I had also become an unpaid contributor of drama and book reviews. "Oh, my God, don't tell Jimmy Baldwin about it," one of them said. "It's the only grant he hasn't tapped." After which, they all promptly sat down and petitioned the foundation for money. New York was awash in penniless authors that year.

Then what Janet had always hoped would happen for me occurred because of a rainy late-July weekend that kept us all indoors one Saturday. Somebody organized a poker game that I dropped in on late that afternoon. One of the players was a tall, affable man named Hollis Alpert, whom I'd met at the *Saturday Review,* where he was one of its two movie critics. Hollis also had a full-time job at *The New Yorker* as a fiction editor and had contributed stories to the magazine, lighthearted first-person accounts, based on actual experiences, that were known as "casuals." He told me that afternoon that he was leaving the magazine to go to work for a Hollywood producer and embark on a career in the movie industry. No one had been hired yet to fill his job, but people were already being interviewed for it. It was a good job, he said, and would leave me plenty of time to work on my own stuff.

I immediately wrote William Shawn a note, telling him who I was and asking for an interview. A few days later, his secretary called me at home and informed me that Mr. Shawn would be glad to see me. Could I come in that Friday afternoon, at about four o'clock?

It was one of the hottest days of the summer, a damp smothering heat of the kind New York specializes in. I showed up at the nineteenth-floor reception desk in the editorial offices at 25 West Forty-third Street dressed in a light khaki suit, announced myself, and sat down in a shabby waiting-room area fronting on the elevator bank. After a few minutes, Shawn's secretary appeared to escort me to his office. She was a tall, slender, attractive woman named Mary Devereux Rudd, who smiled cheerfully at me as she shook my hand and said, "Steel yourself." I had no idea what she meant, as I trailed after her down a long drab corridor toward Shawn's corner office. It was only after she ushered me into Shawn's quarters that I understood what she meant; the windows were open, but the air-conditioning was off and the temperature, with the sun beating in, must have been close to a hundred degrees.

William Shawn was sitting behind a large desk piled high with manuscripts and galley proofs. He was dressed in a dark blue suit, white shirt, bow tie, and a woolen sweater as red as his cheeks. He was a small, pale, bald man with a round kindly face and a manner so deferential and polite that for a moment or two I wasn't sure who was interviewing whom. He shook my hand, smiled, and indicated I should sit down on the brown leather sofa to the left of his desk. When he sat back in his chair only his head appeared above the level of the papers stacked in front of him.

I remember very little about the specifics of the interview, mainly that his extreme good manners only served at first to fuel the terror and awe I felt in his presence. I had heard so much about him for so many years from Janet that he had become almost a mythic figure to me, a divinity so high up in the pantheon of literary excellence that I couldn't imagine talking about writing to him.

For this reason I had resisted sending him anything of mine; I didn't think my work was worthy to be evaluated by him. So I was stunned to hear from him that he had read many of the pieces I had been contributing to the *Saturday Review* and elsewhere. I couldn't imagine how he had found the time, as I gazed at the mass of contributions on his desk. He had liked a number of my articles and reviews, he told me, and he hoped I would be able to find the time to submit my work to *The New Yorker.* He outlined what my duties as a fiction editor would be and then said that he had selected five stories for me to read. Four of them had been typed up on the magazine's yellow copy paper, with the authors' names deleted, and I would be asked to write a brief opinion on each one. The fifth was a long story by Peter Taylor, bought and already in galleys. I would be asked to edit it and suggest any changes in it I might think appropriate. Was this satisfactory to me?

I told him it would be and stood up to leave. Shawn came around from behind his desk to shake my hand. As I stood there saying goodbye I was horrified to realize that the seat of my khaki trousers was soaking wet from perspiration. I didn't dare turn around, so I retreated backwards, bowing and smiling, out of Shawn's office like a courtier dismissing himself from the presence of the Sun King.

I immediately read the stories given to me on my way out by Mary Devereux Rudd and then called up Hollis Alpert for advice. I told him I thought they were all publishable, but that I had found one of them, a casual called "Reunion," nicely written but overly familiar; I would have recommended rejecting it. Hollis warned me to be careful. If these stories had been typed up on yellow copy paper, they had almost certainly been bought. "Let me do a little research," he said, "and I'll call you back." Sure enough, it turned out that all the pieces had indeed been bought and that "Reunion" had been written by Robert Henderson, a senior editor under whom I would be working in the fiction department. I sold out to security; I said I thought all the stories were publishable, even though one of them, "Reunion," seemed a bit familiar, though charmingly written. As for the Peter Taylor story in galleys, I ran it through my typewriter. Taylor was a Southern writer whose style seemed to me full of cornpone mannerisms and offensive grammatical errors.

A few days later I was summoned back to the magazine, this time to meet with Katharine White, then heading the fiction department, and Robert Henderson. Mrs. White was a formidable presence, another legendary figure from the magazine's past, and all the more intimidating because she immediately proved to be an intensely serious person with, I gathered, no taste for small talk. She was a beautiful woman, now heavyset and with a great mass of gray hair coiled in a bun at the nape of her neck. Her eyes were large and clear and focused on me as if to peer straight into my soul. Henderson was middle-aged, with a pleasant round face under a shock of white hair, and he did his best to make me feel at ease. I felt like a churl for not having particularly liked his story.

Mrs. White came straight to the point. She told me I had done a nice job evaluating the material I had been given to read, but that I had overedited the Taylor story. He was a writer with his own distinctive style, Mrs. White informed me, and I should have respected it simply by carefully toning down some of its excesses. Nevertheless I had done a good job on the whole, and they were prepared to offer me an editorial post on a six-week trial basis.

My main task would be to read all the stories submitted for possible publication, most of them unsolicited, select the ones I thought might be good enough to publish and send those on for further readings by other editors higher up on the totem pole. A second favorable opinion would land the piece on Mr. Shawn's desk for a final decision. Obviously, the vast majority of the stories I would be asked to read would be rejected and sent back to their authors with standard printed rejection slips that simply thanked the writers for sending in their work even if it hadn't been found suitable for *The New Yorker*. I could encourage authors who showed promise either by writing them a personal letter or by scribbling a line or two of encouragement on the slips, such as "Thanks and sorry" or "Please try us again," and signing my initials. The only stories I would not be expected to give an opinion on would be those submitted by regular contributors, such as John Cheever, Maeve Brennan, J. D. Salinger, John O'Hara, or S. J. Perelman, to name only a handful, who had their own editors and submitted directly to them. Some of the pieces I would find might be assigned to me to edit, in which case I would become that author's regular editor; in future, their submissions would all come to me directly.

At a time when the short story was already disappearing from most general circulation magazines, *The New Yorker* still published an average of three stories an issue, or about a hundred and fifty a year. It had become the last well-paying market for short fiction in the country. I could expect to receive on my desk every day between eighty and a hundred and twenty stories to read. I think I must have blanched when I heard the figure, because Bob Henderson quickly assured me that I'd almost certainly be able to tell in a paragraph or two whether the author could write at all. The most irritating submissions, he warned me, would be those from established writers, who generally submitted their efforts through agents. These stories were usually meretricious, but written well enough so that they had to be read all the way through, a time-consuming process.

It was nearly seven o'clock in the evening when I left the magazine that day and headed home. Most of the city's office workers had already left the hub and the streets were largely empty, with the setting sun glinting off the window panes of the taller buildings and shadows lengthening over the sidewalks. I decided to walk home and, as I turned up Fifth Avenue, I was suddenly overwhelmed by what had just happened to me. I was now a staff member of *The New Yorker*, admitted as a player into the inner circles of the best magazine in the country. My financial troubles were over. I was being paid a hundred and fifty dollars a week, enough in those days for us to live on, and I had been told that at the end of the year the magazine paid generous bonuses. I was as elated as the day I heard that my first novel had been accepted, and the minute I got home I called Doris out in Amagansett with the news. Now all I had to do to make my job permanent was find at least one publishable story during my tryout period and not make a fool of myself on the opinion sheets.

The New Yorker's policy in those days was to make sure every manuscript received at least two readings, one by a male, the other by a female. My colleague in this enterprise was an outspoken woman named Mildred Wood, who was considerably older than I and an experienced hand at first readings. The submitted manuscripts were divided equally between us to go through, after which we'd pass them on to each other. A favorable opinion on a piece from either one of us would be enough to pass the story on to one of the senior editors. Millie immediately introduced herself to me that first morning and told me not to worry, that it was unlikely I'd find anything worth sending on right away, but that I was more likely to find a publishable story from the unsolicited submissions than from the stuff that came in from the agents.

The New Yorker's editorial offices then occupied three floors of the building, from the eighteenth through the twentieth. The fiction department was located on the twentieth, mostly in a cluster of rooms at one end. Because there were no vacancies at the moment, I was installed in Wolcott Gibbs's office. Gibbs, who had been with the magazine almost from its inception and had worked as an editor as well as drama critic and writer—he was the author of a famous profile of Henry Luce—had pretty much retired; he hadn't been seen around the premises for years, but he had never officially withdrawn. In case he might choose to come in someday, no one had dared formally to evict him from his quarters. His desk was still full of his papers, and a khaki shirt of his hung from one of the three clothes hooks on the wall by the door. I was told I could use the one empty desk drawer, on the right, the typewriter, which belonged to the magazine, and the two empty clothes hooks. The staff referred to the premises as The Shrine.

No sooner had Millie Wood left me alone in my august new surroundings than the door opened again and a cheerful, red-haired man wearing rimless eyeglasses stuck his head into the room. He introduced himself as Tom Gorman, the fiction department secretary. "Here," he said, dumping a stack of manuscripts on the desk. "Now you can go back to sleep. You aren't going to find anything in that rat pile."

He was right. Nor did I find anything even worth reading on the second, the third, or the fourth day. On the fifth and last day of the working week, I did read a piece I thought worth sending on, but it was unceremoniously shot down by the powers above me. "Don't worry about it," Millie reassured me. "I didn't find anything for nearly a year when I came to work." This was small comfort to me, since I was on a tryout period. Janet had every confidence in me. "What fine news that it is in fiction that Bill is working on *The New Yorker*," she wrote Natalia, "his perfect place. Let us pray that the job becomes permanent. I never understand their reasons for not firing some people, so am confused in advance into wondering why they also take on some people, since I do not find logic in either. He would be at his best there and certainly serve them better than most."

I was lucky because eventually I not only found a publishable piece, a nice casual written by a college professor named Dean Doner at Purdue University, but several others as well before the year was out. Nobody ever told me that I had been taken on as a permanent staff member, but the six weeks passed and nobody ordered me not to show up either. By that time I hadn't expected to be officially informed, because the working atmosphere at the magazine was so ruthlessly informal that during my first month there nobody had bothered to introduce me even to my colleagues in the fiction department. Most of the male ones I met in the men's room where, standing at adjoining urinals, we'd nod politely to one another and comment on the weather. We never had formal editorial meetings; business was transacted by passing on brief comments and notes about the work in hand. The office hours were from ten to six, but nobody cared when or even whether you bothered to come in; all that mattered was that the work got done. I was easily able to find the time to spend on my novel and to go on writing for outside publications as well. Then, a week or so before Christmas, I heard a timid knock on my door and opened it to find William Shawn standing in the hall with several envelopes in his hand. Blushing and mumbling something to the effect that the magazine had had a good year, he handed me one of them. It was a bonus check for sixteen hundred dollars, which seemed a fortune to me at the time.

Soon after the first of the year, when I had finished *Best Seller* and sent it off to Julian Muller at Harcourt, Brace, I wrote my first story for the magazine, "L'Americano," a slightly fictionalized account of my boat trip back to Italy after the war and my friendship on board with the old man going home to reunite with his brother in the Abruzzi. *The New Yorker* bought it and then a second one called "Open Season on Turks," another piece based on my postwar experiences in Italy. No one ever told me, of course, that the magazine was *buying* these stories, because the word "buy" was a bit strong for what actually occurred. I was told, as was the custom, that my stories had "worked out" and were "going through," a far more elegant way of describing an otherwise crass transaction. I remember wondering whether when Mr. Shawn retired or died, he'd be described as having worked out and gone through.

I was to remain in my job as a fiction editor for nearly four years, during which I was always able to go on working on my own writing. Wolcott Gibbs never showed up, so I stayed on in The Shrine and even began to think of it as my office, though the desk remained full of Gibbs's things and that shirt continued to hang on its hook in a slightly accusatory way, as if I were an impostor on the premises. I always found enough stories every year, a high of thirteen, a low of five, to justify my salary, though only one of the authors I discovered turned out to be first-rate. This was Paul Brodeur, whose short story "The Sick Fox" landed on my desk one morning. Paul joined the staff as a Talk of the Town reporter soon after and went on to write short stories and several novels, as well as a series of seminal environmental articles that exposed the dangers of asbestos and microwave pollution. Even when I acquired a few authors of my own to edit, I still had plenty of time to write.

After nearly four years of reading short fiction, however, I began to long for even more freedom than I had. I wanted to be a full-time writer only, not just an editor who also happened to write. Besides, I was becoming winded by having to keep up every day with the wave of submissions that washed ceaselessly across my desk. Most of the ones that were publishable were casuals, not real stories, and I began to wonder why we editors in the fiction department didn't make an effort to persuade some of the country's best writers to contribute. I suggested this procedure to Katharine White, who at first said it seemed a good idea to her. I immediately wrote to a few writers I knew, including Norman Mailer and William Styron, urging them to send us some stories. I had told Mrs. White that many writers thought of *The New Yorker* as a closed shop and so never thought of submitting anything; if we could make it clear to them that the magazine was open to anyone, perhaps some of our better established authors would submit their work. No sooner had I sent off my letters, however, than Mrs. White changed her mind. She didn't think the magazine should be put in the position of soliciting contributions. I strongly disagreed, but I was hardly in a position to argue with her.

Perhaps she was right. As Bob Henderson had predicted, the hardest submissions to deal with were those from so-called established authors, whose pieces often required a more careful reading than most of those in the rat pile. Some well-known writers sent in dozens of stories, none of them much good, at least by our standards. Then, too, the magazine had some peculiar taboos, such as prohibitions against pieces about the writers themselves. "Nobody gives a damn about a writer or his problems except another writer," Harold Ross had pronounced early on, and his objection had become a magazine policy. Funny names were out and we were also required to be on the alert for stories about vague little men "helplessly confused by a menacing and complicated civilization," as Wolcott Gibbs put it in an in-house essay he wrote, "Theory and Practice of Editing New Yorker Articles," while still working as an editor. We had to watch out for a gratuitous use of expletives and dirty words, unless absolutely necessary, and we were also told that drunkenness and adultery were not to be treated lightly or be written about admiringly. Graphic sexual descriptions were unacceptable, and as for homosexuality, to quote Gibbs again, it was "definitely out as humor, and dubious, in any case."

Few writers, once rejected, ever tried us again, though I continued to scribble encouraging comments on rejection slips sent to authors who showed some promise or ability. Maybe nobody could read what I was saying. Millie Wood showed up in my office one day to ask why I insisted on writing "Lovey and thumbs" on a number of rejection slips. "That's not 'Lovey and thumbs,'" I said. "That's 'Sorry and thanks.'" I explained to Millie that at the Dalton School I had been taught to print and had had to teach myself to write cursively, something I am so poor at to this day that I sometimes can't read my own writing. After her visit, I went back to printing, but I noticed no increase in the number of resubmissions.

A few would-be contributors never gave up. One man sent in several stories a day for weeks. They were written in longhand on sheets of lined yellow paper, which is the way I still write my own first drafts, but his efforts were pitifully inept. One afternoon my telephone rang. It was the twentieth-floor receptionist, a pretty and naive recent graduate of Bryn Mawr, who could neither type nor take dictation, just the sort of girl the magazine hired in those days. She informed me that there was a man in the lobby who wanted to see me. He had been sending in stories for weeks now and had decided he wanted to talk to an editor in person. I recognized his name as the source of the scribbled pieces I had been turning down. "I don't want to talk to him," I told her. "Send him away. How did he get my name anyhow?" He had asked her who read the unsolicited submissions and she had given him my name, she confessed. I hung up, but twenty minutes later she called me back. The man insisted on seeing me, the girl said, and he was becoming agitated and abusive. She was obviously frightened, so I had no choice but to tell her I would be right out.

As I started down the long corridor toward the reception area, my heart sinking, I met Roger Angell coming in the opposite direction. Angell had only recently come on the magazine, also in the fiction department, but he was older than I and a more experienced editor. He'd know how to handle such a situation. I stopped him and told him what was happening. Angell looked thoughtful, then said, "Don't worry, *The New Yorker* will take care of your family." He smiled and went on his way, abandoning me to my fate.

I now began to get angry; the closer I came to the reception area, the angrier I got. By the time I arrived at the front desk I was in a rage. I swept past the startled receptionist as a pale, thin man in his forties dressed in a rumpled gray suit rose out of a chair to greet me. I grabbed him by the lapels and shouted at him. What the hell did he think he was doing, frightening young women and making threats? He couldn't write a literate sentence, much less an entire story. Why didn't he just go home and take up some other profession? Just then the elevator doors opened and I shoved him inside. My last sight of him was his amazed wide-eyed stare as the doors closed on him and he was whisked away toward the lobby. "Don't ever give my name out again," I told the grateful receptionist as I started back toward my office. "The man is a lunatic." By the time I returned to my desk I was shaking like an aspen leaf in a light breeze. I began to have visions of my rejected author waiting for me in the lobby with a gun. I waited till well after seven that evening before heading home.

Another persistent petitioner was a professor in the English department at Louisiana State University who submitted at least a story a week for months, each one worse than the last. I remember him among so many because he wrote what I still consider to be the single worst opening sentence in the history of English literature: " 'Geez,' she said, undulating toward the jukebox."

When I went to see Shawn about moving onto the writing staff exclusively, he suggested I first try my hand at a long article to see if I could qualify. I suggested I try a piece about a horse trainer bringing one of his young charges up to its first race, and he okayed the project. I began going out to Belmont Park on Long Island very early in the morning, and in six weeks researched and wrote an eight-thousand-word story about a trainer named Pinky Blackburn, who was working with a filly named Lake Moreau. It wasn't a great story, but I tried to convey a feeling of what life was like in the backstretch area of a racetrack, and how much was riding for the men and women there on the talents of the fragile, expensive beasts in their charge.

Shawn told me the piece had worked out and was going through, but that he wasn't sure when he could run it. As soon as somebody could be hired to fill my job, I'd be free to become a full-time staff writer, with a drawing account against earnings instead of a salary. A few weeks later I moved out of The Shrine and into an office on the eighteenth floor, where most of the writers and some of the cartoonists were established. I had finally made it, I told myself. I was a staff writer now on the best magazine in the country, if not the world. I had also established myself as a novelist. *Best Seller* had been published in 1957, again to mostly favorable reviews, and I was working on a third novel. I had also begun to write plays, hoping I could expand my career into the theater. Even though Shawn never did run my article on horse racing, I had been paid for it and I was not too disappointed. More than a few stories, I had been told by my colleagues, were bought but never made it into print. The competition for space in the magazine was fierce, which soon made me realize I would eventually need to develop a particular area or specialty of my own that no one else was writing about.

A few months after I had joined the staff as an editor, I received a check for two hundred and fifty dollars from the Carnegie Foundation. I had forgotten all about my impassioned plea for assistance, made some eight months earlier. My first instinct was to send the check back with a note from my wife, telling the good souls at the Carnegie that unfortunately Mr. Murray had starved to death in his garret while trying to work on his novel and waiting for succor. But I thought better of it. I cashed the check, hired a babysitter, and took Doris out to a gourmet dinner at an exclusive French bistro and then to the theater. We managed to blow most of the money in one night.

TWENTY

A DOLLAR A DAY TO SAY "I LOVE YOU"

It was many years before I realized how important Janet had been in my life. Not only had she served as a role model for me by her absolute and total commitment to the craft of writing well, but she had so often championed me and my aspirations to Natalia that she had each time renewed my mother's faith in me and my future. "Yes, youth is boring and tiresome, as you say about Bill," she wrote at a time when Natalia had complained about my seeming inability to settle gracefully into any kind of career opportunity, "because at your age you know more than he. But he knows an unusual lot for a youth at his age and his theme of not doing what he does not want to do, based ever so firmly on what he considers degrading, has [given] increasingly firmer proofs of something besides mere restlessness and unreliability in it. I was a far more shapeless youth at his age than he is. At any rate what he does he now does on his own feet and on those of his wife, so that is a relief. He does not fall back on your hands nor must you pay to keep him, an ignobility of laziness all too common among young males nowadays, especially some of his dear Rome pals from the states."

Janet hovered in the background of my life like a benevolent angel, observant, sympathetic, providing counsel, guidance, understanding and support whenever asked. She also took an active interest in Doris and my three children, Natalia, Julia, and Bill, Jr., which lasted throughout her lifetime. Her reactions to the births of my children were always jubilantly congratulatory, and she was always amused by my mother's status as a grandmother, delighting in envisioning her as the supreme commander of a growing troop of worthy descendants. "Darlingest head of a new family," she wrote to her on June 26, 1956.

So there is another, littler Natalia in this world. With true and rare praise in such matters of generation, I tell you that if she carries on in her life for her friends, her family and her surrounding civilization the integrities, decisions and truths and honesties, the richness of character and culture which you, her grandmother, have shown, and your fidelities and comprehensions of love and blood ties, those mysteries, you will not have been born in vain, nor your mother, nor your Italy have suffered and flourished in vain, nor the United States having gone through its own retributions without meaning, for she will have enjoyed and will be illustrating and carrying in her brain, heart and hands the greatest gifts you represent, as a magnificent and also, which is rare, a fascinating citizen of this present earth. I can wish her no more fortune than to be like you, Natalia, Natalia I become Natalia II. From general to cadet. . . .

The nineteen-fifties and early sixties were among the most productive in Janet's long career, but she had always worked slowly and now she found herself increasingly struggling to realize what she wanted to say on paper. It often took her many hours merely to write an opening paragraph, and most of the time nothing came easily or fluidly to her. She often spent days in her room, emerging only for a drink or a quick meal, in order not to interrupt her work. Her letters to Natalia were full of accounts of her struggles to get her Letters in on schedule and finish the various longer pieces she had been working on. She also suffered now from various physical ailments: fierce headaches, digestive disorders, mysterious pains in joints and muscles. She saw doctors, again cut down on her smoking and drinking, tried to keep more regular hours, even tried occasionally to exercise. She went to Abano in northern Italy for the mud baths and experimented with various medications, some of which offered relief. Always she rebounded and never stopped writing.

All during the spring of 1956 she had been struggling with a two-part Profile on Georges Braque, which she had been trying to finish in time to come to New York, first in the late spring, then by September. For once my mother had been sympathetic to her efforts and had written her a supporting, encouraging letter about her work. "I tell you now two truths, your letter with its humane patience and understanding gave me a new lease on life and our relation and I shall be in New York in September," Janet wrote,

just as I am sure as I am sitting now in my room, writing to you. If my work has been better in the magazine than I had thought—others, too, have said so—the strain and disorder producing it have been destructive. In any case the question and goal is not that but is you and me, at last, to which you have been sacrificed for ten years of burning and martyrdom. That you still love with only periods of anger and fury and disdain is your miracle. I shall deserve it. The other heartening news is that I worked magnificently over the weekend on the Braque. I had been paralyzed at a certain point, my imagination gave out, tired, flattened with the strain of a visual vocabulary; on that dead point I remained nearly three weeks, never giving up, still trying, still working at it, striking my face

sometimes in a wild physical effort to jolt my brain, to make it re-
vive under outside blows. The hiatus has been bridged, I am going
forward since Saturday with amazing speed, the ground seeming
familiar enough to proceed fast. I was up at 5:30 this morning. . . .

Despite these occasional bursts of clarity and energy, when she
was able to write fluidly, the work went slowly and it became evident she would not be able to leave as planned in September either.
Natalia continued to be supportive and understanding, which was
due in part to satisfactions she was experiencing in her own life and
career. She felt entrenched now in the Mondadori job and had established herself as a forceful and successful executive in New York
publishing. She was happy to see me settled in at *The New Yorker*
and delighted at the birth of her grandchild. Most important,
Mammina Ester had moved back to New York and now shared the
apartment with her on East Eighty-first Street.

Ester was aging rapidly and could no longer live alone, but she
was content to stay at home, taking care of the apartment, cooking occasionally, listening to the radio, and writing verse. When
Janet wrote both to Shawn and Natalia that she would have to de-
lay her departure again, Natalia seemed neither surprised nor angry, but accepted the decision as unavoidable. "I have been more
irrationally disturbed than at any time in my life," Janet confessed.

I enclose a copy of my letter to Shawn to show my plan and my
goal in my September arrival, my resignation. I have been so tor-
tured by the thought of failing you again, and failing me, that my
nights have curiously turned upside down. Sometimes I have to go
to bed at ten o'clock, then I wake at one and read or even work till
six, then sleep till eight; sometimes I do not sleep till four, but this
last week I have been waking regularly at six, even if I have had
nearly no sleep at all. There is always the burden on me, of the anguish of having failed again, of this sacrifice of everything to a
work that cannot be justified as having cost years and flesh. Every-

thing has depended on me in our relation and I have not met nor carried its directions nor its precious weight. . . . I shall try to answer the question of my delayed life in my next letter to you. I am too disorganized, Natalia, to go further than this letter today. I keep thinking of the disappointment I am giving you, but even more, giving me because it is acute, like a paralyzation of constant burden of unhappiness. I shall phone you next week. Tell me what day and where, your house or your office. Forgive me again. . . .

In her letter to Shawn she said that she had another ten pages or so to write in order to finish the Braque and reminded her editor that the magazine would have to publish it before November, when her book, *Men and Monuments,* which would include the Braque, would be published by Harper & Brothers. "I must talk to you, Bill, darling," she continued,

and explain that I think the time now ripe for changing my life, so I may have what is left of it for living much of the time in New York and in traveling in the summer in Europe. I should hope you would let me do Profiles. This is a disorganized letter. I am too emotionally involved with the magazine not to be distraught at my own decision. I am sixty-four. My health is absolutely flawless. But I am slow and confused about my copy, make poor choices of what to use in my Paris Letters, then make better choices too late, though actually the Letters have seemed to me livelier than last year's, even if for the wrong reasons.

The fact was that Janet really loved her writer's life and was deeply disturbed by the prospect of having to abandon it in order to divide her time among New York, Paris, and Italy. The very routines of her working day were pleasing to her, and she adored her familiar surroundings at the Continentale, where the staff waited on her attentively and was impressed by the number of visitors who called on her. Ray Mann, an old friend from Fire Island days, who would drop in on her from time to time on his visits to Paris, remembered how kind she was to the maids who took care of her and how at home she seemed seated at her desk, with its stunning view over the gardens of the Tuilleries and Parisian rooftops. "I get thirty cents a word now," she told him one afternoon. "I'm paid a dollar a day to say 'I love you.' "

I asked her during one of her visits to New York whether she ever intended to give up her career at *The New Yorker*. A look of the most acute distress came over her, as if I had probed a small wound. She didn't answer me. "I could never do that," I added. "I could never give up something I really love to do." She told me she simply had to cut back, that she couldn't go on working as hard as she had, but she didn't sound convinced, as if she were not being quite honest about her feelings. I never raised the subject with her again, but I suspected and hoped she would never retire from *The New Yorker*.

My secret conviction was that her love affair with Natalia had flourished and been nurtured by their frequent separations. My mother was a benevolent tyrant, who through the sheer force of her personality dominated everyone in her immediate orbit. She adored Janet and admired her tremendously, took a fierce pride in her writing, was her greatest champion in the literary world of New York, but she also knew what was best for her, exactly how Janet should structure her life to conform to Natalia's views of a domestic relationship. It was an aspect of my mother's personality that she shared with her two sisters. My cousin Federico, Franca's son, maintained that the Danesi family motto should be "They are always right," and said that it ought to be engraved on their tombstones. Both Janet and I, the two people my mother loved most in the world and who reciprocated that love, had maintained a relationship with her by defending our independence. In my case, through often needless and damaging confrontations; in Janet's, by avoidance, tergiversation, and geographical distance. I could not imagine Janet a beloved captive in my mother's train.

Men and Monuments was published in the fall of 1957. I was immediately enthralled. Here is how Janet presented the book in her preface:

> There are no permanent criteria for declaring what art is and what it is not. Art began remotely as what was not necessary. Nor has it changed over time from that superior and remarkable status. It began in the original civilized gesture of savage man, who started adding and repeating something useless, which in some way pleased him, to the article of need which he was fabricating. His first contribution may have consisted of making some rude decoration on a clay pot which in no way improved that vessel's capacity to function. It was of no aid, but in its own terms it was art. Nothing could be done with it except notice it. Being extraneous, it attracted the eyes. Later this decoration became connected with magic, and, as the world ripened, with religion. Over the ages it developed that gratuitous things like these persistent creations, the miraculously extra, the unneeded, began having a life of their own. They afforded pleasure to bystanders. This was and remains the only utility of art. It is something to be looked at with aesthetic enjoyment and in a way to be deeply thought about, though it remains inexplicable. Words and language do not explain it. What artists say about it usually casts little light. They prove their knowledge of it by creating it.

The five sections of the book consisted of the four profiles of Malraux, Matisse, Picasso, and Braque, and a long section on the Nazi looting of Europe's art treasures during the war. I had read all of the pieces with pleasure when they first appeared in *The New Yorker*, but in book form they made a tremendous impression on me, mainly because of the quality of the writing. I knew how hard she had struggled over the material and what it had cost her, but surely, I thought, the price was worth it in order to be able to write this well. Luckily, the critics mostly agreed with me, and it was this book that finally cemented Janet's place on the American literary scene, elevating her above the category of mere journalism. In Britain the book fared less well, with a number of the English critics pointing out either Janet's lack of credentials to be discussing art at all or complaining about what they considered her discursive style. Janet was dismayed by her reception abroad, but her friend Mary McCarthy assured her that she was paying the price for being a well-paid *New Yorker* contributor. The magazine aroused envy in academic circles, and among an intelligentsia that still regarded even distinguished reportage as an inferior expressive form.

In New York, my mother seemed far more relaxed and contented with her life, less driven to bring Janet permanently into her orbit. She saw a great deal of us and her granddaughter, she had Mammina Ester to go home to every night, and she now also had an old friend and family retainer named Maria Maver as a member of her household. Maria, raised in a working-class family in northern Italy, along the Yugoslav border, had worked for Lea in Rome and had helped to raise Lea's son Stefano. She had come to New York as a governness to an Italian diplomatic family, but soon went to work for us, first helping to take care of Mammina Ester, then my children, and much later Janet, during the last two years of her life. She was intelligent, efficient, and a superb cook, who eventually went on to start a small business of her own, raise a daughter, and become a ferocious fan of the Mets. Her strong presence in the household took a lot of pressure off my mother's shoulders during some difficult years when first Mammina Ester needed to be cared for, then Janet.

As the decade approached its end, the New York literary world began to recognize Janet's achievements. In 1958, she received an honorary degree from Smith College, where the commencement address was delivered by Senator John F. Kennedy. Natalia accompanied her to the event on the Northampton, Massachusetts, campus and took an immense pride in the proceedings, which she recorded in *Darlinghissima*. In early April of 1959, Janet was invited to speak by the Overseas Press Club at a Paris Night Gala. She flew into New York for about ten days during which she was besieged by admirers and received a royal welcome from her colleagues at the magazine. She was also invited to join the National Institute of Arts and Letters, which she did without conceding for a moment that the event was of any lasting significance. She was, as always, modest about her work and also not unaware that many in the literary establishment still regarded journalism as an inferior form of creativity. In 1966, when Janet won a National Book Award after the publication in two volumes of her *Paris Journals,* edited by William Shawn, she commented to Natalia, "It seems I have won some sort of prize." Grandiloquence was not her style.

The pattern of my mother's life had become deeply satisfying to her. She and Janet continued to see each other at least twice a year, with Janet coming for longer periods to New York and Natalia going off to Europe for both business and pleasure. They would meet in Paris or Milan or Rome, then head for Sperlonga or perhaps go off together to some new destination "to be refreshed by new sights," my mother wrote, "and to find ourselves again, in terms of each other."

Although she worked far more slowly and laboriously than before, Janet never gave up her work. It took her many months to finish a profile of Bernard Buffet, which *The New Yorker* published two years after she had begun it, much to the painter's annoyance. But "writing for her was an overwhelming urge—a real, deep pleasure, like eating or drinking," Natalia recorded. She had resented it earlier in their relationship, but now at last accepted it, even as Janet's age began to take its toll on her abilities. In 1960, Janet was sixty-eight years old, still able to write well but less committed to her work than before. "She became more relaxed, more conscious of my needs and wishes," Natalia observed.

My mother, deeply involved in her own career, was also no longer as troubled as she had been by the public front she and Janet had had to put up for so many years. To the outside world they

were merely two single women who were old friends, lived sepa-
rately, and traveled together. The reality of their relationship, a love
affair as strong and enduring as any marriage, was still not something society accepted. Janet had never been troubled by this double view, but Natalia, still a product of her strong Roman
bourgeois outlook, had always been uncomfortable with it. Now,
after so many years, she began at last to accept the rules of this
game, reassured to a large extent by her family's acceptance of the
relationship. She felt warmed by our love and that of Hildegarde,
who exuded a poetic sensibility that my mother found "gentle,
warm, tender, humorous, with a superior intellect and in love with
nature."

Surrounded and supported by such affection, with Mammina
Ester a constant presence in her daily routines, my mother's life
had become full and satisfying. Even when I told her during the
summer of 1961 that Doris and I planned to move to Italy that fall
for at least a year, she didn't seem unduly upset. She understood
that it was probably a necessary move with regard to my career at
The New Yorker, and she would not be losing touch with us. We
would be in Rome when she visited in the summer. Air travel had
begun to shorten the distances between continents to the extent
that within a few years the passenger trade on transatlantic liners
would almost cease to exist. In any case, from my point of view I
had little choice. I had drifted at the magazine into that large unsatisfying category of the staff writer with no specific topic of his
own to write about, merely another would-be contributor compet-
ing for space with a couple of dozen other writers. As I pointed out
to my mother, Janet had always had Paris; I now proposed to carve
out a niche for myself in Italy.

TWENTY-ONE

THE
ITALIAN
CONNECTION

In early October of 1961 I went to talk to Shawn about my situation at the magazine. Nearly two years had passed since I had joined the writing staff and I had yet to see anything of mine in print. That winter I had written a long article, a so-called Onward and Upward with the Arts, about the production of a big industrial show, a musical celebration of the launching of a new line of automobiles. The piece had been scheduled several times for publication, but was always bumped at the last minute to accommodate some other article Shawn considered more timely. This was a common practice at the magazine, but that didn't make it easier to accept. Shawn had praised the piece highly, told me that it had made him laugh out loud several times when he read it, but that was small comfort to me. Now so much time had passed that it seemed unlikely my effort would ever be published; the show had long since closed and the car models it celebrated had already been launched onto the market.

I had also recently handed in another effort on the arts, this one about an extraordinary woman named Josephine La Puma who ran an opera company out of her apartment on the Upper West Side, but Shawn had given no indication that he was about to publish that piece either. In fact, it had been sitting on his desk for weeks and it was evident that he hadn't yet read it. I had decided that my only chance of surviving at *The New Yorker* was to go back to Italy, from where I could write Letters and Profiles without having to compete with anybody else on the staff. Janet no longer wrote from there, and I knew I could do better than the two or three other articles the magazine had recently published out of Italy, written by people who didn't speak the language and knew little about the country. I felt I was uniquely qualified to become *The New Yorker*'s man in Rome.

To my delight, Shawn agreed. He also pointed out that Italy could become a cornucopia of good stories for me. Unlike every other major European country, Italy was a conglomeration of ex–city-states and regions, each with its own culture and politically united for less than a century. If one wrote out of France or England, for instance, one had to be based in Paris or London. But what did Milan, Rome, Venice, Florence, Naples, and Palermo have in common? Very little, not even a language, since most Italians communicated with one another in their local dialects. I told Shawn I'd stay in Italy for a year or more, depending on how successful I would be, and suggested first a Rome Letter, to be followed perhaps by others from Milan and Palermo, also a possible profile of Enrico Mattei, the highly controversial head of the Italian state-run oil cartel. With all that settled, Doris and I began to make plans to leave New York for Rome before the end of the year.

Until the last few months I hadn't worried too much about my status as a staff writer. Everywhere in the magazine world but at

The New Yorker my career had flourished. The nineteen-fifties and -sixties were golden years for magazines, and I had begun to write for many of them, including *Esquire,* the Sunday *New York Times, Venture, McCall's, Cosmopolitan,* the *Saturday Evening Post, Holiday,* and others. I knew by then that I could make a comfortable living freelancing, but none of these publications paid as well as *The New Yorker* or provided the essential perks, such as medical insurance and a pension plan. Nor did being published elsewhere matter as much in terms of sheer prestige as being a staff writer for William Shawn. The position all but guaranteed acceptance anywhere else and enabled my agent to secure better fees and contracts for out-side work. I would be foolish not to try to guarantee my future at the magazine, especially as I was no longer sure of myself as a writer of fiction. My third novel, *The Self-Starting Wheel,* had been a failure, due mostly to my own stupidity. I had allowed myself to be wooed away from Julian Muller and Harcourt by another editor and publisher, after Julian had warned me that the novel needed ei-ther to be vastly revised or put aside. I had ignored him, with disas-trous consequences; I was no longer considered a hot new author in the increasingly fickle world of book publishing, and I would have to rebuild my career as a novelist practically from scratch.

It had occurred to me, too, that I was spreading myself too thin. I was deeply involved in the theater. I had coproduced and directed a bill of one-acters by Bernard Shaw, *Press Cuttings* and *O'Flaherty, V.C.,* for a limited run Off-Broadway. I had adapted my first novel for the stage and had begun to translate several of the plays of Luigi Pirandello, which were published and went on to be pro-duced all over the country, including New York and Los Angeles. In the spring of 1962, I had been invited to join the playwrights' unit of the Actors Studio, and I also was working on two other plays of my own. Unfortunately, none of these ventures enriched me and hardly justified the time and effort I put into them. The theater, I discovered, is a treacherous world in which, as Neil Simon once ob-served, it's possible to make a killing but hard to make a living.

None of my theatrical and other activities had anything to do with *The New Yorker,* and it's astonishing to me now that Shawn kept me on the staff. Other writers worked on books and for other magazines, but none had as many outside conflicting interests as I did. The move to Italy was my way of recommitting myself to the magazine. Here, after all, was an editor considered by nearly every-one to be the greatest of his era who wanted to publish my work. Both Janet and my mother believed fervently in this venue as the best in the world for a young writer of promise. What was I doing wasting my efforts in all these other frivolities? It was time to stop being such a dabbler in so many different fields and settle down to serious work at last. This was how these older women in my life saw my situation and I realized they were almost certainly right. We booked passage on the Italian luxury liner *Cristoforo Colombo,* sailing in late November for Naples.

It wasn't easy to uproot ourselves from our comfortable life in New York, especially for Doris. I, after all, spoke Italian, and going back to Rome was a homecoming for me; but for her, the change posed huge logistical as well as emotional problems. We now had two children, after the birth of a second daughter, Julia, in the sum-mer of 1960. And Doris was an American woman, used to her in-dependence and deeply involved in close relationships with her American family and friends. She had found living in Italy difficult in 1952, after our marriage, but I hoped that she'd be more easily able to adapt to life in a Latin country now and that Rome would turn out to be more pleasurable for her. In any case, we were not going back to live there permanently, we assured each other; I was going to create for myself in Italy a career along the same lines that Janet had in Paris, but in a much more modest way, with an eye merely to establishing myself, at least for Shawn, as the correspon-dent who would write for the magazine out of this second country of mine that I loved as much as my own.

●

Our first few weeks back in Rome were entirely occupied with getting ourselves settled—finding an apartment, hiring a cook and a maid, enrolling Natalia in a private school, buying a car, looking up our relatives, joining the Foreign Press Club, taking care of some family business for my mother. By the first of the year, however, I was at work on my first Letter from Rome. And there was much to write about.

In fact, I was all but overwhelmed by what I found in this city I had known so well. Nearly seven years had passed since I had last visited and everything, it seemed to me, had changed. The country was in the throes of what it called *il benessere,* an American-style economic boom that was in the process of creating an entirely new middle class, ordinary citizens earning well enough to afford at last all the household appliances and machines created by a newly industrialized society based on freewheeling capitalism. People who never before had been able to afford even a home of their own were now buying apartments and villas and stocking them with goods acquired on the installment plan and other forms of credit. Most immediately in evidence was the triumph of the automobile, which had become the focus of the boom and a growing source of concern to the authorities, as well as to people simply trying to get around without finding themselves stuck for hours in huge traffic jams.

It seemed to me that Rome, once the greatest walking city in the world, had all but disappeared beneath this daily tidal flow of cars. The ancient capital's narrow cobblestoned streets in the *centro* were clogged by cars, with pedestrians and cyclists forced to weave their way precariously in and out between the long rows of honking vehicles and lines of cars often parked two and three deep, up on sidewalks, against the sides of buildings, in courtyards, around the fountains, even on church steps. The air of the *centro* had become almost unbreathable and the noise deafening. Every local newspaper seemed to be entirely concerned with the problem, while no one cared about political events or foreign affairs. A steady drumbeat of vitriolic criticism in the press was levelled at the ministerial types who seemed to be unable to solve the problem; yet at the same time the country as a whole was embarked on a crusade to become rich, with everybody's goal being the acquisition of at least two cars as well as a motor scooter or two for the kids. The chaotic situation of Rome's traffic and *il benessere* in general provided me with the central theme of my first Letter.

With Janet as my model, I worked ferociously hard, up to twelve hours a day, and airmailed my copy to Shawn on January 12, 1962. I expected to hear from him in a week or two at most, since part of the article dealt with topical events, the atmosphere of the city at holiday time. To distract myself, I began to adapt an Italian play into English and then went up to Milan for a few days to sniff out what I might write about in a Milan Letter and to see Mondadori on behalf of my mother, who wanted to be able to spend more time in Italy every year.

Mammina Ester could no longer be left alone during the day, as both her sight and hearing were failing. She was also pining to return to Italy, where my mother and Franca would try to settle her, preferably in an apartment of her own and with a full-time housekeeper to take care of her, an arrangement that in New York would have proved too costly. What my grandmother most wanted was to be able to live with my mother, her favorite daughter—but in Italy, her own country. The problem was an agonizing one for my mother, who was in no position to give up the Mondadori job and who had by then become a passionate New Yorker, far more at home there than in her native land. I had assured both her and Mondadori in person that I would fill in and run the office for her in New York during her absences, assuming that I would be going back there by the end of the year. This began to seem more and more likely as time passed with no word from Shawn.

By January 23, I still hadn't heard anything and was becoming agitated. My mother wrote, counseling patience, to which I responded angrily. "I would like to go on with the magazine," I wrote to her, but not on any terms. Either they will read and publish my stuff, or I will, of course, have to find something else to do. I can assure you, without too much rancor, that if I were a blind Hindu [a reference to Ved Mehta, whose very long articles seemed to get into print as soon as he finished them], a three-named English lady authoress or a friend of Edith Oliver's [Edith, a close friend of Shawn's, seemed to have his ear on whom to publish and when], my pieces would get read quicker. Impatience, you talk about! I've been waiting two years now for a piece of mine to appear and you dare mention impatience to me! It makes the blood rush to my head! *Santo cielo! Pazienza,* the stupidest word in almost any language. The situation is perfectly simple: either I am a *New Yorker* writer or I am not; all I can do is turn in the work, but the burden of the decision does not lie on me, but on the magazine. For Christ's sake, you talk as if *The New Yorker* were some sort of shrine at which everyone should worship. It is a good magazine, the best around, and I hope to be able to contribute to it regularly, but if I can't, surely the end of the world has not come. Enough said. I'm sorry to sound so ill-tempered, but there's a certain strain in waiting around to hear from Shawn, which seems to be all I've been doing for two years.

At the end of this diatribe I apologized again for sounding so ill-tempered, but begged her to try and understand.

By the end of February, I still hadn't heard from Shawn and I had just about given up hope. Doris and I planned to return to New York in late summer. Then, in early March, I received a wire from Shawn asking me rather testily for a rewrite; I would need a whole new opening, since the holiday season was now well behind us. I immediately set to work and spent a week finishing up a revision, this time not pegging the contents of the Letter to any specific time or event. I also decided to relax, to stop worrying too much about "facts" and simply to report what I personally saw and felt about Rome after such a long absence from it. I found it easier

to write, putting much more of myself into the work. I was determined not just to be a reporter, but to create a personal style, as
Janet had done for herself after years of writing for the magazine.
Then I sent the article back to Shawn and steeled myself for another long wait.

After a couple of weeks had passed and I had heard nothing
from Shawn, Janet confided to my mother in a letter of March 27
that she was worried about the trouble I seemed to be having with
the piece. "Those long Letters, or even the short ones, are very
tricky to do, and I am the one who knows it, having more or less
invented the formula which Bill would not like to have to follow, he
being very independent," she wrote. "But some similar formula
which combined special writing and a treatment of news both illuminating yet with a certain mixed light and dark touch will have to
be invented to replace mine." She was right, of course; my whole
problem with this first piece, I realized later, had been an initial inability to find my own voice.

My mother continued to counsel patience, but by that time I
had begun to think of myself as "an unwanted contributor." Never
again, I vowed, would I put myself in the position of having to
wait endlessly on an editor. I finished up my adaptation of the Italian play and set to work on a novel.

No sooner had I resigned myself to a possible rejection than I
heard from Shawn, who wired me early in April that he was now
enthusiastic about the Rome Letter and would publish it the following week. I cabled The General, who replied by letter on April
13. "You can't imagine how happy I was to receive your cablegram
with the magnificent news of *The New Yorker*," she wrote to me in
Italian.

I was sure, as I had already written you, that you would succeed
very well. And now that you've found your personal formula,
you'll feel more sure of yourself and you'll be able to write the
other pieces knowing that you've found the right way. Always, in

everything new, one must try and try again. Only when talent doesn't exist, in whatever field, does one fail. What is most needed and more than talent is constancy, a working discipline, and a control over impetuosity and rebellions of one's own character that, even if sometimes justified, can play nasty tricks.

It was just the sort of homily I'd been hearing from her all my life, but on this occasion I did not rise to the bait to argue with her. I had to admit for once that, as usual, she was right.

She wrote to me again on April 25, after the piece had appeared in the magazine, to tell me how pleased she was. "It was a very beautiful Letter, brilliant, intelligent, personal, amusing, and without the usual clichés." Her Italian friends in New York, including all the foreign correspondents, had read it and had only kind words for it. And my success was assured when Janet wrote to me from Paris:

> Bill, dear, your Rome Letter is excellent; I read it with all the reactions with which I think a foreign letter must be read—interest for news, personality of the writer in his presentation, intelligence and concentration on one or more subjects (in your case *il benessere*) which give the dateline and political comprehension that establish the letter as a true *report*. I was very glad to see it in print because writing the first one for the magazine is not too easy a task for the writer.

I felt I had finally arrived, even more so than after the publication of *The Fugitive Romans*. The two people whose opinions most mattered to me had at last found me worthy, and all because of *The New Yorker*.

While still basking in my success, I went up to Milan and wrote my second Letter for the magazine from there. I did not make the mistake this time of grounding the piece on current events, but made it general. I wrote primarily about the city's status as the coun-

try's commercial hub and the character of its people, resolutely op-
timistic, open to new ideas, hard-working, and exasperated by the
backwardness and the bureaucratic incompetence of Rome. "Politics is a Roman industry," I quoted a Milanese friend of mine, "the
only one they have. We make the money and they steal it."

Shawn took only two weeks this time to let me hear that this article had also "worked out" and would be "going through," without my having to make any revisions. It was published in the issue
of September 8 and pretty much established me as exactly what I
had aspired to become, the magazine's man in Italy. The irony was,
however, that we would be going back to New York in the fall.
Doris had become pregnant and would be giving birth to our third
child in mid- or late January. It was a surprise to us because we
hadn't planned to have any more children, but we never even considered the possibility of an abortion. We would accept with some
trepidation, due to our permanently shaky finances, this new arrival. We wanted, however, to have the baby in New York, under
the same medical supervision we had had with our daughters. We
would spend the rest of the winter there, after which I could always come back to Italy to write again for the magazine. If this
meant frequent separations from my wife and family for periods of
a month or two at a time, it was the price we were both willing to
pay. I had at last found my niche at the magazine.

TWENTY-TWO

AN END
AND
A BEGINNING

I remained on the writing staff of *The New Yorker* for the next thirty-three years. The pattern of contribution I had established in Italy in 1962 remained a constant, although I also later wrote several pieces from California. Every year, often twice a year, in spring and fall, I would go back to Italy for stays usually of four to six weeks. Every year I contributed no more than two or three articles—Letters from Rome, Naples, Milan, Tuscany, Venice, or elsewhere, or reportage on such matters as the day-to-day life of a piazza or the depredations caused by earthquakes, volcanic eruptions, environmental neglect, or the misadventures of politics and terrorism. I didn't earn enough from these contributions to support myself fully, but I didn't want to make the mistake of relying entirely on *The New Yorker* for my well-being as a writer. I continued to write novels, I remained active in the theater, and I also wrote for quite a number of other magazines. I considered myself essentially a man of letters. I also didn't trust the magazine to guarantee me a career. One of my mother's most valuable legacies to me was her love of Roman proverbs, all of them cynical and coldly appraising of human follies and cupidity. My favorite one was, "It is good to trust, but it is better not to trust." The fact that she herself was constantly being victimized by placing too much faith in institutions and people only served to make me all the more wary in the pursuit of my own interests.

I never understood Shawn nor became close to him, though I was one of the few staff writers who called him by his first name. One day, in his office, after we had pirouetted through another of those excruciatingly polite conversations in which we always addressed each other formally, I asked him please to call me Bill. He blushed and said, "Then you must please call *me* Bill." After that I always did, to the surprise of most of my colleagues, some of whom had known him for many years and never achieved even that degree of intimacy with him. But it didn't bring us any closer and may, in fact, have served to distance us even more. I always felt in dealing with him that he would have been happier to communicate with all of us by brief typed memos of the sort that bounced from office to office regarding the merits, or lack of same, of various pieces under consideration. He gave the impression of being so painfully shy that, if pressed, he would vanish behind his scarlet blushes, leaving in his wake only a hazy aura of regret.

The bitter fact is that I also learned not to trust him completely. He was by far the best editor I ever worked for, but his deepest loyalty was to his personal concept of what *The New Yorker* was: not just another magazine, but, for him, a mystique bordering on religious belief. His favorites on the staff were those he considered most in concert with his feelings, and he protected them with an eye always on how they could best serve his fierce dedication. He fought a long campaign to install the writer Jonathan Schell as his designated successor, even though Schell was probably not suited to the task, if only because he seemed to lack a sense of humor. Shawn persisted for several years and gave in only because of the united opposition of most of the staff and all of the senior editors, though in the light of what happened to the magazine after Shawn's forced retirement, Schell might not have been such a disastrous choice. When one of my Letters from Rome went unpublished because Schell had picked that same time to go to Italy and write a story for the Talk of the Town that dealt almost exclusively with some of the same topics I had covered, I realized I wasn't high enough in the pecking order at the magazine to feel secure. My polite but strong letter of protest to Shawn went unanswered. I considered the careers of other staff writers at the magazine who had eventually vanished from its pages and decided, after that incident, never to rely exclusively on any one source of income. I've always played the field.

Shawn, of course, knew what I was doing, but never objected. Even in the years when, for one reason or another, I failed to write for him, I always received a renewal of my contract, which did not guarantee me an income but merely stated what I would be paid for my work upon its acceptance. He was extraordinarily patient with his staff writers and never put pressure on any of us to perform except at our own pace. Once he happened to mention to me that he would have been very happy to have published a long cover story I wrote for the Saturday Evening Post on the Hell's Angels. I told him I had no idea he might be interested in the subject, but that, in any case, the Post had commissioned the piece from me. He only nodded and mumbled that I had done a good job, and I thanked him, secretly amazed that he had read it. The magazine had someone on staff whose job it was to keep track of what we were all doing for other publications, which is how Shawn must have been made aware of the piece. Even so, I was flattered that he had taken the trouble to read it and seen fit to compliment me on it.

One of the reasons I loved working for The New Yorker was its editing process, which others have complained about for being excessively finicky and insanely fact-oriented. I never found it so. The procedure was admittedly meticulous and the fact checking could become exasperating, but I never had reason to complain about it. Every article I wrote for the magazine was to some extent improved by it; just knowing what I would have to confront if I didn't do my best work made me a better writer, just as it had Janet. Only once did I object to what I considered needless meddling with a paragraph of my text, but over such a trifle that I'm sure the offending editor, Roger Angell, would not remember it. Most of the corrections and suggested changes seemed to improve the articles; no one ever simply took my copy and mangled it to suit his own vision of how the piece should have been written. Some pieces, especially the casuals, had to be run through some editor's typewriter to make them publishable, but this was because they had been written by amateurs or by correspondents too lazy to submit anything but rough copy. I had learned from Janet to take great care to rewrite and polish before submitting anything, which is why, when dealing with other magazines, I often found myself in heated confrontations with editors who thought they could improve on my work and sometimes edited with a meat cleaver. Not once at *The New Yorker* did I ever feel that my work had been damaged by someone's heavy pencil. And every time a piece of mine appeared somewhere in the magazine it would be greeted with words of praise from Paris, where Janet, perched vigilantly in her hotel room overlooking the Tuilleries, kept a benevolent and watchful eye on my literary career, as reflected for her in the pages of the magazine she considered the best in the world.

Janet's own life had begun to suffer the losses inflicted by age. She had now to maintain a more careful watch over her health, and friends noticed that she suffered occasionally from memory lapses. She was also dismayed by the illnesses and disappearances of friends, especially by that of Nancy Cunard, who died alone in a Paris hospital ward. Gallant, unrepentant, fiercely outraged to the end, Nancy had, according to Janet in a letter to Solita, slipped out of sight, "so violent in her febrile rage against the life she made."

Janet had also been distressed by the drama of Alice B. Toklas's old age, long after the death of Gertrude Stein in 1946. Suddenly stripped, due to legal action taken by the Stein heirs, of the remarkable collection of paintings that had graced the walls of their apartment, Alice had been left practically penniless. Janet and other friends had had to rally to her support, paying hospital bills, contributing to her household expenses, writing letters on her behalf to lawyers for the estate and to the French government. The pictures wound up in a bank vault in Paris for safekeeping, leaving Alice surrounded by bare walls. "Miss Toklas's eyesight is, naturally, not what it once was," Janet wrote in her account of the affair in *The New Yorker.* "Of the disappearance of Miss Stein's familiar pictures from her salon and foyer, she only says, 'I'm not unhappy about it. I remember them better than I could see them now.' "

As her friends slipped away and she was left increasingly alone, the city Janet had loved and written so trenchantly about over the years began to seem hostile to her, and she was greatly distressed by the so-called improvements that were being made all around her. "The uglification of Paris," she observed in the magazine,

> the most famously beautiful city of relatively modern Europe, goes on apace, and more is being carefully planned. Already, one of the enormous square blocks of skyscraper office buildings on the Boulevard de Vaugirard, which forms the first part of a huge complex of modern buildings that will be composed around and will include the new Montparnasse railroad station, is, with its eighteen stories of unmitigated cement, a solid, high eyesore on the southern skyline of Paris. It disgraces the horizon as seen from the city's upper windows giving on the Tuilleries gardens, which were formerly possessed of one of the capital's most elegant perspectives. For these ignoble changes, big business and the automobile, either squatting by the curbs or crawling or racing along the boulevards, are responsible.

•

Inevitably, as the years passed, I saw less of Janet, especially after Doris and I moved to California, first for a long stay of nine months in 1964, then definitively in the early summer of 1966. She always kept in touch with me, however, and never failed to comment on our activities. After the birth of my son in January 1963, she had written to Natalia, "I sail tomorrow and so I shall soon see you and the masculine new member of the family. I am delighted it is a boy. You will have done well in consideration of the female difficulties in life, but after two daughters, a son is a psychological change you and I can appreciate, being part of a trio of daughters."

She was less sanguine about our projected move to the Los Angeles area. "I cannot comprehend why Bill wants to live in California, despite its occasional geographic beauties like a park that has become half-urban in most cases except in the deep ranch country, where, except for Hildegarde in her valley, there is deep mourning this spring because of lack of rain. . . ." She saw us as departing by covered wagon to live in "a civilization so-called which is appalling and tragic and only less violent and cow-minded than Texas." She also worried that my mother, deprived of our presence and that of her grandchildren, would feel abandoned and lonely. She continued to reassure her that soon now, very soon, she would be giving up her full-time career in Paris and come to live with her in New York, but Natalia had heard that siren song before and learned not to pay much attention to it.

In 1966, Janet did come to New York for an extended stay of three months, during which she and Natalia bought a small two-bedroom apartment at 785 Park Avenue, on the corner of Seventy-third Street, where she eventually spent the last three years of her life and from which Natalia never strayed until the last two years of her own life.

Janet was then at the height of her popularity. Her *Paris Journal, 1944–1965*, edited by William Shawn, won the National Book Award for "the most distinguished work in the field of Arts and Letters."

She found herself in demand for interviews and was pleased to note that her "spatter of writing" had finally been recognized by the literary establishment as something more than mere magazine journalism. Nevertheless, she never thought that her work had much substance, and she believed she had thrown away her talent through her devotion to churning out the Paris Letter year after year "as if it were one of the important communications of mankind instead of merely the rather disgraceful means to an end—my livelihood—which when handed to me I stuck to in my laziness." She believed that by limiting herself to articles she had denied herself the chance to develop her literary talent, and she was puzzled when her *Paris Journal* produced a prize and recognition, until she realized that in book form her work had acquired substance and weight.

> A book is positive and even a book of reprints gave me more size than the appearance of fortnightly letters, I now know and agree to. I thought that writing in the first place was more important than a book publisher's focus: wrong. I have deformed my life and yours. I am the occasion of our happiness and our middle-aged love, when we started. My constant unfaithfulness has been to my love of writing, my instinct for preserving my small but precious career and my love for Paris. I think I love it in part because I am a stranger, a foreigner, who still speaks bad French as a form of sloth. In geography it is the only place I have ever loved, and Fire Island. . . ."

Mea culpa had long been a recurrent theme in her relationship to Natalia and my mother accepted Janet's professions of regret as her due, but she had mostly stopped putting pressure on Janet to change. Every now and then Natalia would explode in anger or bitterness, but these were minor crises compared to the ones that had afflicted them earlier in their relationship. The last serious one occurred in the spring of 1967, when Natalia paid a brief visit to Paris at the end of a tour of Venice and the Palladian villas sponsored by an Italian hotel chain. Janet, who had been looking forward to seeing her, found herself under attack for her selfishness and was so distressed by the episode that she could hardly sleep for several nights and wondered whether Natalia actually wanted her to come to New York as she had planned in early summer. Natalia, of course, quickly rebounded from her bout of unhappiness, exacerbated, I'm sure, by having found herself so alone in New York after our departure for California. Janet did show up, as planned, at the end of June and they spent the rest of that summer together, shuttling between Manhattan and Cherry Grove on Fire Island.

Although Janet's situation had become fairly static, this was a period in Natalia's life full of change and drama. Her job at Mondadori, now being run by Giorgio, the younger son of the old presidente, was coming to an end. Giorgio was more of a businessman than a publisher, and he had surrounded himself with younger associates who evidently believed that the New York office should be run by someone younger, preferably male. Natalia could sense the pressure building for her removal after fourteen years on the job, but she had been hoping to hang on in some sort of consulting capacity, possibly based in Rome. She didn't want to leave New York, but she was worried about Mammina Ester, whom she had helped to settle in Rome in a small apartment below Franca's on the Campo dei Fiori.

By 1963 my grandmother's sight and hearing were failing and she was becoming incapable of caring for herself. Worst of all, her memory was going, too, and she seemed to be deteriorating at a pace that threatened to leave her without defenses and helpless. No one could be found in New York to take care of her, at least at a cost Natalia could afford, and Franca had suggested returning her to Italy, where there were other members of our family on hand to help and where a full-time caretaker could possibly be found for her. Natalia at first resisted the move. She and Mammina Ester were so close and she knew that her mother wanted most of all to be with her, whether in New York or Rome. But in the spring of 1963, she brought Mammina Ester back to Italy and settled her in a Rome apartment, where she was being cared for by a wonderful woman named Maria Ronconi, the sort of loyal retainer Italy seems always to provide to families in distress.

The move took an enormous amount of immediate pressure off Natalia, but nevertheless she missed Ester terribly and continued to worry about her. When my grandmother nearly died of pneumonia in the early winter of 1965, Natalia began to think seriously about moving back to Italy, a step Janet warned her to consider very carefully. "News of your darling mother is both good and, of course, bad," she wrote to her.

> I feel it is my duty, since you are so emotionally knitted with your insistence that your mother live forever because you love her beyond the limits of rational relations, that I point out what I have already known—that the heart may go on beating like an engine producing no work, except the extension of life itself, but which can be an extension of existence without full faculties. The antibiotic which saved her from double pneumonia cannot have saved her from the destruction of her faculties or may even have contributed to it, as you now report. That she sends word to you daily that she is waiting for you to fetch her to go away and that she is ready, with her fur coat! She is old and magnificent in her resistance, for God's sake do not once again insist upon keeping her alive as a memento of your love for her, in your youth, and in your sense of what you have owed her so that as a result she lives on in the humiliation of a beating heart and lost faculties. . . .

She urged Natalia to seek my advice, but I was hardly in a position to be helpful, since Doris and I were planning our own permanent move to California. If Natalia did decide to move to Rome, Janet assured her she would be able to spend half the year with her in Italy and offered to contribute to the expenses. "That is not the point," she cautioned her, however. "The point is, will you mourn for the rest of your days, beloved, for Manhattan?"

As it became clear to her that her tenure at Mondadori was coming to an end, at least as head of the New York office, Natalia did begin to negotiate a move that would take her back to Rome. Then, in early October, she was contacted by Andrea Rizzoli, whose father Angelo had founded Italy's other major publishing company, Mondadori's great rival. Angelo had heard that Natalia was unhappy with the way things were going at Mondadori, Andrea said. Would she consider becoming the head of Rizzoli's New York office, located above their newly opened elegant bookstore at 712 Fifth Avenue, in the old Cartier building? They had to have an answer by the next day, but Natalia accepted at once and resigned from Mondadori that afternoon. Years later, when old Arnoldo Mondadori stopped by her offices to see her, he looked around, smiled, and congratulated her. "*Cara* Natalia," he said, "one makes mistakes in life!"

The problem remained of having to break the news to Mammina Ester, who was waiting for Natalia in Rome, though we weren't sure she'd even be able to understand what was going on. During my own last visit to her a few months previously she had at first failed to recognize me, and we had eaten together in silence, her memory rooted then only in the remote past. While my mother was still in New York in early November 1965 and preparing to go, my telephone rang in Princeton, where Doris, the children, and I were spending the winter. It was Franca. Mammina Ester was very ill. "You must come at once," she said. I heard the cold anguish in her voice. "Franca, tell me, you must tell me," I answered. "Is she alive?" The silence at the other end told me all I needed to know. I promised Franca I would break the news to my mother and that we'd be in Rome the next day. I would wire her details as soon as we could book our flight.

I couldn't tell my mother the truth right away, only that Mammina Ester was desperately ill. We booked a flight out of JFK airport that evening. As we flew in over the Italian coast early the next morning, with the city of Rome lying beneath us in the distance like a scene out of a cheerful travelogue, my mother said, "I hope we are not too late." I took her hand. "Don't hope for too much," I said. "Is she dead?" my mother asked. I nodded and we sat together in silence, holding hands, until the plane landed.

My mother maintained a fierce, desperate control over her emotions until the taxi dropped us off in front of Franca's palazzo. Then she bounded up the stairs in front of me and burst into the room where Mammina Ester lay on her back in her bed, her eyes closed and her mouth, twisted by the effect of the massive stroke that had killed her, hidden by a handkerchief. My mother fell to her knees by Ester's side and cried out in her grief, "I have come too late, I have come too late!" rocking back and forth over her body while I held her shoulders from behind and tried to offer what comfort I could.

A simple funeral service was held in the chapel of the Palazzo della Cancelleria, the vast Renaissance structure next door belonging to the Vatican, and was attended only by family members and a few friends, after which Mammina Ester's body was taken to the Campo Verano, Rome's vast and ancient cemetery, and lowered into our family tomb. She was eighty-seven when she died, leaving behind her in memory an image of light and warmth that had illuminated my childhood. "This has certainly been the saddest day of your life," Janet wrote to Natalia from Paris. "There can be no loss like that of the mother, if she is still loved and was so meriting of devotion as yours."

I flew back to New York in a few days, while my mother remained in Rome, where she was joined by Janet on November 19. They stayed together until Thanksgiving, after which Janet went back to Paris and Natalia returned to New York and her new job at Rizzoli.

TWENTY-THREE

LITTLE
CELEBRATIONS

Janet finally achieved the status of a celebrity in December 1971 with her appearance on a TV talk show hosted by Dick Cavett. Two other guests, Norman Mailer and Gore Vidal, spent much of the broadcast nastily belaboring each other until Janet exploded. "I've had enough of you!" she snapped, addressing them as a couple of spoiled children, much to the delight and approval of the live audience. Looking elegant in one of her beautifully tailored dark suits and wearing white gloves, she established herself as a public performer, which, in fact, she had always been. Later she made an equally successful appearance on *60 Minutes*, where she was interviewed in Paris by Mike Wallace and chatted wittily about her days in the City of Light. Irving Drutman, a retired publicity man and an old friend from Fire Island, had edited a collection of her pieces under the title *Paris Was Yesterday* that was published in

July 1972, and immediately became a best-seller. Her preface to the book appeared in *The New Yorker* in March, by her own estimate the most popular piece she had ever written for the magazine. "Write, write, write, that's what I wanted to do; that's always what I wanted to do," she informed a reporter who interviewed her about the book. And she echoed that theme when she showed up for a second time on the Dick Cavett show, even though she despised television in general: "I think it is drivel, a waste of time and brain. It is merely a way to entertain people who don't buy books, so far as I am concerned!!!" Irritated by what she thought were needless redecorating changes and poorer service at the Continentale, Janet had moved in 1969 to the Ritz, whose luxurious appointments and chic cachet now seemed more suited to her new status as an international literary celebrity, even though she wasn't sure she could afford it.

She finally came to live with Natalia in New York in early October 1975, a few weeks after the publication in *The New Yorker* of her last Letter from Paris. Unable to get around on her own anymore, she had spent the spring and summer in Orgeval and had written mainly about "the flowers in our valley, mostly roses. Never did I see so many; it has been a great rose year and thus a pleasure to the eyes." Her health, fortified for so long by martinis and a judicious absence of exercise, had begun at last to break down these past few years. She suffered from high blood pressure and severe angina attacks, for which she took nitroglycerine tablets, and had difficulty walking for more than a few yards. Her mind, however, was still clear, though she had memory lapses and occasionally dozed off for minutes at a time during the course of the day. She had become increasingly dependent in Paris on the kindness of her friends, especially Noel, whose own health, however, had begun to deteriorate. By the time Janet settled permanently in Natalia's apartment on October 10 she had, in effect, become an invalid.

Natalia saw no irony in the fact that Janet's so-long-delayed move to New York should have taken place only when Janet could no longer live alone or even work. My mother had waited thirty-five years for this moment, when she could at last bring Janet under her maternal wing and take full control over her life. She immediately set about organizing Janet's day by limiting her alcohol intake to a single light Scotch and water before dinner, and got her to cut down on her smoking, a major achievement. She also made sure that Janet ate properly and took her various medications on time. And she screened all requests for interviews and social engagements to make certain Janet wouldn't be exhausted by the now fairly numerous requests for her presence. "I am learning a great many things," Janet commented soon after moving into the New York apartment, "obedience and patience." But she didn't chafe under Natalia's benevolent tyranny; indeed she seemed to thrive under it. "Such felicity!" she said to Natalia one evening, as they sat in their living room before dinner. "Love is full of little celebrations."

Their favorite times together were in the morning, when they shared the newspaper, gossiped, and drank tea, which Janet called "a valiant potion for salvation." Janet's mind was at its clearest then and she adored the sharing of news, the exchange of opinions and the comments on friends and family that Natalia never failed to provide. "Our mornings are very intimate and rich in our perceptions," Janet observed. "The presence of love in our lives makes a special atmosphere in the apartment, as if one could smell it and feel it as a scent of warmth."

After breakfast Natalia would depart for her office at Rizzoli and Janet would sit down at her desk to go through the paper, marking with a colored pencil items that particularly interested her and clipping some to store away in her files. It was a routine she had followed for most of her working life, constructing out of these bits and pieces of daily life a mosaic of events to form the backbone of her narratives for *The New Yorker*. Sometimes she would spend several hours rereading her own stories, often commenting aloud on them, judging them anew. "Oh, that was good!" she would say.

"Yes, I handled that rather well, I think." Occasionally, she would squawk in protest like an indignant bird over a passage or a paragraph that she felt had been mutilated in the editing. Once, when I was visiting her in New York one afternoon, she was angered by the recollection of what she considered a brutal piece of editing at the hands of somebody, not Shawn, at the magazine. "It is always wrong to cut a part of a thought or an incident out," she once explained. "In cutting a part it is like serving the chicken's neck, having cut off the rest of its toasted carcass. There must always be taste in carving."

She liked to sing the spirituals and old Methodist hymns she had heard growing up in Indianapolis, and she and Audrey, the handsome Jamaican woman my mother had hired to take care of her, could sometimes be heard warbling away from the bathroom or the kitchen. In the afternoons, if the weather was fine, Audrey would try to take her out for a walk, to which Janet objected on the grounds that her feet were too small. She preferred to let Audrey push her about in a wheelchair through the park or past the storefronts on Madison Avenue. "One often gets the impression that New York is constructed around drugstores, bars and banks," she observed one day, while riding back home in a taxi from lower Fifth Avenue.

Irving Drutman, although already ill from the cancer that would kill him within a few months of Janet's death, had begun to assemble and edit another volume of her writings, published in November 1979, under the title *Janet Flanner's World*. It included her profile of Adolf Hitler, as well as many of her reminiscences of all those extraordinary characters on the Parisian scene whom she had brought so vividly to life in the pages of *The New Yorker*. As Irving began to work on the book, Janet limited herself to approving his selections, but noted sadly that all of the people she had written about over so many years had disappeared; she had outlived them all, including Solita Solano, who died in Paris a month after Janet's final departure for New York. Solita had remained faithful in her loving friendship for Janet until the very end. The two women had seen each other often in Paris and Orgeval and continued to carry on a correspondence over the years despite Natalia's opposition. Janet could never turn her back on anyone who had once been close to her, a trait that infuriated my mother, who had never forgiven Solita for her behavior in the early months of her relationship with Janet. "She was not a generous enemy," Janet said about Solita, but then the same observation could have been made in this instance about Natalia. After Solita died, Janet observed sorrowfully that these deaths were "like leaves falling from the tree." On her last birthday, March 13, 1978, she commented, "The highs and lows of life tear one apart."

Although Janet ceased to be as much of an influence on my life and career as before, once we had moved to California, Natalia remained a powerful and loving presence in my life. The days of our power struggles and my often overheated rebellions were long behind us. She came at least once a year to visit us for a period of several weeks, usually at Christmas. I went to New York several times a year and saw her every day. She continued to question, challenge, and support me in every way and to comment, not always positively, on my literary efforts. She couldn't understand why I couldn't seem to grab off chunks of that easy Hollywood money that she believed was just lying around for someone with a minimum of talent to pick up; but when I consulted her about possibly trying my hand at a screenplay, she would turn pessimistic. She was contemptuous of almost everything that came out of California, especially the Los Angeles area, and would recall her time spent with Anna Magnani working with people she regarded as profoundly corrupt and artistically highly overrated as well as overpaid. She was always secretly relieved whenever one of my attempts to break into movies or television failed.

The closest I ever came to the easy Hollywood money had been in 1967, when Twentieth Century–Fox bought my novel *The Sweet Ride*. We were living in Malibu in a rented house east of the Malibu Colony, on flat land along the shoreline of Malibu Creek. "Why don't you ask if you can write the film?" my mother suggested. "Who could do it better than you?"

I called up my agent in Hollywood and asked him if anybody had been signed to do the screenplay. When he said no, I asked him to set up an appointment for me with Joe Pasternak, the producer the studio had hired to bring the project to fruition. A couple of days later I drove in from Malibu to the Fox lot on Pico Boulevard and was ushered into the presence of Pasternak, who was in the studio barbershop having his nails done. The producer was a small, bald man with a thick Hungarian-Jewish accent. He was a survivor of dozens of studio wars and had earned his reputation as the producer of a series of highly profitable but forgettable films starring Deanna Durbin and Esther Williams. "In the vater she vas a star," he had once commented about the latter. I stood by his barber's chair and introduced myself over the head of the young woman bending over his cuticles. I thought it was entirely appropriate that a writer in Hollywood should be kept standing during a public interview like a supplicant at the throne of a minor Roman emperor. "So vat haff you written?" he asked me.

I told him, and added that I had a reputation for churning out excellent dialogue. "Ah, but haff you written a screenplay?" he inquired. I told him that I hadn't, but that I had written for the theater and translated several plays by Luigi Pirandello. "My God, Pirandello! But you haffn't written a screenplay," the producer said. No, I hadn't, I admitted, but pointed out that two of the three stars signed for his project, Jacqueline Bisset and Michael Sarrazin, had never been in a movie before and that his director, Harvey Hart, came out of Canadian television. "That's right," Pasternak said, "but there's a limit to the amount of inexperience ve can haff on this film."

I laughed and had to agree with him. I didn't get the job, but Pasternak and I became friends, especially when I found out he liked to play the horses. I would see him from time to time at Santa Anita or Hollywood Park and we'd confer over the merits or lack of them of the animals running that afternoon. A few months later, while my mother was visiting us in Malibu over the Christmas holidays, my children expressed a desire to go and watch the filming of a scene or two of the movie being made out of my book.

I called up the producer's secretary and made arrangements to go onto the lot to watch a big indoor party scene being shot on one of the main soundstages. We walked into preparations for a huge nightclub affair featuring a rock band and several hundred extras, all milling about under flashing multicolored lights. We stood clustered at the edge of the proceedings, watching the preparations for an event I had not written about in my novel. My characters were people living by their wits on the fringes of the Hollywood scene; they could not have afforded to go to any kind of expensive nightclub. As we stood there, gawking at the goings-on, Pasternak spotted us from across the way. Dressed in a long, dark gray overcoat against the early morning chill, he came tottering toward us across a great snarl of cables, waving his arms and smiling. "Don't vorry, Bill," he said, "ve didn't keep nothing but the title."

This was the closest I ever came to making a breakthrough in Hollywood, and my mother stopped urging me to solve my periodic financial problems by picking up that easy studio loot. I think she was secretly pleased by my failures in this department, even though she longed to see me happy, financially successful and not so dependent on magazine assignments to pay my monthly bills.

The last months of Janet's life were mostly peaceful and easy, her routines punctuated by visits from old friends. Her mind sometimes wandered and there were moments when she would grieve over her inability to write, but she was always aroused by her visitors and, like an old trouper confronted by an audience, would rise to the occasion, stimulated by company and the memories of the past that crowded in upon her. The editor and novelist William Maxwell, an old colleague from the magazine, dropped in on her one day to find her "like a caged animal. Only instead of pacing back and forth behind bars she picked up a copy of *Time* and turned the pages, without looking at them. Or me." Maxwell went right on talking, however, and eventually Janet dropped the copy of *Time* on the coffee table and began to talk back. "Marvelously," Maxwell recalled. "As well as I have ever heard her. About *The New Yorker*, about Paris, about writing and the life of writers. I came away feeling how privileged I had been to know her."

Helen Bishop, another old friend, went to see her in October, while Natalia was away at the yearly Frankfurt book fair in Germany. She found her with a copy of *The New Yorker* open on her lap, staring at a full-page ad. "When I'm not up to reading, I look at the ads," Janet told her. "They're very revealing." She pointed to a picture of a beautiful woman with a drink in her hand and tried to look indignant. "Do you have to look like that to enjoy gin? I certainly didn't . . . and yet I did."

Bishop asked her about Natalia, wanting to know if she were at ease with her absence and whether she had heard from her. Yes, there had been phone calls, letters and cards, lots of news. "We've been separated much longer than this, in more critical times than these," Janet said. "We always get together again. She's been part of my life for so long, it almost seems forever. I'll be here when she gets back and she will get back."

Bishop read aloud to her for a while, a short story by Edna Ferber, talked a bit longer, then left, relieved by the visit because of "the clarity of her thoughts, the emotion she stirred in herself and me when she spoke of [Natalia], the impish humor which pervaded all, made it one of her better days, I'm sure. She was in fine form and it was a joy to be with her." Bishop had been alarmed a few days earlier by having spoken to Janet on the phone and finding her conversation "disjointed and faltering."

I was in New York for a week in October, during my mother's

absence, and saw Janet nearly every day, even though I wasn't staying in the apartment. I would find her sitting in her favorite chair in the living room, close to a window that provided enough light for her to read by. Sometimes she would be simply sitting there, her head slumped against the back of the chair, seemingly nearly comatose. The sight of me would rouse her and her face would beam with pleasure. "Bill, dear," she would say, "what are you doing in New York?" Or, "Bill, how nice to see you," as if it had been months since our last meeting. I'd tell her, as I did every day, that I was in town to see my editors and agent and then we'd talk, always about the past, *The New Yorker,* Paris, old friends—never about the present, which seemed ephemeral and confusing to her, of no possible significance or interest. Once we talked about God and religion and I told her about Pirandello's view of the church as a construction built to house the highest of human sentiments, to embody, with its domes, naves, columns, gold, marble, and great works of art, "the spirit of man in adoration of the divine mystery." But by building itself such a home, the playwright had maintained, the spirit itself had been diminished, made to seem vain. She was fascinated by the concept, her brain stimulated, as always, by the impact of an idea, a view of the human condition considered from an angle that had not occurred to her. I told my mother about this conversation when she returned, and she was amused by it. It wasn't that Janet didn't believe in God or some form of immortality, she said, but she simply didn't believe that any religious order could claim a monopoly on the truth regarding it.

I remembered this conversation with Janet, my last serious one with her, years later, when I was going through my mother's papers. In a letter dated April 6, 1955, Janet wrote about seeing an article in *Life* on India and its religious systems. "I was brought up to go to Sunday school, to believe in Christianity," she said.

But as I look back I never had any belief at all in any religious inspiration or entity; was not quite able to turn with that angry radicalism of youth against Jesus, it being easier to deny God as a principle because he was both impersonal, without a face and representative of authority. But the human inherited visage of Jesus, looking nothing like anybody specially except a gentle bearded man who was a mere artistic convention, nevertheless touched me too much, as did the horror of his physical suffering, his crucifixion, for me not to believe that surely he must have lived historically. But I never believed in the doctrine of virgin birth, rising from the dead, etc. Today they seem all natural uses of the abnormal, of the special, of the non-possible that mankind naturally invents to give significance to a religion which of itself must be different than man himself. That is religion's meaning. I think of these things at Easter, that lovely festival of rebirth, of spring, of new hopes, of new determinations to be better in heart and soul and acts. For in the soul I believe, in some element of mysterious entity within us when civilization offers it as a means of upward growth. It is an attainment, not necessarily an endowment. Plato more surely had a soul than I because superior in civilization and I more surely have a soul than a Nazi soldier because he did wicked deeds of cruelty, no matter whether from duty or obedience; the acts remained, when personal, part of his individual damnation on earth. Should we think to meet after death? I do not see or feel this to be possible. But if so I shall be yours with love there, too.

In a postscript scrawled in pencil at the end of this letter, Janet observed that Natalia would probably be going to church on Easter. "Pray for me, too," she urged her.

TWENTY-FOUR

"WE ENJOYED THEM"

My mother never quite recovered from Janet's death. Does anyone recover from the quintessential losses? But she continued to work, and gradually her life again became full of friends and projects and aspirations. From across the country she kept a watchful, often reproving eye on my successes and misadventures. She never accepted my move to California and blamed it for the breakup of my marriage in 1973, when Doris and I drifted carelessly apart and I moved a few miles down the coast into an apartment in Santa Monica, but at least she adapted to it. (Alice, whom I'd met after the split, moved in with me the following year.) I would go to New York several times a year, usually on my way to and from Italy for *The New Yorker,* and I would stay with her, sleeping in the small narrow bed that had been my grandmother's and later Janet's. In late December, a week or so before Christmas, she would arrive to spend the holidays with Doris and the children. No sooner off the plane than she would assert that she couldn't stay very long, that she also had a number of people—old friends, business acquaintances—she would have to see and that she couldn't simply waste her time sitting around Doris's house in Malibu, isolated from her world of publishing, theater, and the arts in general. My children thought of her as a flashy comet that dazzled their horizons once a year, then vanished.

She considered southern California a wasteland, a cultural desert in the hands of the philistines who ran the movie and TV industry. When my translations of Pirandello were produced in L.A., she assumed they would not be successful or even understood because the public there was not sophisticated enough to respond to them. Even in 1987, when Gordon Davidson, the artistic director of Center Theatre Group, produced a one-hour dramatized version of Natalia and Janet's book of their letters, *Darlinghissima,* at a small dinner theater downtown, with my mother reading her own commentary and the fine English actress Christina Pickles reading from Janet's letters, she couldn't quite believe in the enthusiastic local reception the piece received from critics and public alike. It was the hot ticket of that season and could have run much longer than its allotted seven weeks. My mother assumed that its success was due to the presence in Los Angeles of a great many New Yorkers unhappily transplanted to the entertainment factories of the West. As far as she was concerned, southern California did not and could not nurture an indigenous artistic and intellectual life, not in the part of the country that had given us Richard Nixon and Ronald Reagan.

Darlinghissima, published in 1985, was the great event of her later years. The book was splendidly reviewed everywhere and revealed to the world a softer, far more intimate personality than Janet had ever before disclosed in her published work. My mother had had her doubts about publishing the book, afraid mainly that her grandchildren might be shocked or offended by the revelation of their beloved Nonna's emotional relationship with another woman. Had I objected, on my own or their behalf, she would not have gone through with the project. As it was, she left out much that was revelatory of the difficulties they had, of their quarrels, doubts, complaints and fears, the letters I have chosen to quote from in this book. I worked with her on the manuscript mainly as a copy editor, and sometimes she became indignant at my suggested changes, what she considered a smoothing out of her lively Italian voice. "You are destroying my style!" she trumpeted at me one afternoon from New York, thus establishing herself as a true outraged author subverted by overediting. I contented myself mainly with suggesting cuts, correcting grammar, spelling, phraseology that sounded clumsy to my American ear. I never pushed, always yielded to what she demanded, and she trusted me, as she did her editor, Jonathan Galassi, at Random House. It wasn't his fault that the book didn't sweep up the best-seller lists. Random House made no effort to promote, advertise, or reprint, even as the first modest printing of ten thousand copies was quickly selling out. My mother knew a potential best-seller when she saw one. What gave her the most pleasure from the book was those evenings when she and Christina Pickles were able to bring Janet's words and their world together to life in front of a live, appreciative audience. It was a vindication of all they had lived through together and what they stood for, as two women who had, as my mother put it, "surmounted obstacles, trying to lead their personal and professional lives with dignity and feeling."

Even before Janet's death, my mother's career in publishing was in decline. As in the case of Mondadori, the Rizzoli empire began to fall apart after the death of its founder. Old Angelo's son Andrea gambled away his time and money in the casinos of the French Riviera, and young Angelo, his son, took over the firm. He was a witty, enthusiastic innovator who quickly overreached himself with costly acquisitions and new projects, such as the purchase of a leading daily newspaper, the *Corriere della Sera,* and the launching of the Italian edition of *Playboy.* I was involved with the latter, as its American editor, and it didn't take me long to figure out that the project was squandering millions of dollars with little hope of an adequate return. Trusted old hands departed or were fired, and the new executives proved to be speculators on a massive scale, with political connections in Rome to whom money had to be funneled in vast amounts to buy political support for the firm's risky ventures. My mother sniffed the new atmosphere and soon realized her days as director of the New York office were numbered. By the end of 1976, she had been shunted aside to make way for the cronies of the new regime in Milan. In 1977 she resigned to take a job as representative for the much smaller Milanese publisher Sperling and Kupfer, to which she lent her prestige and provided the contacts that enabled it to acquire a number of American books that became best-sellers in Italy.

As she grew older my mother seemed physically to shrink into herself. She became tiny, but seemed to compensate for it by increased energy and her lifelong proclivity for embarking on and nourishing several projects at once. She seemed always to be on the run, here, there, everywhere, commenting fearlessly on all subjects of public interest and lavishing withering scorn on the developments in the American spectrum that seemed to her to be corrupting the values she had stood for all her life. She was uncompromising in her judgments of personalities and merciless in her criticism of the ways in which I and my children were choosing to conduct our own lives. She could still wound to the bone, a talent she had shared with her sisters and which my cousin Flavia, Lea's daughter, had once defined for me by explaining that "the Danesis bite." This gift had never failed to enrage me whenever I happened to be the victim of it, which was often, but as I grew older and surer of myself, it often failed to incite me. The thrusts would come most often out of the clear blue, like flashes of lightning from an unseen source, and they never failed to astonish.

A typical example was the day the phone rang at my office at the magazine. I happened to be in town, on my way back from Italy. Our old friend Cheryl Crawford, the Broadway producer and one of the original founders of the Actors Studio, had recently died. The Studio was holding a gathering in her honor, a function devoted to celebrating her career and life and at which old colleagues and friends would rise to reminisce about her. My mother wanted to know if I would escort her there. I told her I would, and we met that afternoon at the entrance to the Studio and headed together up the narrow flight of stairs leading to the main quarters on the second floor. "I haven't been in here since 1962," I observed, as we climbed the steps, "the year I was in the playwrights' unit." "Another thing you started and quit," my mother said, without missing a beat. As a young man struggling to master his life, this remark would once have enraged me. This time it merely stopped me in my tracks, left me leaning against the wall in helpless laughter.

Her health remained superb until the summer of 1992, when she had taken a house for a month at Cherry Grove with one of Janet's old friends from Paris, the photographer Giselle Freund. My mother had sold her own place there some years before, having found it too difficult and expensive to go on caring for the house simply in order to be able to enjoy it for a few weeks every summer. Afterwards she had refused to return to the island, so as not to have to walk past her cottage where she and Janet had spent such good times together. This last summer, however, the pain of loss had lessened sufficiently for the island to reclaim her. Most of her older friends had long since died, but she had become an icon in the community, a sort of living monument to its establishment as a homosexual sanctuary. Now there were young women who had befriended her and for whom she had become a beloved symbol for the freedom to be themselves that they, too, had fought so hard to attain. She and Giselle reigned there that summer as queens, befriended and nurtured by a small tribe of admirers and acolytes.

Sometime in August she began to complain of stomach pains, but characteristically refused to do anything about them. She had

rarely been sick, never been hospitalized, and refused to yield her
freedom to any medical judgment. She told me nothing, not until
September when she was at last compelled to see her doctor in
New York, a gentle, scholarly man who had also been our family
physician during the years Doris and I had lived in New York. He
sent her for tests and X rays and reported the finding of a large,
probably malignant tumor in her colon. Only then did she consent
to inform me, and I came to New York to be with her for the
surgery she would have to undergo.

She swept into it with the fearless panache that had character-
ized her whole life. Everything at the teaching hospital she entered
amazed and outraged her. She mocked the parade of doctors who
gathered periodically at her bedside, and her judgments on the
nursing staff were uncompromisingly severe. The nurses dreaded
going near her, and once she was left alone on a gurney in a corridor outside an X-ray room for five and a half hours. I went to
protest to an administrator, a pompous young man who assured
me that his establishment was the finest health-care facility in the
Western world and that my mother must have done something
herself to cause the incident. I told him that his hospital would indeed have been considered the marvel he said it was had it been located in Bosnia-Herzegovina or the Sudan, but that it couldn't
qualify for such honors in our part of the world. I then went and
hired private nurses to watch over my mother's welfare, at the im-
modest cost of a thousand dollars a day. "Have you gone mad?" my
mother asked me from her hospital bed shortly before being
wheeled off to the operating room. Not mad enough to allow her
to be abused in her old age in a badly run private institution, I told
her. She laughed. Not at my remark, I realized later, but because I
had at last taken charge of her life; she was proud of me.

The surgeon who operated on her was skillful but proved to be
what my wife, Alice, my resident medical expert, described as a
cowboy. He operated too often and allowed subordinates to clean
up after him, which resulted in my mother failing to heal properly.

I took her home, but she continued intermittently to run a low-grade fever for weeks after the surgery. Shortly before Christmas, Alice and I came East to whisk her out to California, where we were certain she could obtain the best care available and we could supervise her recovery at close hand. She didn't want to come. She insisted that she could go on controlling her fevers with aspirin and home nursing care. I asserted my newfound power over her and she began to refer to me as "the Boss," a considerable upgrade in rank from my once lowly status as the only private in her army.

We went straight from the airport in San Diego to the emergency ward of Scripps Memorial Hospital, where my mother was promptly assigned a private room and entrusted to the care of physicians Alice knew and trusted. The nervous energy we had been operating on for weeks banished jet lag. My mother remained in the hospital for forty-nine days, during which she underwent two more surgeries to correct the errors perpetrated on her in New York. She barely survived the second one, which left her that night hooked up to tubes and machines in the intensive care unit and looking like the subject of an experiment in a bad science fiction film. I leaned over her to say good night and urged her to try and get some sleep. "Fat chance," she murmured in my ear.

She began to recover and we brought her home. Her heart, however, had been fatally weakened. A cardiologist informed us that she had perhaps a year and a half to live. She recovered so quickly that we deigned to shrug off his prediction of impending congenital heart failure and to hope for something like a full recovery. Natalia was ninety-one years old, but she had the will of a lioness in her prime and we hoped for five, maybe six more years. She would live with us in our house in the San Diego suburb of Del Mar, where we could watch over her, and her grandchildren could visit her frequently from Los Angeles.

As she became stronger, we became weaker. She began to order us about, to establish her rule in what had been, in her eyes, a sloppily managed household carelessly ruled over by a woman far too tolerant of my penchant for going to movies, attending racetracks, and playing tennis. She chided Alice about her laxness in my regard. "Why don't you just *tell* him what to do!" she urged her one day. Alice sat at her feet, took her hand in hers and looked earnestly up into her eyes. "Natalia, I've been married twice," she said, "and both my marriages lasted longer than yours." She pleaded with my mother for understanding and tolerance of our undoubtedly slipshod ways, but in vain. It was like asking Louis XIV to lighten up on court etiquette or persuading Alexander the Great to slow down in his march toward India.

The struggle for dominance began to batter at our marriage. My mother enlisted the children on her side. She began secretly to telephone them from her room, to inform them that she had been isolated in her quarters, that she wasn't even being fed properly. I became aware of this tactic when the children would call and hardly say hello, ask to speak only to Nonna, never inquire about Alice or me. I confronted my mother, asked her to desist, offered to engage a full-time helper to take care of her needs. She refused. She wasn't going to squander money on strangers. I offered to sell the house, buy a larger one with a separate apartment for her so she could reign over her own small kingdom. She dismissed my offer as impractical, unnecessary, typical of my irresponsible approach to all practical problems. Alice said she would have to go away, go stay for a while with a friend who lived across the freeway from us, a half mile away. Unable to sleep and fueled by caffeine and decongestants, I developed a heart problem of my own, an atrial fibrillation that eventually would require cardioversion (a restoration of normal rhythm by electrical shock) and would put me on medication for several years.

I took Alice off to Hawaii for ten days to rest, and to see if we could salvage our situation, formulate a plan. When we returned I confronted my mother on our patio, where she liked to sit and enjoy the view of our garden that Alice had willed into existence out of the desert sand. My mother had already formulated a plan of her own. She would move into an apartment in a senior residential complex two miles away from us. She planned to remain there a few months, then move back to New York.

The place she had chosen was pleasant enough, a large, well-managed facility catering exclusively to the needs of the elderly. Her ground floor apartment consisted of a bedroom, living room, dining alcove, and a small kitchen. From the tiny patio off the living room she could look out on a bank of flowers across the way, and she bought plants of her own to nurture. The children drove down periodically from Los Angeles to see her; her friends in New York came, too, and followed up their visits with frequent phone calls. I dropped in on her every day, and two or three nights a week we would dine together, either at our house or in the facility's main dining room, where the food proved to be adequate. She made friends with several of the other women in the complex, one of them the widow of a well-known sculptor. Giselle Freund spent a month with her, stirring my mother into action through her inability to manage money or even her travel arrangements. Nothing made my mother happier than the opportunity to correct someone else's mistakes and dictate courses of action that she approved of. I went into family therapy with my children in L.A., driving up there once a week for sessions that allowed us at last to pick at the bones of contention between us, to explain ourselves to one another, to listen to one another's grievances. Some of the damage caused by the war my mother had fought to take over our lives was mended, though traces of bitterness and anger remained. Alice withdrew from the scene as much as possible, afraid to risk finding herself permanently cast in the role of wicked stepmother. All she'd ever wanted from my children was their friendship. It had been granted, withdrawn, and now was again being tentatively proffered. I had a very hard time forgiving my mother for the damage she had caused in our lives. I knew that she had no insight into any of her own motives. She had never had any, I realized. The Danesis were always right.

In the fall of 1993, accompanied by a young woman we had hired

to help care for her, she went back to New York, but not to stay. She
had become too dependent on the skills of the doctors we had engaged to take care of her, and dependent on us. She realized that
New York was too far away from us, and I think she knew now that
her days were numbered. From time to time she experienced difficulty in breathing, and oxygen had to be administered. She wanted
to be near us and to be available to the children, who visited regularly and who for the first time in their relationship with her were
able to command her full attention. They fell in love with her. She
had always had the magical ability to make everyone within her immediate orbit become entranced by her. She again asserted her
dominance within the confines of her new living quarters and she
participated actively in the facility's public events, going off with her
new friends to concerts, shopping expeditions, art exhibits, even during the summer racing season to the Del Mar racetrack where, luckily, I was able to produce a few winners for her. "I will bid [sic] on
this horse," she would declare, then inform her new friends that this
paragon of a beast had been selected for her by her son, the racing
expert. She wrote letters back to her old friends in the East and to
Franca in Rome. She wrote poems in Italian—about her past, about
Fire Island, about Rome, about New York—that I translated for her.
She referred to her present situation as life in a golden cage.

Giselle came again for another long visit, this time so exasperating
my mother that Natalia forced her temporarily to move out, into a
guest apartment in another part of the building. My daughter Julia,
who witnessed one of her grandmother's outbursts against her old
friend, remonstrated with her. Giselle had come to see her all the
way from Paris, how could she treat her this way, heap such abuse on
her? My mother relented, Giselle moved back in with her. At Thanksgiving, Franca came and stayed with her through the holidays. Flavia
had accompanied her from Rome and we both feared the worst;
whenever Franca had visited my mother in the past in New York they

had fought fierce territorial wars, forcing Franca often to depart prematurely from the apartment in the mornings in order to avoid daily confrontations. This time, however, they adjusted immediately to each other's needs. Franca's sunny personality bloomed in California. We took them to a Thanksgiving dinner in the great sprawling rococo vastness of the Del Coronado Hotel, where we ate in the huge fin-de-siècle dining room that made both of them giggle with outrage and delight. About ten days before Christmas, in an atmosphere of drama, Franca left to return to Rome. That night my mother had suffered a serious attack necessitating the arrival of a crew of firemen to administer oxygen and rush her to the hospital. Franca said goodbye to her as she lay recovering in her room, in some ways a blessing because it meant they would have no time to grieve over what they both suspected would be their last embrace.

The phone call from Rome came two months later, early in the morning. Federico's voice sounded calm, strangely cold at the other end, as if he had willed all emotion out of it. "Bill, my mother died yesterday," he said, as if announcing a change in the weather or a train schedule. She had not responded to phone calls and the police had had to break into her apartment, where they found her sitting in her living room in an armchair facing the television set, a dinner tray on her lap. "She didn't suffer at all," Federico said. "A heart attack." I shouted in disbelief. Alice came running into the kitchen and we fell into each other's arms. We had both loved her deeply, but now we had no time to grieve for her. We would have to tell my mother before she would inevitably begin to receive condolences from Rome and New York.

An hour later Alice and I stood in the corridor outside her apartment while she finished getting dressed. She smiled with pleasure at the unexpected sight of us as she emerged from her bedroom. "I have very bad news, darling," I said, pulling her into my arms. "It's Franca." She cried out in an agony of grief, her arms flailing helplessly about as I held her tightly. "Why not me? Why not me?" she cried. There was no answer to such a question. Alice gave her a sedative and we stayed with her throughout the day until well into the night, when at last she fell into a sleep dark with pain and irreparable loss.

I think it was then that she began to long actively for death. The attacks came more frequently now, every two or three weeks, but by late April she seemed to have recovered; the children came regularly to see her, she was surrounded by love, she resumed an active life within her golden cage. I decided to go to Italy for a month. There were matters to be settled concerning taxes and the house in Sperlonga.

The phone rang in Sperlonga in the middle of the night. It was Alice, who told me that my mother had suffered a very bad attack and was not expected this time to recover. She was in the intensive care unit, hooked up to the inevitable machines. Alice was with her, the children were on their way. My mother couldn't talk, but she could hear me; Alice held the phone to her ear. "Darling, I love you," I said into the receiver. "Wait for me, I'm coming. *Aspettami!*"

I drove directly to the airport at Fiumicino, arriving there at dawn, and threw myself onto the mercy of the airlines. An hour and a half later I boarded a flight to London, then one to Boston, then another directly to San Diego. Alice met me at the airport. My mother had rallied after my call, she reported, to the extent that she had been transferred back to a private room. The children had arrived and clustered about the bed. My mother's feet had begun to kick out at the covers. Why wasn't she dying, she wanted to know. She looked at Alice and took her hand, spoke to the children. Together, she told them, this is the way you must be from now on, together, always. It was her way of apologizing for the pain she had caused. Then she sent the children off to dinner and lay back, her eyes closed, to wait for me.

When I came bursting into the room later that evening, Alice in my wake, the children were lined up against the wall. "Oh," I said, falsely cheerful as I rushed into her arms, "I'm sorry, I forgot to bring you a mozzarella." The children left us alone and I sat down beside her to bring her up to date on all the goings-on in Italy.

Two days later we took her home and settled her in the downstairs bedroom, where she had stayed before, with a view out the window of white roses in full bloom. We had contacted the local hospice, which dispatched nurses to settle her and rig up a morphine drip she could activate herself simply by pressing a button. I hired young women to take care of her around the clock, so she would never be alone, and we resigned ourselves to waiting. It would be a matter of days, perhaps at most a few weeks until the next attack.

She slept well at night, was alert and cheerful during the days. The children took turns coming down. Hooked up to an oxygen tank, she was able to get as far as the patio one morning, where she could sit and see nearly the whole garden, in bloom under a perpetual blue sky. We began to hope the doctors were wrong, that she would cheat death one more time and linger on in our lives a while longer, her mind clear and lucid, teeming with memories of people and events long forgotten by the rest of us.

Then came the morning, after twelve days, when she couldn't rouse herself from sleep. I spent the day with her, talking constantly, reminiscing about the past. We played music she could hear from the living room, Verdi's great chorus "Va, pensiero" from *Nabucco* that she had used as her signature piece during her wartime broadcasts to Italy. Late that afternoon I put my head on the pillow next to hers and again began to ramble on about the spectacular life she had led, all the interesting people she had known and loved, all the places she had graced with her presence. I knew she could hear me, though her eyes never opened. "We enjoyed them," she murmured in Italian, "we enjoyed them."

I finally went upstairs well after nine that night, leaving her seemingly safely asleep once again. A cry in the darkness awakened us. We stood at the head of the stairs and looked down on the frightened face of the girl who had been sitting beside her. "She's trying to get up," she said. I rushed into her bedroom and held her as she thrashed blindly, wildly about, her eyes open but seeing nothing. She emitted a flat, high wail, the sound of something not quite human, lost and far away. Alice pressed the button of the morphine and she sank back down on the bed, silent now, departing from us. Alice knelt beside her, her hand on her pulse. "She's gone," she said a few seconds later. I kissed her and her heart resumed beating, fluttered as if bent on one last thrust at life, then ceased. I sat there holding her hand, her eyes closed, her face turned toward the window, until the hearse arrived an hour later to take her away. The last I remember of that morning was the pale faces of my children at our front door three hours later. "She went in her sleep," I said. "It was very quick."

We threw one last party for her in New York. Doris and the children and Alice came with me. We lined up wonderful photographs I had found of her from different periods of her life around the walls of her living room and invited everyone who had known her to come and celebrate her life with us. About sixty friends came, of all ages and backgrounds, and we toasted her and spoke of her and laughed a lot. She would have loved it, because it was the kind of gathering she had always specialized in, bringing people together who perhaps had little in common besides their love for her. Only one person cried, but we forgave her because she had had too much to drink and tended toward tears on awkward occasions.

Two days later we took her ashes and Janet's out to Cherry Grove, where that night another, smaller gathering came to honor her. In the morning a small group of us took the ashes down to the beach. The Atlantic surf was calm under a blue sky, and in warm sunlight my son Bill and I walked into the ocean up to our waists carrying the twin pewter boxes containing all that was physically left of these two remarkable women. Together we scattered their ashes into the waves and stood there for a few moments watching wind and water do their work of taking them both back into the bosom of the world. On the beach I fell into my daughter Natalia's arms, the one full moment of unconstrained grief I had allowed myself since my mother's death. I understood now why Federico had frozen himself into a dispassionate accounting of his own mother's sudden death. Something of the old Roman ways survived in us, too.

My mother had finished *Darlinghissima* on a day in June 1984, at Sperlonga. Now I, too, on another June day fourteen years later, sit in the tiny whitewashed stone house she built on the hillside overlooking the ancient beach stretching to the dark mouth of the Grotto of Tiberius. The green and rocky mountains end here at the sea, peppered on their crests by the upthrust arms of lone pine trees. Swifts dart above my terrace on their ceaseless pursuit of insects, and late tonight a pale sliver of a new moon should rise above the darkened sea. I like the idea of Janet and my mother floating endlessly together in another sea thousands of miles away. I can hear their voices still in endless conversation and a timeless search for truth and love and dignity in an imperfect world.

INDEX

In the index, "Natalia" refers to Natalia Danesi Murray, "Janet" to Janet Flanner, and "William" to William Murray.